SWORD AND PLOUGHSHARE

THE CASTLE, AERIEL VIEW

reproduced with the consent of Terence Soames (Cardiff) Ltd.

SWORD AND PLOUGHSHARE

THE STORY OF THE DE BOHUNS AND CALDICOT

BY

THOS. T. BIRBECK

(Author of *The Foudroyant*)

THE CHEPSTOW SOCIETY
CHEPSTOW, MON.

© T. T. BIRBECK

ISBN 0 900278 15 3

MADE IN GREAT BRITAIN
Printed by
R. H. JOHNS LIMITED
NEWPORT . MON.

iv

CONTENTS

	PREFACE	.	.	.	.	.	.	ix
I	INTRODUCTION	.	.	.	.	.	1
II	THE DE BOHUNS AND HOLDERS OF THE CASTLE AND MANOR	.	.	.	.	.	5
III	THE LESSEES OF THE MANOR OF CALDICOT AND NEWTON						54
IV	THE MANOR OF CALDICOT AND NEWTON UNTIL 1421	.					57
V	THE MANOR AND THE DUCHY OF LANCASTER, 1422–1857						63
VI	THE CASTLE	.	.	.	.	.	74
VII	THE MILL	.	.	.	.	.	.	86
VIII	THE CROSS AND THE COURTS	.	.	.	.	88
IX	THE CHURCH AND THE BELLS	.	.	.	91
X	THE NONCONFORMISTS	.	.	.	.	97
XI	THE CHARITIES	.	.	.	.	.	99
XII	THE POOR AND THE OVERSEERS	.	.	.	100
XIII	THE VILLAGE CONSTABLE	.	.	.	.	103
XIV	MILITARY SERVICE	.	.	.	.	.	105
XV	THE ROADS	.	.	.	.	.	.	107
XVI	THE RAILWAYS AND WORKS	.	.	.	.	109
XVII	THE SCHOOL	.	.	.	.	.	.	112
XVIII	THE INNS AND SOCIETIES	.	.	.	.	114
XIX	NEWTON	.	.	.	.	.	.	118
XX	THE OTHER MANORS:	.	.	.	.	
	(i) Caldicot-by-Caerwent or West End	.	.	139
	(ii) The Priory	.	.	.	.	.	141
	(iii) Dewstow	.	.	.	.	.	144
XXI	LIFE AND CHANGES IN THE NINETEENTH CENTURY	.	145

APPENDICES:

(a) Extract from Liber Landavensis . . . 149
(b) Survey of the Manor of Caldicot and Newton, 1613 149
(c) Holders of Castle and Manor . . . 157
(d) Lessees of Castle and Manor . . . 158
(e) Pedigrees:
    (i) Herberts and Somersets . . . 159
    (ii) Gamages and Vans . . . 161
(f) Division of de Bohun Inheritance between Alianore
    and Maria 162
(g) Vicars of Caldicot and Rectors of Newton . 164
(h) Census Statistics. . . . 165
REFERENCES AND ACKNOWLEDGEMENTS . 166
INDEX 168

ILLUSTRATIONS

THE CASTLE, AERIAL VIEW, reproduced with the consent
of Terence Soames (Cardiff) Ltd. . . . *Frontispiece*
SEAL OF MILO FITZWALTER 8
THE DE BOHUN COAT OF ARMS AND CREST . . 29
THE WOODSTOCK COAT OF ARMS . . . *facing page* 38
WOODSTOCK'S FRENCH CAMPAIGN. Drawing by Bryan Wood-
field 38
WOODSTOCK'S BIBLE, reproduced by permission of the British
Museum . . . . *facing page* 39
EFFIGY OF SIR WILLIAM AP THOMAS, in Priory Church, Aber-
gavenny . . . . *facing page* 54
CHARLES SOMERSET, 1ST EARL OF WORCESTER, AND FIRST LESSEE
OF CALDICOT MANOR IN 1507, reproduced by permission of
the Duke of Beaufort . . . . *facing page* 55
MAP: CALDICOT, drawn by Bryan Woodfield . . . 64
PLAN OF THE CASTLE 75
SECTION OF THE KEEP, OR N.W. TOWER, based upon a drawing
made for the Caerleon Antiquarian Society in 1853 . 77
CALDICOT CHURCH 92
INTERIOR OF CALDICOT CHURCH, from a drawing in the National
Library of Wales . . . . . *facing page* 94
THE OLD WHITE HART INN AT THE CROSS . . . 115
MAP: NEWTON, drawn by Bryan Woodfield . . . 119
SHIRENEWTON CHURCH 121
EARLSWOOD WESLEYAN CHAPEL 122
MAP: EARLSWOOD IN 1608, from a drawing in the Public
Record Office 129
SHIRENEWTON HALL 131
PROPOSED OBSERVATORY AT SHIRENEWTON (Chepstow Museum) 132
CALDICOT HALL, OR GREAT HOUSE, built by Henry Wise . 140
CHURCH, OR PRIORY, FARM-HOUSE 143

The line drawings are by the author.

PREFACE

C ALDICOT is now a parish within the Rural District of Chepstow in the County of Monmouth; a straggling area centred upon the silent ruins of a medieval Castle, but for four hundred years after the Norman conquest an industrious agricultural community linked with Shirenewton and dominated by the administration of the lords of the Castle. Whilst the noble holders of the manor were wielding the sword in pursuance of their principles in national, as well as their own, affairs the tenants were assiduously carrying out their agricultural activities on behalf of their lord and for their own subsistence. On one hand there was the militance of the de Bohuns, and on the other hand the quiet pastoral pursuits of the manor.

In 1948 when the Chepstow Rural District Council was making plans for post-war development it was decided to concentrate mainly upon Caldicot to provide the services for an increase of population from 1770 to 3000. Shortly after this, however, a decision was made to establish the important and extensive Steel Works at Llanwern, a few miles from Caldicot. The County Planning Authority then decided that a large proportion of the steelworkers should be accommodated at Caldicot, and additional services and amenities were provided there to serve an ultimate population of 14,000. The building of new estates and roads has resulted in the disappearance of much of the old Caldicot, and it seems appropriate that some record should be made of its past history, hence the preparation of this book. It is hoped that it will prove a reasonably correct and interesting account of Caldicot and the de Bohuns.

I record my appreciation of all the help I have received from many people in unearthing information, and I would in particular acknowledge the guidance and encouragement given to me by my friend Ivor Waters.

Thos. T. Birbeck

I

INTRODUCTION

A BRONZE axe head, made before 2000 B.C., is to be seen in the National Museum of Wales. It was found in Upper Rodge Wood, in the Parish of Caldicot, and indicates that there was in the bronze age some human activity in the Caldicot area.

Opinion is divided upon the derivation of the name Caldicot or Caldecote. Archdeacon Coxe in his "Historical Tour through Monmouthshire" expressed the opinion that the name was a corruption of Cil-y-Coed, or the skirt of the wood. On the other hand Sir Joseph Bradney, in his "History of Monmouthshire" writes: "The name of Caldicot, which is not uncommon in England, is most rare in Wales. The meaning of the word is generally considered to be cold cot, a place erected by the Romans on a main road where a traveller could obtain rough shelter." Both interpretations were apt descriptions of Caldicot in the past.

The first hamlet at Caldicot of any importance would be that which developed as a result of the Roman occupation of Monmouthshire and the establishment of the settlements at Caerleon and Caerwent.

At the time of the Roman invasion the Caldicot area was inhabited by the Silures who had a large encampment on Llanmellin Hill, just north of Caerwent. They also had a settlement at Sudbrook, a mile from Caldicot. The Silures had attained a high degree of culture, excelling in artistic bronze, iron, and gold work. Pottery was found at Sudbrook. Although Frontinus, the Roman, defeated the Silures they so impressed him that he induced them to leave Llanmellin and live like Romans in the new town of Venta Silurum (Caerwent).

The Roman way from Silchester to Bath and from thence over the Severn, reached one of the Pills near Caldicot and then passed through the latter to Caerwent. The Castroggy Brook rising on the ridge of Wentwood passed Maesgwyneth, rounded Caerwent and before reaching Caldicot became known as the Neddern. At Deepweir in Caldicot the brook divided, the main stream entering the Severn at Sudbrook Pill with a minor discharge from Caldicot Pill. In later years a new cut was made for the improvement of drainage by which the Neddern was turned direct into Caldicot Pill and Sudbrook Pill became silted up.

1

At the time of the Romans, however, Sudbrook Pill and St. Pierre Pill were the harbours and landing places used by the Romans on their passage from the West of England to Caerwent and Caerleon.

Liber Landavensis, the Book of Llandaff, quotes that about A.D. 900 Brockwael, son of Meurig, sacrificed two churches for the redemption of his soul, and restored to Bishop Cyfeiliawg both the churches of Caldicot and St. Brides with land and commonage in field, wood, water, and pastures, and with free approach for ships at the mouth of the Troggy and all its weirs for fisheries without any payment besides to the Church of Llandaff.

Offa, the King of Mercia, who died in 795, built his famous dyke along the Welsh border terminating at Beachley on the opposite side of the Wye to Chepstow and this established Caldicot in the Welsh sphere of influence.

Harold, the son of Godwin, on attaining his powerful position in England was confronted with unusual difficulties on the Welsh border, for the Welsh, under the vigorous and warlike Gruffydd ap Llewelyn, had united all their forces to become a serious menace to England. Gruffydd's power extended from Chester to Chepstow, and Offa's Dyke no longer served the purpose of a national barrier.

Harold's first campaign into Wales was in 1055, but it was not until 1063 that he was able to overthrow his enemy. Gruffydd lost his life and Harold married his widow Ealdgyth.

Harold's forces were in the Caldicot-Portskewett area and a short passage in the Saxon Chronicle reads: "1065—In this year just before Lammas, Earl Harold gave orders for a building in Wales at Portascith when he had taken possession of it and there he collected much material and thought to have King Edward there for the hunting. And when it was almost all collected then Caradoc, son of Griffin, went there with all the men be could put together, and slew almost all those who were building and took away the material that had been collected. And this slaughter was on St. Bartholomew's Day."

It was probable that Caradoc retained control of the Caldicot area until the Norman Conquest.

After Saxon Harold had made his incursion into South Wales he was followed by the adventurous Normans. William the Conqueror, on gaining control of England by the decisive battle at Hastings, granted manors and estates to the nobles who had supported him, but he took good care that they should not become independent of the crown of England. The Welsh, however, were of different calibre to the English. They were hardy and active and employed guerilla tactics, using their wild mountains as havens for retreat if things went badly for them. If they were beaten in one battle they would return again. William, therefore, applied other methods to subdue them. He permitted certain Norman lords to conquer as much of Wales as they could and hold as their own what they had conquered. This resulted in a number of fortresses being erected in the marches of Wales for the protection of these new lands. The lords enjoyed the excitement of their encounters with the Welsh and, furthermore, they were their own masters, not being so tied to their sovereign as the barons of England.

The barons could not commence to conquer in the march without the King's leave, but being once allowed to go they had a free hand.

One of the most powerful supporters of William of Normandy in his invasion of England, in 1066, was his kinsman, William FitzOsbern, who had volunteered sixty ships with their armament for the expedition. Shortly after the conquest, in 1067, FitzOsbern was created Earl of Hereford, and he was enriched with vast possessions in various parts of the Kingdom. The Earldom of Hereford comprised not only the modern county, but so much of Gloucestershire as lay between the Severn and the Wye. It also included portions of the territory on the Welsh side of the Wye previously conquered by Harold from the Princes of South Wales. FitzOsbern entered into an alliance with Caradoc ap Griffin by means of which he consolidated his powers along the whole of the eastern portion of Gwent including Caldicot.

Lordship Marchers were formed and they were under the obligation of erecting and maintaining castles for the defence of the realm against their turbulent neighbours. They were singularly free from the jurisdiction of the King's courts, enacting their own laws and appointing their seneschals, chancellors, and other high officers. They also created mesne lords or petty barons having feudal obligatons.

FitzOsbern introduced laws and customs for the administration of his territory mainly based upon laws and customs of his Norman possessions which were to regulate the life of the manors for centuries thereafter. He also had his position in national affairs. He was placed in charge of the royal castle of Winchester, and on the Conqueror's visit to Normandy he was entrusted jointly with Odo, Bishop of Bayeux, with the government of the realm as justiciaries. Unfortunately, however, he had a difference with the King and he was sent to Normandy to assist Queen Matilda in the defence of the duchy. FitzOsbern was killed in battle there on the 20th February 1071, and was buried in his own Abbey at Cormeilles.

William, the elder son of FitzOsbern, succeeded to his father's Norman estates, and the second son, Roger de Breteuil, succeeded to the English possessions. He thus became Earl of Hereford and the holder of lands in south-east Monmouthshire.

Roger was in good credit at King William's Court, having assisted in obtaining revenue for the King's treasury from the Abbeys of England. In his private capacity he was, however, a benefactor rather than a plunderer of the Church.

In the year 1074 he joined the Earl of Norfolk and others in the rebellion against King William in his absence. When the King returned to England he summoned Roger to attend court and as he did not deny his treason he was adjudged to have forfeited his lands, and imprisoned.

King William on his deathbed, in 1087, expressed his foregiveness of Roger and ordered his release from prison, but his successor, his son William Rufus, declined to be bound by his father's arrangements and Roger de Breteuil remained in prison until his death.

The lands of the Earldom of Hereford were thus in the King's hands from 1074, and the affairs of the estates of Caldicot and other parts of South East Monmouthshire were administered by the Sheriff of Gloucester.

In 1086 King William instructed his royal commissioners to gather the facts to ascertain the ownership of each estate of land and its value for taxation. To get these facts the commissioners were sent to each circuit and a court was summoned to meet them. The members of the court, or jury, were required to tell the name of each manor and its holder, the number of hides it contained, the number of ploughs employed on the lord's domain, and the number on the lands of the tenants. Then they gave the population of the manor in classes: freemen, villeins, cottars, and serfs; the amount of forest and meadow; the number of pastures, mills, and fishponds; and what the value of the manor was. The facts thus gathered together were put into permanent form in Domesday Book and provide a storehouse of valuable information on the economic conditions in the country of 1086.

At the time of Domesday the sheriff's duties were to see that the King's lands were let and properly stocked and cultivated, and that their returns came in at the proper times. He also had to collect and pay over certain judicial fines and fees which belonged to the King from the local administration of justice. He assumed some of the military duties in calling out and commanding local levies. He was entrusted with the care of all the interests of central government from which he took his orders, and was a close connecting link binding the King with every locality in the kingdom.

THE DE BOHUNS AND HOLDERS OF THE CASTLE
AND MANOR

Durand and Roger de Pistres

D URAND, known as de Pistres from the Norman village from whence he came, was appointed by FitzOsbern to assist in the government of the West of England and he was granted the office of Sheriff of Gloucester.

On the defection of the second Earl of Hereford, the duties of the Sheriff became onerous and the wide range of his activities can be seen from Domesday Book.

The entry in the book relating to Caldicot reads as follows: "The sheriff Durand holds of the King in Caerwent one tenement called Caldicote. He has there in demesne three ploughs and fifteen semi villeins, and four serfs, and one man-at-arms. All these have twelve ploughs. Here is a mill of 10/–. All this is worth £6."

This is the first glimpse of Caldicot as a community of living persons. Village life had been organized on the Norman pattern and agricultural operations were in progress. It was a modest beginning prior to the erection of the castle and the influx of knights and men of substance. It can be seen from the entry in Domesday Book relating to Chepstow what effect the building of the castle of FitzOsbern had had upon the growth of the community and their activities.

From other records in Domesday Book it is learned that Durand had a brother Roger who had been in the same office, and was moreover, Lord High Constable of England.

Durand is said in Domesday to have held a house in Gloucester, wherein he most probably resided. The man-at-arms referred to in Domesday Book may have been a person to whom Durand had given some portion of land in return for supervising the tenants, and receiving the rents. Durand died in 1096 and was buried in St. Peter's Abbey, Gloucester.

Walter Fitzroger

Walter, the son of Roger, and nephew of Durand, was created sheriff on the death of his uncle, and four years after this there was a change in the government of the country. William Rufus died and his younger brother Henry received the support of the barons to his coronation on his promise that he would abandon the arbitrary acts of his brother and sign a charter for the good government of the country.

Walter married Emma, sister of Hamelin de Balun, Lord of Abergavenny. He built the castle of Gloucester upon his own demesne land in 1122 and he either built or superintended the building of the castles of Bristol, Rochester, and part of the Tower of London. Although there is no documentary evidence it can be assumed that he built the Caldicot Keep by employing the same workmen as had carried out the other work for him.

In Walter's time the holding of the lands in Gwent was much more secure, but the site selected for the castle was nevertheless a strong one, surrounded by a marsh, and well suited to meet any attacks from the Welsh, overland or from the Severn.

The formation of the Lordship with the two areas of Caldicot and Newton may be ascribed to Walter. Sheriff's Newton indicates that the land was cleared and the village built by one who held the office of sheriff at the time.

In his later years Walter became a monk at Llantony Priory in the Welsh mountains and there he died about the year 1127.

A great deal had been accomplished by Walter, during his service as sheriff, in stabilizing the economy of his region.

Milo FitzWalter

When Walter FitzRoger retired to become a monk at Llantony, in 1123, his only son and heir, Milo, was appointed by Henry I as Sheriff of Gloucester and Staffordshire, and he was granted all the lands and privileges of his father, including the office of Constable of England. He was also the holder of Brecknock.

Milo held Caldicot, as his grandfather had done, as a small agricultural unit. The castle was not completed and the only part which may have existed was the Keep which could accommodate a very small garrison.

A Bull of Pope Honorius, dated 19th April 1128, ordered Milo to restore land and other property which had been taken unjustly from the Church. This may have referred to land at Caldicot.

Milo's relations with the Church improved and he founded a Priory at Gloucester, on 25th May 1135, which he called Llantony Secunda, to receive those who had fled from the old Llantony Priory in Wales.

Milo married Sybilla, the daughter of Bernard Newmarch, by gift of King Henry in 1121, and he continued the administration of his estates, being a loyal subject of the King. By charter signed at Rouen he was confirmed in all his father's lands held in chief with the office of Constable.

He accounted to the King for the counties of Gloucester and Stafford in 1130.

In 1135, however, the King died, and this concluded the long peace of Norman rule. Henry's only legitimate son died in 1120, and he had, therefore, declared his daughter Maud as his heir. Stephen, the son of Adela, the sister of Henry, lost no time in making an attempt to snatch the crown of the English portion of his uncle's kingdom. He crossed to England from Normandy, and appeared at the gates of London whilst Maud was still in Normandy. The Norman barons and the Pope accepted Stephen, but Robert, Earl of Gloucester, the half brother of Maud, formed a party to support her.

Milo did not acknowledge Stephen with any enthusiasm, but after threats and persuasion he did homage to the new King, in 1136, at Reading, in consideration for which he received two charters granting to him his whole honour of Gloucester and Brecknock, and all his land held in shrievalties, together with his constableship of Gloucester Castle, as he had held them at the death of King Henry I.

He attended the Easter Court of 1136 as Constable of England and witnessed Stephen's Charter of Liberties.

In May 1138, Milo received Stephen, amid great rejoicing, in Gloucester.

Robert, the Earl of Gloucester, had then renounced any allegiance to Stephen and was in open rebellion in support of Maud.

In August 1138, Milo assisted Stephen, at Shrewsbury, in an attempt to crush the revolt, and six months later he obtained from the King the Abbacy of Gloucester for his kinsman Gilbert Foliot, but when Maud landed at Arundel, in August 1139, and proceeded to Bristol, where Milo was Constable of the Castle, he there acknowledged her claim to the crown.   Thereafter he was one of her ablest and most faithful supporters.

Owing to lawlessness at Bristol Milo persuaded Maud to leave for Gloucester where he had collected a strong garrison and a large supply of provisions. By extracting ransoms from his captives he had replenished his exchequer. It was here that Maud granted Milo the constableship of St. Briavels Castle, and the whole of the extensive Forest of Dean.

Stephen marched towards Gloucester, but Milo met him and routed his forces completely. Shortly after this Milo made sorties into Worcestershire and returned to Gloucester with much plunder.

Stephen then deprived Milo of the Constableship of England, which he conferred upon William de Beauchamp.

In 1141 Maud's fortunes were at their zenith. She was victorious at the battle at Lincoln where Stephen was captured and taken a prisoner to Gloucester and thence to Bristol Castle.

In the same year Maud made royal progress through Cirencester and Winchester to London where she hoped to be crowned. Her haughty bearing and arbitrary government, however, raised the anger of the

Londoners, and she retreated to Oxford. It was here on 25th July 1141 that she created Milo Earl of Hereford, giving him the Mote of Hereford with the whole castle in fee, and to his heirs and their heirs, also the 3 penny of the pleas of the whole county of Hereford, three manors, the Hay of Hereford, and the forest of Trevella. The witnesses to this grant were David, King of Scotland, Robert of Gloucester, Bernard the Bishop of St. Davids and Humphrey de Bohun.

Maud's position rapidly deteriorated from this point. She moved to Winchester where she was besieged and escaped with difficulty escorted by Milo. They passed in great haste, and in disguise, from Winchester, Andover, to Gloucester. Milo's seal of silver was found at Andover in 1795, when labourers were digging, and it is now in the British Museum. He probably threw it away with his armour to escape recognition; and he arrived at Gloucester exhausted with hardly a rag to his back.

SEAL OF MILO FITZWALTER
drawing by Thos. T. Birbeck

The cause of Maud was lost, but Milo remained faithful to her. He had spent all his money in her cause and in 1143 he levied large sums from Church lands in Hereford to pay troops recruited in Maud's support. For this he was ex-communicated by the Pope.

Milo's active support of Maud appeared to decrease for he spent more of his time hunting, and on Christmas Eve, 1143, whilst hunting in the Forest of Dean, he was accidentally hit by an arrow shot at a deer. He was removed to Gloucester Castle where he died shortly afterwards.

He directed that his body should be buried in Llantony Priory, at Gloucester, which he had founded, but the monks of St. Peter's Abbey interposed, and cited a prescriptive right of burying all who died within the Castle precincts, referring to Milo's great uncle, Durand. The dispute was passed to the Bishop of Worcester who, being entreated by the Bishop of Hereford, decided to respect the dead man's wishes, and the monks consented to forego their rights. Milo was accordingly buried in the Chapter House of Llantony Priory in Gloucester.

Milo was the first of the Caldicot lords to be a national martial figure. He was esteemed by his contemporaries, including his opponents. Very few men of his times were comparable to him in counsel or in action.

Milo had five sons and three daughters by his wife Sybilla. All the sons, Roger, Walter, Henry, William, and Mahel, were martial men, and redoubtable knights, but they died without issue. Their inheritance was ultimately divided amongst their three sisters.

In the Chapter House, at Llantony, at the head of Milo, were buried his sons Roger, Henry, and Mahel. On his right was his wife Sybilla, and on her right, Margaret de Bohun, whilst the latter's husband Humphrey lay at the foot of Sybilla.

After the death of her kinsman, Robert, Earl of Gloucester, in 1147, Maud abandoned all attempt to gain the crown, and returned to Normandy where she joined her son Henry. He had received four years tuition under Master Matthew, at Bristol, who cultivated in him a love for learning which in later days made him a worthy successor to his scholarly grandfather. Stephen, easy going and chivalrous by nature made no attempt to interfere with Henry's movements.

Henry, in 1149, came back to England to receive the honour of knighthood from King David of Scotland. He landed at Wareham and had a brief stay at Devizes where Roger Fitzwalter, eldest son of Milo, was in attendance.

Roger FitzWalter and his brothers
Roger, born about 1121, had married Cicily, daughter of Payne FitzJohn, Lord of Ewyas.

It was agreed by Stephen that provided he should remain King for his lifetime he would recognize Henry as his heir. In 1154 Stephen died and Henry II was crowned at Canterbury.

Henry recognized the claims of Roger Fitzwalter to his gratitude and confirmed to him all the fee of Earl Milo, his father, and of Bernard Newmarch, and all the lordships which King Henry I his grandfather had between Severn and Wye except the castle of St. Briavels, the town of Newnham, and the Forest of Dean. He also gave "the mote of Hereford and all the castles and the 3 penny of the Borough and the 3 penny of the pleas of the whole county of Hereford with which I have made him Earl and all the justiciarships which were his fathers as his father held of King Henry I and the town of Gloucester and the office of sheriff of Gloucestershire by the same rent which Milo his father used to pay to the King." Roger thus held Caldicot.

He shortly afterwards joined Mortimer in disobeying the King's orders and he had to surrender the Earldom of Hereford and his castles to the King who granted them to Geoffrey Ridel. The lands and earldom were, however, regranted to Roger in 1155, but he then entered Llantony Priory, in Gloucester, where he died in the same year, and was buried in the Chapter House. The King again took possession of the estates.

Roger had been active and valiant, but unequal to his father. He, however, greatly respected Milo's memory for he erected Flaxley Abbey on the spot where Milo had received his mortal wound. He also caused William, the Prior of Llantony, to resign because he had blemished Milo's character.

After the death of Roger his three brothers were successively holders of his estates, including Caldicot. Walter eventually became a monk at Llantony. Henry was killed by one of his own men at Gwentllwch. Mahel was killed by a fall of stone at one of his castles. William also ended his days at Llantony. As they all died without issue the estates were divided between their three sisters, Margaret, the eldest, who married Humphrey de Bohun, Berta who married Philip de Braose, and Lucy who became the wife of Herbert FitzHerbert. The division of the estates was the origin of the separate manors of Caldicot West End and Caldicot East End and Newton.

Humphrey de Bohun (*Third*)
Margaret brought to her husband the titles of Earl of Hereford and Constable of England, together with the manor of Caldicot and Newton in 1158.

Humphrey was the third de Bohun of that Christian name. His grandfather, Humphrey with the Long Beard, was a cousin of William the Conqueror, with whom he came to England. His father Humphrey, called the Great, was steward to William Rufus.

The de Bohun estates were in Wiltshire.

Humphrey de Bohun had been a friend of the Fitzwalters and had witnessed the grant of the Earldom of Hereford to Milo. He had also witnessed King Stephen's charter of Liberties in 1136. Humphrey was later Master of the Horse to the Empress Maud.

Humphrey the third was a loyal supporter of Henry II after his coronation in 1154. He was steward to the King in 1158, and witnessed the sealing of the Clarendon Bill of Rights, in 1164.

In 1173 the King's three sons rebelled against him. The King had the support of the best part of the baronage including those of the military

ability of de Bohun. The latter fought for the King with a detachment
of mercenary cavalry and he pursued the Scots, who were supporting
the insurgents, across the border, and burnt Berwick.   News then
reached Humphrey that the Earl of Leicester had landed with a force
of Flemings at Walton.   Humphrey at once turned southwards and
reached Bury St. Edmunds where he was joined by royalist troops under
the Earls of Cornwall and Arundel, and Roger le Bigod.   Setting out
with the banner of St. Edmunds at their head they met Leicester's forces
at Farnham St. Genevere.   Leicester was defeated, but bought a truce
to enable him and his Flemish mercenaries to leave England.

Humphrey died in 1182 during the lifetime of his wife. Until he had
taken over the estates Caldicot Castle had been merely an outwork of
the Earldom.   The keep was all of the castle which existed.   By the
time of his death Humphrey had strengthened the keep and added the
curtain walls and other towers, making the Castle a suitable home for
a great and powerful baron. He was also the founder of Monk Farleigh
Priory in Somerset.

Humphrey de Bohun (Fourth)

Margaret de Bohun bought the wardship of her young son, Humphrey
the Fourth, from King Henry II for 400 marks. She died in 1187, and
was buried in the Chapter House, at Llantony in Wales, of which she
had the patronage.

Henry II died in 1189. His reign had been of particular importance
in English constitutional and legal history. It is interesting to note
that he had improved the controlling machinery of the exchequer
instituted by his grandfather. The exchequer derived its name from
the great table covered with a black chequered cloth on which the
revenue accounts were set out by means of counters.

The only coin in circulation at that time was the silver penny, twelve
were a shilling, 160 a mark, and 240 a pound.

Henry had agreed with Philip of France that he would recognize
his son Richard as his heir although he had a higher regard for his
son John.   Neither, however, had the attributes to make a good
ruler.   Richard was arrogant and quarrelsome.   John was vain and
vicious.

Richard spent most of his short reign, from 1189 to 1199, at war on
the continent, and he was killed by an arrow at Limousin.

In Richard's reign young Humphrey de Bohun, the Fourth, died in
France assisting Philip, the French King, against the Earl of Flanders.
He was buried at Llantony in Wales, about 1197.

Humphrey had married Margaret, the daughter of the Earl of
Huntingdon, and they had a son, Henry. On the death of her husband
Margaret bought the wardship of her young son from King Richard for
400 marks. She died in 1201.

Henry de Bohun

When Henry de Bohun succeeded his father in 1197 he owed the King 300 marks for the fine of the Gloucester land of his grandmother Margaret de Bohun.

King John, who succeeded to the crown when his brother died in 1199, almost immediately confirmed to Henry, Milo's grant to Llantony (Gloucester) and whatsoever was given by King Henry, inter alia, the church of Caldicot, and whatsoever was given by Margaret de Bohun. On the 28th April 1200, the King, by charter at Porchester, granted to Henry the Earldom of Hereford. Henry paid John 300 marks for the grant of his mother's lands.

After John's coronation Henry de Bohun was sent with the Bishop of Durham and the Earl of Norfolk, to conduct King William of Scotland to do homage at Lincoln. On the 21st November the two kings met, and on a hill outside Lincoln, in sight of all the people, the King of the Scots did homage for his English lands, among the witnesses being Henry de Bohun.

Henry married Maud, the daughter of Geoffrey St. Piers, Earl of Essex.

King John received no support from the barons and had to rely on mercenaries to carry out his military ventures. He made no effort to abide by the charters of his predecessors for the good government of his kingdom, and the barons and clergy were united against him. They granted the King little money and he resorted to any method open to him to extort revenue from his subjects. Matters came to a head in 1215 when John, without means and support, agreed to meet the barons to consider the terms of a charter they wished him to seal. This was based upon the charters of Henry I and Henry II. The place chosen for the conference was an island in the Thames between Staines and Windsor. The King encamped on one bank while the barons covered the marshy flat, still known by the name of Runnymede, on the other side of the river. Their delegates met on the island between them. The Great Charter, also known as Magna Carta, was discussed, agreed to, and signed in a single day.

Henry de Bohun had been a steadfast opponent of the King who had seized Caldicot Castle and committed it to the custody of Engelramus de Prattelus during the King's pleasure. Henry was one of the twenty-five earls who undertook to compel the King to observe the charter and he was amongst those excommunicated by the Pope.

John was reluctant to observe the conditions he had agreed to and the barons appealed to the French for military assistance. This was forthcoming and a joint army of French and the barons (including Henry de Bohun) was formed. John by a series of rapid marches distracted the plans of the barons and took Lincoln. On proceeding southward, however, he was crossing the Wash when he was surprised by the tide and his baggage with the Royal treasures was washed away.

John entered Newark in a raging fever and died there, in 1216.

John's ten year old son Henry was in the care of William, the Earl Marshal. The coronation of the boy King was immediately followed by the solemn acceptance of the Great Charter. At this time a joint army of French and the English barons, including Henry de Bohun were besieging Lincoln, but the Earl Marshal fell upon them with a bold stroke and utterly routed them. He took captive Henry de Bohun and many others. The Earl Marshal showed moderation and wisdom in the terms of submission. By the Treaty of Lambeth in 1217, the French were permitted to return home, the prisoners released, and their possessions restored.

Henry de Bohun thus returned to his estates. He started on a pilgrimage to Jerusalem, but died on the way on 1st June 1220. He was buried at Llantony, Wales.

Henry's wife Maud inherited the estates of the Earldom of Essex when her brother died in 1227. When she died in 1236 she was buried beside her husband at Llantony (Wales).

On the 11th June 1220, King Henry III sent the following order to the Constable of Caldicot Castle: "The King to the Constable of Caldicot greeting. Since we have heard that the Earl of Hereford, your lord, is dead, we have ordered all his land to be seized into our hand, and have committed it to our beloved and faithful William de Putot and Ralph de Norwich, clerk, with the Castle of Caldicot, to be kept until we order otherwise thereof. And therefore we order you without delay to deliver to them the castle aforesaid with all its appurtenances and with all the chattels and things which belonged to the same earl found there, and in testimony of this thing, witness Hubert de Burgh, etc at York, on the 11th day of June, 1220, by the Lord King's Council.

"And all knights and free tenants of the honour of the castle of Caldicot are ordered to be attentive and respondent to the same in all things which belong to the aforesaid castle until the Lord King orders otherwise thereof."

This clearly indicates that the Castle was completed by 1220.

The long reign of Henry III from 1216 to 1272, was divided into three periods, (1) The ministerial period when the government was in the hands of men who had grown up under the influence of the administrators trained in the reign of Henry II, (2) the period of misgovernment when the King sought to rule himself, influenced by foreign friends, (3) the period of great crisis when revolution broke out.

In the first phase the regency of the Earl Marshal ceased at his death in 1219, and Hubert de Burgh continued an efficient administration until the King cast him into the Tower in 1232.

Humphrey de Bohun (Fifth)

Humphrey (5) the son of Henry de Bohun did not suceed immediately to his father's estate which, as we have seen, was in the custody of

William de Putot, Ralph de Norwich, and William de Briwer. After an intercession on Humphrey's behalf the King sent the following order: "Concerning the Castle of Caldicot. The King to William Briwer greeting. Know that at the instance of the illustrious King of the Scots, and our magnates of England, we have received the homage of Humphrey de Bohun for all the lands which he ought to hold of us, which were of Henry de Bohun, Earl of Hereford, his father, whose heir he is. And, therefore, we order you without delay to deliver the Castle of Caldicot with appurtenances which was of the aforesaid Earl of Hereford, and is in your custody, to the same Humphrey, saving to you the grain and your chattels which you have there. Signed at Salisbury, 17 June 1221."

Humphrey was then granted the Earldom of Hereford with all its estates, together with Caldicot, and the Constableship of England. He had married Maud, the daughter of the Earl of Eu, and by her he had one son and four daughters.

Humphrey joined the Earl of Cornwall in his quarrel with the King in 1227, but a year later he was acquitted upon payment of $15\frac{1}{5}$ fees of the moiety of the fees of the town of Trowbridge which he held as part of his inheritance.

In 1235 Humphrey was Marshal of the King's Household at the coronation of Henry's Queen, Eleanor of Provence.

He went on a pilgrimage to Santiago in 1238, and when he returned he was appointed Constable of Dover Castle until 1241. During this period he was Sheriff of Kent.

Humphrey was godfather to young Prince Edward who was born in 1239.

In 1242 he accompanied an expedition to France, but returned because he could not tolerate the King's foreign favourites. In the same year there was a Welsh rising and the blame was assigned to Humphrey because he had kept in his hand the inheritance of the sister of Llewellyn, the Prince of Wales.

Humphrey's uncle, Geoffrey de Mandeville, had agreed to pay King John 20,000 marks for the privilege of marrying the King's sister, Isabella of Gloucester. The obligation of meeting a proportion of this sum had descended to Humphrey, but King Henry released him from this debt in 1244, and confirmed the Earldom of Essex, with Pleshy Castle, upon him: He then became one of the wealthiest of the barons.

In 1246 he was among the barons who signed a letter to the Pope complaining of the oppression the kingdom suffered under the Court of Rome, threatening the withdrawal of their tribute unless their grievances were redressed. He was present at the Great Council, in 1248, and also at the sentence of excommunication against the transgressors of the Charters in 1253.

Humphrey was with the King in Gascony in 1254, but received permission to withdraw after failing to obtain satisfaction in a matter concerning his jurisdiction as Constable, and he returned to England to assist Prince Edward against a Welsh uprising.

He and his son Humphrey had license to hunt hare, fox, cat, and other wild beasts in the forests of Bradon and Savarnake, in Wiltshire.

In 1258 Simon de Montfort, who had married the King's sister, Eleanor, and had been created Earl of Leicester, headed the opposition of the barons against the King's administration. Henry had to submit to the barons' demands, and the Provisions of Oxford were drawn up. Humphrey de Bohun was one of the twenty-four councillors to carry out this task, being chosen among the Baron's twelve, and he was, thereafter, one of the fifteen chosen to advise the King on all points. He was also one of the twelve elected by the Barons to represent the community in three annual parliaments, and one of the twenty-four who were concerned in treating of aids.

In 1259 Humphrey was the King's representative, with the Count of Aumâle, for the preservation of peace between England and France, and he was one of the commissioners who ratified the Peace Treaty.

He was sent, in 1260, to treat for peace with Llewellyn in Wales, and in 1262 he was one of the commissioners to meet Llewellyn's commissioners at the Ford of Montgomery. It was at this time that de Montfort returned from a visit to France and a period of turbulence emerged. In the struggle of 1263 Earl Humphrey de Bohun took the side of the King whilst his son Humphrey was with de Montfort and the barons. Neither side was strong enough to get the better of the other so they submitted their differences to the King of France who ruled in favour of Henry III. De Montfort would not accept this decision so a civil war developed between him and Prince Edward who had espoused his father's cause. Edward joined the Lords Marchers and established himself in Gloucester Castle. In 1264 the battle of Lewes was won by de Montfort, and Edward was taken as a hostage for the good behaviour of the Lords Marchers. Edward, however, escaped and rejoined his friends in the Marches, signing the Treaty of Ludlow whereby he made formal acceptance of a popular programme for government.

In 1265 Humphrey was one of the keepers of the City of London, and a plenipotentiary for the Dictum of Kenilworth.

De Montfort made his final stand, in 1265, at Evesham, where after a brave resistance he was killed and his army defeated. Humphrey de Bohun, junior, was at the side of De Montfort, and was taken prisoner, but was soon afterwards pardoned.

A period of peace followed, and in 1267 the statute of Marlborough was signed re-enacting the reforms desired by the barons. The King had become a puppet of his son, and so remained until his death, in 1272, when Edward was crowned King.

Humphrey de Bohun had been a national figure for over forty years

and, as age was telling upon him, he led a less active life. When the
Earl of Gloucester died in 1263 Humphrey assumed the guardianship
of his young son but in 1266 he resigned that duty.

Maud, the wife of Humphrey, died in 1241, and was buried at
Llantony, Gloucester. He married a second wife, Maud of Avenbuiy,
and she died in Gascony in 1273. In 1290 her remains were taken from
there by her son John de Bohun, of Haresfield, and interred beside those
of her husband.

Humphrey died on 24th September 1275, and was buried before the
high altar at Llantony, Gloucester. He was called "the Good Earl"
having followed his father in endeavouring to curb the power of the
Crown, and striving for the liberties of the people. He was patron of
Walden Abbey, and had founded Austin Friars. His lands, including
Caldicot, were taken into the King's hands on 27th September 1275.

The Good Earl's son, Humphrey (Sixth), predeceased his father in
1265. The King had provided him with the annual sum of 80 maiks
from the Exchequer. He assisted his father to keep order in the Marches
but he was at times on the opposite side in the conflict between the King
and de Montfort. He married firstly Eleanor, daughter of William
de Braose, Loid of Abergavenny, and secondly Joan, daughter of
Robert de Quincy, Earl of Winchester. He died at Beeston Castle,
Chester, after the battle of Evesham, and was buried at Combermere
Abbey.

On the 9th October 1275 at Windsor, the King issued the following
order: "To all tenants of the Castle of Caldicot to be intendent to
Bartholemew le Juvene to whom the King has committed the castle and
all lands pertaining thereto late of Humphrey de Bohun, sometime Earl
of Hereford and Essex, tenant-in-chief, he to hold during pleasure."

Humphrey de Bohun (Seventh)

Humphrey (Seventh) de Bohun, the grandson of the Good Earl, and the
son of Humphrey (Sixth) and his wife Eleanor, was born about 1249.
The King took his homage, and he had livery of his mother's lands of
Brecknock and Haverford West in 1270. On 14th January 1270, he had
a grant of 40 marks a year as long as he remained in the King's service.
During the last few weeks of his grandfather's life he was deputy Constable of England. On the 26th October 1275, he had livery of his
grandfather's land and was granted the Earldoms of Hereford and
Essex, and created Constable of England. In the same year he married
Maud de Fiennes who was a cousin of Queen Eleanor, and by her had
one son.

Edward I had a vigorous and active reign. He had an imposing
figure and was nicknamed Longshanks. In 1254 he had married
Eleanor, daughter of Alphonso of Spain. He was thirty-three years old
when he was proclaimed King and his aims were to strengthen the

Royal power and to take the people into partnership with him in the administration of the country. The lack of good laws impressed upon him the need for legislation.

Edward found the feudal system of providing his army was unsatisfactory. The troops he obtained had divided loyalties between the King and the lord whose servants they were, and in some cases the persons liable for service paid scutage or money in lieu of personal attendance. It was sometimes comical how the feudal system worked. In one instance a tenant was liable to provide a soldier who was bound to remain in the army as long as his provisions lasted. He turned up with a piece of bacon, ate it forthwith, and then retired. Edward found that he received more reliable and loyal service from the troops he himself paid.

As soon as he was crowned Edward was faced with difficulties on the Welsh border. Llewelyn ap Gruffydd had refused to pay homage to the new King and Edward knew he would encounter great obstacles to subdue the lawless Welshman. Llewelyn's men employed guerilla tactics. They avoided pitched battles, sought cover in the forests and mountains, and loved to pounce upon convoys. They were active and difficult to reach. Their chief weapon was a long spear. Gilbert of Gloucester endeavoured to make peace with Llewelyn, but it was more of a truce and the Welsh continued to make trouble on the border.

Llewelyn had made incursions into the de Bohun lands at Brecknock, but when Humphrey complained to the King the latter decided that the matter did not justify a war.

In 1276 the King decided that action must be taken against Llewelyn and he mustered a large force at Worcester preparatory to advancing into Snowdonia. Meanwhile Humphrey de Bohun was fighting alone with his own resources at Brecknock. He had not been supported in his protest to the King against Llewelyn's occupation of Brecknock so he took advantage of the pressure in the north to occupy the land he claimed. Having done this he was free to appear in person at the feudal muster at Worcester to do his duty as constable.

There were dense forests between Chester and Llewelyn's country and the King's first action was to cut down trees to make a roadway for his troops to advance. Llewelyn was deserted by a number of his followers and retreated to his inner mountain hideaway. Negotiations for peace followed and when Llewelyn yielded Edward took the land as far as Conway. The King was merciful to Llewelyn. He remitted a heavy fine and arranged the wedding of the Welshman to Eleanor, the daughter of Simon de Montfort.

Humphrey returned to his Welsh castles, and in 1278 he made a pilgrimage to Santiago.

In 1282 Llewelyn and his followers again penetrated into South Wales. The Earl of Gloucester was appointed commander-in-chief, and Humphrey de Bohun was asked to support him. Humphrey, however,

demanded the emoluments of his office as constable. The King ordered
the barons of the exchequer to investigate the precedents and they
reported that the Earl was entitled to certain payments.

De Bohun had been so busily engaged in holding Brecknock in the
midst of a revolt of his own tenants that he was unable to join the King
at the feudal muster at Rhuddlan. As Llewelyn moved northwards
Hereford took up his duties with the King and drew his pay of 5s. a day
for his office, and the King sent him to Anglesey.

When Humphrey was engaged at Brecknock he deputed his uncle,
John de Bohun, to act as constable until he was able to take up the
duties at the King's side.

The final battle with Llewelyn was at Builth, on a hill above the
Yrfon, a tributary of the Wye. He expected Welsh support from Builth,
but he did not get it. A treacherous Welshman shewed the English the
way to Llewelyn's camp. They surprised him, and one Stephen de
Frankton came upon him, not knowing who he was, and ran him
through the body as he was without armour.

In June 1283, the Earl of Hereford left Hugh de Turberville as deputy
constable with the King and went back to Brecknock. He then stamped
out the embers of the war on the upper Towy, and it was to him that
Gruffydd and Llewelyn Vychan finally surrendered in the summer.

From July 1283, Edward released his army and turned to castle
building at Caernarvon, Conway, and Caerphilly.

In 1284 a definite peace settlement was made by the passing of the
Statute of Wales. The birth of Prince Edward at Caernarvon eased the
tension. In this year Humphrey de Bohun had a dispute with John
Giffard regarding the ownership of land at Isgenen on the borders of
the march of Brecknock. The King appointed judges to settle the
matter, and much to the chagrin of Humphrey they favoured Giffard.

Humphrey was on the continent in 1285, but he returned in the
following year, and in February 1287, he was commissioned by the
King to see that peace was kept in the land beyond his Brecknock
border towards Carmarthen. Whilst he was away his Brecknock tenants
again revolted, and the King sent the Earl of Gloucester to subdue the
uprising. It was not strictly etiquette for Gloucester to enter the de
Bohun lands, but there was no alternative as he was the nearest available
for the task. He took 200 trained woodmen from the Forest of Dean to
cut ways through the forests for his troops. His large force quickly
subdued the insurgents. The Earl of Gloucester was a prominent figure
in the marches and he married the King's sister Joan.

The other chief marcher was Humphrey de Bohun, Earl of Hereford,
who was rather sullenly obedient to the crown. He knew that he had
not the strong status of Gloucester, but he had served in the wars of
1277 and 1282, with his quota of knights, at his own expense. Like
Gloucester he never took the King's pay for himself, except as constable.

Though he was a man who insisted on his rights, and claimed the custom of the marches to settle disputes by private war, he was not powerful enough alone to defy the crown.

De Bohun again attracted attention in 1289. Giffard held Llandovery and Builth and the march of Isgenen which bordered on Hereford's land. The Earl's grievance was that he had conquered the Vychans and ought to have had Isgenen. Giffard's lands were the chief theatre of the war with Rhys which the King had ordered Hereford to conduct. He quelled the revolt and the King commissioned him to guard Carmarthen, but he made an attempt by force of arms to assert his claims against Giffard. The King intervened and the judge he appointed confirmed the ownership of Giffard.

Gloucester had been building a castle at Morlaix which lay on a tributary of the Taff, and he was claiming a debatable strip of land between his and Hereford's marches. On the 25th January 1290, the King sent a strongly worded proclamation calling on Gloucester to abstain from active hostilities, but in February Gloucester's men raided into Brecknock, killed some of Hereford's men and carried off spoil. They were led by the Earl's bailiffs. Gloucester made a second raid in June, and a third was made in November.

Hereford was the plaintiff at law. He had suffered considerably, but he had obeyed the King's orders not to wage private war. There was general lawlessness, and the King saw an opportunity to upset the laws of the marches by appointing judges to settle the dispute. They were set up in 1291, and were the Bishop of Ely, William de Valers, and two regular judges, together with a jury. On the appointed day Hereford appeared, but Gloucester did not, and at an adjourned court Gloucester again failed to appear. At a third attempt the case proceeded without him. The finding was that Gloucester was cognizant of the raids. An unknown number of Hereford's men had been killed, 1,070 head of cattle, 50 horses and bulls, and countless sheep and pigs were taken.

After the judges reported to the King he sat in judgement at Abergavenny. Since the judges verdict Hereford's bailiff had, very unwisely, attacked Gloucester's men near Brecon. The King, therefore, had a case against Hereford also. He pronounced that Hereford had acted contumaciously and he was committed to prison and his lands confiscated into the King's hands.

The King and his court proceeded to examine Gloucester, who was this time present. He made trivial excuses which the court brushed aside and then pronounced that he was responsible for the three raids and had received a share of the spoil. The sentence was couched in the same terms as in Hereford's case, and he was committed to prison and his lands confiscated. Certain nobles promptly offered themselves as sureties and the King consented to release the Earls after they had been in prison for some months. This was later commuted to fines of 10,000 marks by Gloucester and 1,000 marks by Hereford as the King considered that the Earls had then been duly humbled.

Hereford lived with a rankling sense of injury, but the two earls were reconciled before the Archbishop of Canterbury, the Bishop of Durham, and the Earl of Cornwall in the King's Chapel at Westminster.

In 1294, the King was making preparations to send a force to Gascony in which was included the Earl of Hereford. The Welsh took advantage of the withdrawal of the nobles and their followers by mounting another uprising; but Edward sent Humphrey de Bohun with a detachment back to South Wales. The rising was quelled and de Bohun then joined the King to defeat the Welsh, at a battle at Conway in 1295. In this year Gloucester died and the leadership of the barons passed to Roger Bigod, Earl of Norfolk, as marshal, and Humphrey de Bohun, Earl of Hereford, as constable. Bigod was lord of Striguil, holder of Chepstow Castle, and, therefore, a near neighbour of de Bohun who held Caldicot and Brecknock.

In 1297 Humphrey de Bohun conducted the Princess Elizabeth, and her husband the Count of Holland, from England to the continent.

The year 1297 was marked with disaffection. The clergy began by refusing to grant the King money in January, and later when the King was anxious to send an army to Gascony to support the Count of Flanders against the King he ordered Norfolk and Hereford to head the force whilst he went on another mission. Both earls resented this. Norfolk had been promised that he would always serve by the King's side, and Hereford was still embittered by his imprisonment after the Gloucester case. They insisted on the strict letter of the feudal law that they should be at the King's side. Edward might have avoided a crisis if he had dealt tactfully with the earls instead of adopting an air of strong insistence. The earls had numerous allies amongst the barons.

Hereford and Norfolk withdrew from Court and they sent a message to the King, who was on the point of sailing for Flanders, that they demanded the confirmation of the Charters. The King replied that he could not discuss the Charters without a full council which he could not call as many members were abroad. He said, "If the earls choose to accompany me it will please me much; but if not, I request that they will not injure me, or at any rate my kingdom, in my absence."

After he had sailed the two earls formed a party to insist upon confirmation of the Charters, and to prevent by arms the collection of taxes which they declared was contrary to the Charter of Liberties. The King had left behind a number of loyal nobles and good warriors in case the recalcitrant earls became too aggressive. A council of the barons was convened ostensibly to deal with the defence of the coast, but it resulted in the gathering of a large military force. A further meeting was ordered to be held in London at which the loyal barons advised the Prince of Wales, who was acting as regent, to confirm Magna Carta and the

Charter of the Forests. On the 6th October, Hereford and Norfolk appeared at the city gates with 1,500 mounted followers and choice infantry. They received the Charter and returned to their estates in the Marches.

Meanwhile William Wallace was heading a rebellion in Scotland. Hereford then went north to assist the King's forces, but he did not display much enthusiasm for the fray.

Although there were quarrels between the English and Welsh soldiers they united in the face of battle and heavily defeated the Scots at Linlithgow and Falkirk. When the English army retired to Carlisle Hereford and Norfolk set their faces against an autumn campaign alleging fatigue and loss of men and horses. The King gave way and agreed for a new muster at Carlisle in the following June, 1299.

Humphrey (Seventh) de Bohun retired to his castle at Pleshy. He died on the 31st December 1298, and was buried at Walden Abbey, where his wife already lay. He had been a steadfast supporter of the rights and liberties of the people, and, although Edward was one of our greatest Kings, Humphrey had been strong enough to withstand him to his face. It was at his insistence that the Statute of Tallages was passed providing that no tax be levied without the consent of Parliament. The tenants of the Brecknock estates, which Humphrey had inherited through the de Braose family, had been very troublesome to him, but there is no record of friction between the Earl and his Caldicot tenants.

Humphrey de Bohun (Eighth)

Humphrey (Eighth), the son of Humphrey (Seventh) was born about 1276 and succeeded his father. He appears to have been as pliable and unstable as his father had been unbending and patriotic. The King took his homage and he had livery of his father's lands, including Caldicot, on the 16th February 1298. Humphrey was in attendance at the marriage of Edward I to Queen Margaret, at Canterbury, on the 9th September 1299.

Humphrey was present at the siege of Carlaverock in the campaign against the Scots in July 1300. Walter of Exeter recorded this and stated that "the companion of the Earl of Lincoln was the Constable, who was the Earl of Hereford, a rich and elegant young man. He had a banner of deep blue silk, with a white bend between two cotises of fine gold, on the outside of which he had six lioncels rampant. By birth, titles and possessions Humphrey de Bohun was perhaps the most distinguished of his age, being 25 years old at the time of the siege."

Humphrey's seal was appended to the barons letter to the Pope, dated 12th February 1300. The seal depicted the de Bohun arms, and the counterseal had the arms hung by a strap from the back of the de Bohun swan.

THE DE BOHUN COAT OF ARMS AND CREST
drawings by Thos. T. Birbeck

The Earldom at that time was the highest rank in the peerage. The number of earls was scanty and each individual earl was important as the people saw in him their natural leader. For this reason, and also because of the trouble caused to him by the operation of the law of the Marches, the King decided to bring the Earldom of Hereford more under his control, and he married Humphrey to his seventh daughter Elizabeth Plantagenet, widow of John, Count of Holland, on 14th November 1302. On the 8th October 1302, the King had compelled Humphrey to surrender to the Crown his castles, towns, manors, and lands in Essex, Hertfordshire, Middlesex, Huntingdonshire, Buckinghamshire, Wiltshire, counties of Gloucester and Hereford, and in Wales, also the Constableship of England.

John de Barham, who had been sent by Edward I to Caldicot, sent the following letter to the King on the 3rd November 1302: "I and Nicholas de Wedergrave, sub escheator, came to the Castle of Caldicot, near Strugoil, on Wednesday after St. Luke early in the morning and took seisin thereof to your use and fealty of the people and tenants of Caldicot and Newton so solemnly that no one small or great of competent understanding failed to do fealty. Master Rees ap Howel delivered seisin on behalf of the Earl.

"Whereas the tenants by knights service alleged that they ought not, and were not, accustomed at any time, to seek their lord beyond the water of the Severn to do homage, after reasoning with them I made them do fealty on the following terms: 'I will be faithful and loyal, and bear faith and loyalty to King Edward and his heirs, Kings of England, of life and member, and of earthly honour against all people who may live or die, and will loyally recognise and do the customs and services belonging to the tenements which I claim to hold of him, and have held of Humphrey de Bohun, Earl of Hereford and Essex. So help me God and His saints.' "

The knights at Caldicot were Thomas de Huntley, John ap Adam, John Maral, Leyson ap Morgan, Jevan ap Belyn, Meurice de Redmayn, Jevan ap Wronow Wyne, and William de Valers.

After Humphrey's marriage Caldicot and his other estates were restored to him, and his wife, to be held as fully as he held them before quitclaiming to the King. There was a condition that if Humphrey and Elizabeth had no issue the estates should pass to Elizabeth's issue by any other marriage. No complications arose in this connection, however, as they had six sons and four daughters.

Humphrey accompanied the King's son to the continent in 1304, and in 1306 he was appointed to treat on the affairs in Scotland. Shortly afterwards he had a grant of Annandale, with the Castle of Lochmaben, late of Robert of Bruce.

At the knighting of Prince Edward, in 1306, the Earls of Hereford and Lincoln fastened his spurs. In the same year Humphrey served in

C

Scotland passing through the mountains, with the Earl of Lancaster, and investing the Castle of Kildrummie.

In the last year of Edward's reign Humphrey incurred the King's displeasure for having left the Scottish war without license, but he obtained pardon after the solicitation of the Queen, his mother-in-law.

On the 7th July 1307, King Edward I died. He had been responsible for bringing into effect a number of statutes to strengthen and improve the government of the country and is recognized as one of the greatest and wisest of rulers.

He was succeeded by his worthless son Edward II, and Humphrey de Bohun carried the sceptre with cross at his coronation.

It was the new King's objective to throw off the hold of the barons upon him, and he chose as his ministers men of an inferior position who were wholly dependent upon him for their power. Piers Gaveston had been his friend and companion, and he was created Earl of Cornwall, at the head of the administration.

In 1308 a grant of Edward II to Humphrey de Bohun recited the surrender to Edward I of the de Bohun estates to the crown, and their regranting was confirmed. It was made clear in the grant that the office of Constable of England was the right of the de Bohuns and their heirs, and not connected with the Earldom of Hereford.

At the demand of the barons in 1308 the King reluctantly exiled Gaveston. He, none-the-less, returned the following year, and he was the chief object of hatred when the barons, in 1310, forced Edward to appoint a commission to reform the government. Humphrey de Bohun was one of the Lords Ordainers appointed to carry out this task. It was again a condition that Gaveston should be exiled, but his stay abroad was even shorter than before. On landing in England he marched north to Scarborough where he was besieged whilst the King skulked at York. Gaveston surrendered to the barons, who included de Bohun, on condition that he would be brought before a Council of Barons, but the Earl of Warwick, with the approval of the Earl of Lancaster executed him in 1312. Humphrey de Bohun had assisted the barons, but a year later he was pardoned by the King.

The death of Gaveston resulted in the formation of a middle party more partial to the King's cause. Lancaster, however, was still hostile to the King, and the six years following were among the darkest in the country's history. There was a succession of famines, and continual dissension between the King and the barons.

De Bohun had been changing sides during this turmoil, and had been deprived of his office of Constable, but, in 1312, Edward had regranted it to him, "as fully as the same Earl and his ancestors held it before the taking of the same into our hands for certain causes."

In the following year he was the chief person in a commission to continue a treaty with Lodovick, Earl of Evreux, the Bishop of Poitou and others.

The Scots had again risen under Robert Bruce, and in 1314 Edward took a large force north to meet the threat thus imposed. Humphrey de Bohun, and his kinsman Henry, accompanied the King.

The vital meeting of the two forces took place at Bannockburn. Just prior to the onslaught Henry de Bohun bore down upon Bruce as he was riding along the front of his army. Robert was mounted on a small hackney, and held only a light battle axe in his hand, but, warding off his opponent's spear, he cleft his skull with so terrible a blow that the handle of his axe was shattered in his grasp. This incident dispirited the English forces, and in the following battle the Scots triumphed.

Humphrey de Bohun and the Earl of Gloucester had disagreed as the forces assembled for battle. Humphrey considered he should take precedence in the line as Constable of England, whilst Gloucester claimed the privilege on the grounds that his ancestors had always been first. As they disputed the Scottish line drew near and Gloucester dashed forward, but his horse fell and he was killed. De Bohun retreated to Bothwell, where he was betrayed by the Governor, Sir Walter Gilberton, and captured by the Scots. He was, however exchanged for Bruce's wife, Elizabeth, who had been in the hands of the English for some time, and the Bishop of St. Andrews.

Humphrey's wife, Elizabeth, died in 1316. She was the King's sister, and had been born at Rhuddlan Castle, in Carnarvonshire. She was buried at Walden Abbey. At the Parliament which met at Lancaster in 1315, Humphrey delivered the King's answer to a petition of the Bishops, and he was one of the peers appointed to regulate the King's household.

In 1315–16 Humphrey was appointed as captain of all forces against Llewellyn Bren in a Welsh uprising, but later in 1316 he was again in Scotland on the King's service.

He went to the continent in 1318 on behalf of the King to treat for peace with the Count of Flanders and the Count of Hainault, Holland, and Zealand.

He was named a commissioner, in 1320, to treat with Robert the Bruce.

Humphrey was summoned by the King to attend the Council at Gloucester, but he refused to do so while Hugh le Despenser, the King's new favourite, was also his adviser. The King was aware that de Bohun was preparing to attack Despenser, and he ordered him to abstain, but despite this Despenser's lands were ravaged. Humphrey received a pardon in 1321, but a year later it was annulled in a Parliament held at York. His lands were taken into the King's hands and various orders for his arrest were issued.

The Earl of Lancaster had come out of retirement to oppose the King, and de Bohun and a number of other barons joined him. They took Gloucester, burnt Bridgenorth, and then proceeded north. The King and Despenser also marched north and the two armies met at Boroughbridge on 6th March 1321. There Humphrey de Bohun lost his life. He was endeavouring to force the bridge accompanied by his standard bearer Sir Ralf de Applinsdene when one of the King's Welshmen got under the bridge and thrust his lance upward through a hole. It pierced a joint in Humphrey's armour, and he died instantly at the age of forty-five. He was buried in the church of Friars Preachers at York despite his wish to be buried beside his wife at Walden. He made many pious bequests and remembered those in his employ. His estates passed into the hands of the King. An inquisition held at Gloucester in 1324 stated: "the land and tenement in Caldicot, late of Humphrey de Bohun, a rebel, are valued at £25/3/4¼."

Lancaster and many of his adherents were executed.

The King's temporary popularity soon faded owing to the arrogance of Despenser, the failure of campaigns against the Scots, and the King's domestic vices. The Queen took her son, Edward, to the continent and refused to return.

The Queen, however, had a secret conspiracy with the barons, and she later landed at Orwell where the barons hastened to her standard. Deserted by all, the King fled to the Marches of Wales where he fell into the hands of the new Earl of Lancaster. Despenser was at once hanged and the King was held until Parliament decided what should be done to him. He was eventually most cruelly put to death at Berkeley Castle by Sir John Maltravers and Sir John Gournay.

In 1327 the young Prince was proclaimed King Edward III.

Edward was a boy of fourteen when he ascended the throne. He had a splendid physique and his energies took the form of striving after military glory. He had been under the tutelage of his mother, Queen Isabella, and her lover, Roger Mortimer, Earl of March, who for three years ruled the country as he willed. Mortimer accumulated estates and roused the hostility of the barons. His foreign policy was declared despicable and he was accused of the murder of the late King. Baronial movements against him appeared. The first, under the Earl of Lancaster, collapsed. The second resulted in the execution of the King's uncle, the Earl of Kent, but in the third, the young King himself, desiring to rid himself of Mortimer's influence, sided with the barons.

The King issued an order on the 19th February 1322, shortly after the death of the eighth Humphrey, to the keeper of Caldicot Castle to be intendent to the king's cleık, John Walewayn, whom he had appointed during his pleasure as surveyor and chief keeper of the castle.

John de Bohun

Humphrey the eighth's first son, born in 1304, was named Humphrey, but he died in infancy, so the second son John, born in 1306, became the heir to the de Bohun property when his father died in 1321. The estates, however, were in the King's hands, and it was not until Edward III became King, in 1327, that John was granted his inheritance. In the roll of liveries of cloth and other things for the apparelling of new knights issued by the Clerk of the King's Great Wardrobe it states that John de Bohun received a tunic and cloak of brown cloth, materials for his bed and bedding, cloth of gold, a robe of scarlet cloth, and another of green cloth.

John had married Alice, the daughter of the Earl of Arundel. He was a prey to ill health and often struck down with sickness.

After the troubled times preceding his coronation King Edward had prohibited tournaments and feats of arms. He wrote to this effect to John de Bohun, but the latter was disobedient and the King again wrote to him expressing surprise that his command had been ignored and bidding the Earl to come to him at Stamford. De Bohun was one of the great men of the Council, and by his disobedience to the King's orders had set a bad example to others.

In the same year (1327) the King requested the barons, including de Bohun, to assist him in a campaign against the Scots by providing him with troops equipped with carts, wagons, tents, and pavilions. The army gathered at York and then proceeded north. At Carlisle was a considerable body of Welsh under the command of John de Bohun to defend the passage of the Eden to prevent the Scots entering England by that route. The King made John a Knight of the Bath.

When the King went to Amiens in Picardy in 1329, to pay homage to the French King, John de Bohun accompanied him, and they were royally entertained for fifteen days.

John's infirmity became more acute in 1330 and at his request the King substituted his younger brother Edward as his deputy to carry out the arduous duties of Constable of England. John then went on a pilgrimage to Santiago.

His last duty for the King was in 1335 when he proceeded with letters of attorney to Scotland.

John de Bohun died in 1336 at Kirkby Thore, in Westmorland, and was buried at Stratford Abbey, near London. His wife Alice had predeceased him and he had married a second wife, Margaret, daughter of Ralph, Lord Basset. His lands were taken into the King's hands.

Humphrey (Ninth) and William de Bohun

When John de Bohun had been struggling to overcome his infirmities he had been ably supported by his brothers, Humphrey, William and Edward. Humphrey had received the family name as his father's first born son named Humphrey had died in infancy.

Humphrey was born about 1309, and Mr. J. R. Cobb has recorded in his notes that William and Edward, twins, were born at Caldicot Castle in 1312.

Humphrey did not wed and it is doubtful whether Edward did so, but William married Elizabeth, the daugher of Bartholemew de Bladesmere, and widow of Edmund Mortimer.

Whereas the de Bohuns of the past were not consistently supporters of the crown, there was never any doubt about the loyalty of Humphrey, William, and Edward to King Edward III. They were invariably by his side and carried out all his commands without question.

Their first assignment was in 1330. Mortimer, the Queen Mother's paramour, had been created Earl of March and, as he was in a very powerful position, the barons regarded him as a menace to their positions. They accused him of complicity in the death of Edward II, and they decided that it would be expedient to get rid of him when an opportunity should occur. Parliament had been summoned at Nottingham on the advice of Mortimer, and the Queen Mother took into her hands the keys of the Castle so that none might enter except Mortimer or herself. When Sir Edward de Bohun, who was then Deputy Constable, endeavoured to secure lodgings in the Castle for the King's cousin and other nobles, Mortimer roughly refused, and the barons found quarters a mile out of town where they were able to confer together. With the King's consent Lord Montagu was instructed to take some trusty persons to bring Mortimer to account. He, therefore, took as his associates Humphrey, William, and Edward de Bohun with five other nobles. They were unable to obtain direct access to the Castle as the Queen Mother had the keys, but the King commanded Sir William Eland, the Constable of the Castle, to assist them. Eland informed the plotters that Queen Isabelle had fixed new locks and slept with the keys under her pillow, so that he could not help them to enter by the gate by any means, but he knew of a hole that passed under the wall of the Castle, which neither Queen Isabelle, Mortimer, or any of their company knew of.

Montagu and his followers took horse and left town, giving Mortimer the impression that they had fled, but at about midnight on the 19th October 1330, they returned and met Sir William Eland at the hole near the wall, where they entered a dismal cave and went through an uneven passage which gave access to the Keep.

Without any great noise they took Mortimer in the company of the Lord Bishop of Lincoln. The next day he was taken to the Tower of London, and he was executed at Tyburn on the 29th November. His great possessions of land passed into the King's hands.

Queen Isabelle was deprived of her property and confined by the King at Risings, near London. William de Bohun escorted her.

The King not unmindful of the services rendered by Edward de Bohun awarded him 400 marks per annum together with two lordships in Wiltshire.

In 1333/4 William and Edward were with the King's expedition into Scotland when Edward unfortunately lost his life. Joshua Barnes (1688) records this as follows: "A noble young lord unhappily was taken away about the close of this year. It was Sir Edward Bohun, a right valiant and worthy gentleman, being brother to John, Earl of Hereford and Essex, and the King's cousin, who as he was driving a great booty of cattle over the Solway Firth, in the Marches of Scotland, was lost in this manner. For causing his guide to ride softly before him through the water he presently saw that what with the slipperiness of the stone whereon they were, and the strength of the current through which they passed, his servant together with his horse, was overwhelmed in the water. When Sir Edward out of compassion endeavouring to recover the man chanced in the like manner to lose his right ground, and so, being oppressed with the weight of his armour, perished in the channel, leaving no issue behind him."

On the death of John de Bohun in 1335, his brother Humphrey was granted the earldoms of Hereford and Essex, and was created Constable of England. In the same year William married Mortimer's widowed daughter-in-law. In the Papal Letters Mortimer was described as having been murdered by William and his accomplices, and the marriage was said to be arranged to put an end to the enmity between the two families.

In 1336 William was again in Scotland at the head of the men of Cumberland and Westmorland, and he was one of the Commissioners to treat with the Scots for a truce. The King recognized his services in the following year by creating him, with the consent of Parliament, by girding him with a sword, Earl of Northampton. He was granted the reversion of the castles and manors of Stamford, Fotheringhay, and Oakham, the manor of Grantham, and the shrievalty of Rutland. An income of £1,000 per year was promised him.

Between October 1337, and March 1338, William was one of the Commissioners to the French King to declare Edward's rightful claim to the crown of France. They first visited continental princes to obtain their support to Edward's claim. The King of France, however, made plans to attack them, but Edward sent a fleet of forty ships to secure their safe return to England.

Also in 1338 the King sent the Bishop of Lincoln, and the Earls of Northampton and Suffolk with 10,000 sacks of wool to sell in Brabant, and William was a commissioner to treat with the Duke of Brabant, as to the marriage of Prince Edward (the Black Prince).

On 12th June 1338, William became Constable of England by grant of his brother Humphrey which was accepted and confirmed by the King.

In the following year King Edward met the German lords at Mechlin, in Brabant, and they started a campaign against the French. There were three English divisions and William de Bohun was captain of one.

They were faced by a similar number of French forces. Joshua Barnes describes the event: "It was a glorious and ravishing sight to behold these two armies standing thus regularly embattled in the field, their banners and standards waving, their proud horses barbed, and Kings, lords, knights and esquires richly armed, and all shining in their sur-coated satin and embroidery." The French, however, retreated and there was no battle, so Edward with his followers returned to Antwerp to join his queen and young son Lionel.

In 1340 King Edward then twenty-eight years of age, set sail from Southampton for Flanders with a fleet of 260 vessels. Both Humphrey de Bohun and his brother William, who was the same age as the King, were present. When they reached the coast of Blankenburg they saw before them a fleet of 400 ships. The masts were so numerous that they resembled a great wood. On the 23rd June the fleets engaged in battle, in which the de Bohuns distinguished themselves, and finally the French were defeated and retired. This combat, in which the King was wounded in the leg by a spear, is known as the Battle of Sluys.

The King's force duly landed in Flanders and advanced to Tourney to which they laid siege. William de Bohun was present and when the King decided to return to England with the Queen, William accom-panied them.

When Queen Philippa gave birth to her fifth son, Edmund, his christening was the occasion for a Feast and Tournament in London. A proclamation was issued inviting knights and gentlemen to come from France, Scotland, Hainalt, Brabant and Flanders to attend the gathering. Joshua Barnes stated that: "there were many ladies and virgins of prime quality present all dressed and set off in the best manner." All the knights took part in the jousts and the ladies sang and danced. The de Bohuns excelled in the tournament.

After a short spell of service in Scotland in 1341, William de Bohun was appointed the King's lieutenant in Brittany in June 1342, and Edward wrote to the mayors and bailiffs of thirty-nine ports ordering them to provide ships for the passage of William, Earl of Northampton and his troops. The King also ordered for their use 8,970 sheaves of arrows with iron heads, and 1,600 bowstrings. He asked the Irish lords to join the Earl with 116 men-at-arms and 250 hobelers (lightly armed horsemen).

The French fleet endeavoured to intercept the English fleet but they were separated by a storm and William was able to land his forces near Vannes. He relieved Brest, and defeated Charles of Blois at Morlaix. Of a personal combat between Charles and William de Bohun Hollins-head wrote: "The French General, Charles de Bois, and William de Bohun fought so long with hand strokes that day that no man but a liar could give more praise to one than the other. Three times being both weary they withdrew to take breath and then fell to it again, with spear and shield, sword and target but the French being routed, the right worthy and stout Charles de Blois was forced to fly."

In October the King left Sandwich to join the forces in Brittany, and William was sent to besiege Nantes.

At the intercession of the Pope, in January 1343, a truce was agreed on, and Edward and his forces returned to England. William then made a rapid visit to Scotland to relieve his castle of Lochmaben. He returned to England and engaged on the King's administrative business. He had the Great Seal from the Chancellor, by the King's order, to seal three pardons.

In this period was the first instance of two houses of Government. The Bishops, Prelates, and Barons sat in the White Chamber, and the Knights of the Shires, and the Commons, or Burgesses, met in the Painted Chamber. The days in which the King himself was present were called Parliament days. They then all met in one house, and about 250 members were present.

Humphrey de Bohun and his household spent the whole year from September 1344 to October 1345, at Caldicot and during that period he paid for a man with a horse to carry a stag from Brecon to Caldicot.

Edward could not negotiate a permanent peace with France so, after strengthening his defences in England, he prepared for war, and he commissioned William de Bohun to defy Philip as a violator of the truce. He wrote to the Mayor and Sheriffs of London ordering them to proclaim that all persons who were going with the Earl of Northampton to Brittany should proceed to Portsmouth without delay, and on the 11th June 1345, he again wrote to the Sheriffs to say that the Earl had sailed.

William duly marched into Brittany to assist in the defence of the Duchy, and was there joined by the King and the Black Prince. When this affair was settled, and they had appointed captains to control the places they had won, the English contingent returned to England in July. The King then wrote to the Sheriffs of the various counties ordering all barons, bannerets, soldiers and persons capable of bearing arms between the ages of sixteen and twenty to prepare without delay to go to Gascony and Brittany. The Prince of Wales was directed to gather 2,000 troops from the north and 2,000 from South Wales, half lances and half bowmen.

Edward and the Black Prince, and the cream of the nobility, including Humphrey and William de Bohun, left England for Normandy on the 2nd July 1346. The force pillaged Caen and the King sent William back to England with a spoil laden fleet, together with documents for the Archbishop of Canterbury. William then rejoined the King in the fields near Crecy with his large force of Irishmen, Welshmen, and men-at-arms, numbering 32,000 in all.

The French army under King Philip greatly outnumbered the English forces, but Edward arranged his plans for the imminent battle with great care and forethought, whereas Philip, relying upon his superiority of numbers, neglected to consider the comfort of his troops, and was careless in his arrangements.

Edward divided his army into three divisions, the first under the Black Prince with Humphrey de Bohun at his side; the second under William de Bohun, and the Earl of Arundel; and the third under the King himself. Each had his banner before him and the red dragon of Wales floated before the Welshmen. Men of Caldicot, the manor of Humphrey de Bohun, were almost certainly in the fray.

The ground sloped towards the south east, and the Black Prince was placed on the right with the bowmen in front. William de Bohun was placed on the left protected by the river Maie and a deep ditch. The King took up his position above and behind the others.

At about midnight the King rode through his ranks speaking cheerily to his men, ordering them to eat at their ease and drink a cup, after which they sat and waited patiently for the French.

Philip advanced and ordered his 15,000 Genoese cross-bowmen to attack, but they were weary after marching six leagues and refused to go forward. Then came a storm of rain which wet and slackened their bowstrings. When the storm ceased the Genoese were persuaded to advance, and as they got near to the English line they set off loud shouts to scare their enemy. The English remained silent, but advanced one step, took their bows from their cases in which they had been protected from the rain, and shot quickly a thick cloud of arrows. The Genoese rapidly retreated and upset the ranks of the troops behind them. Whilst this commotion proceeded the English bowmen poured their arrows in relentlessly, wounding the horses, and increasing confusion. The Counts of Alencon and Flanders made a simultaneous attack on the Black Prince and a body of German and Savoyard knights broke through the bowmen and engaged in hand to hand fighting with the Prince's men-at-arms. The Prince was in difficulties and William de Bohun rushed to his support. A fierce battle ensued.

The Prince killed King John of Bohemia, whose arms were ostrich feathers with the motto "Ich dien" (I serve) which were taken by the Black Prince, and ever since have been the arms of the Princes of Wales. James, the King of Majorica, fell by the hands of that incomparable warrior, William de Bohun. The Counts of Alencon and Flanders were also slain.

Philip of France retreated from the field on a borrowed horse, defeated and demoralized, and thus ended the battle of Crecy.

After the battle William accompanied the King to the siege of Calais. A French army approached and William went out against them, slaying a large number, the remainder fleeing.

Two Cardinals appointed by the Pope endeavoured to procure a truce between the English and French Kings. Four lords from each side were nominated to attempt to find a solution. Those representing England were, William de Bohun, Earl of Northampton, the Earl of Derby, Lord Reginald Cobham, and Sir Walter Manny. Their efforts were unsuccessful, the Cardinals departed, and the English and French forces dispersed from Calais.

Edward wished to secure the friendship of Flanders and hoped to marry his daughter Isabella to the young Count of Flanders. Philip of France also had ideas of marrying his nominee to the Count. Edward sent William de Bohun and the Earls of Arundel and Cobham as ambassadors to the Flemings. They stressed the fact that the manufactories of Flanders were dependent upon England for supplies of wool. The Count would not agree because his father had been killed by the English, but the Flemings imprisoned him until he promised to accept the marriage. The Count, however, escaped, and joined the French.

Edward's large army had remained in France and, as the French army retreated, they advanced through Picardy towards Rheims. William de Bohun had rejoined the army and his brother Humphrey was also present. Much booty was taken.

In June 1347, the Earls of Northampton and Pembroke put to sea and near Crotoye they defeated and dispersed a French fleet going to the support of Calais.

Calais surrendered to Edward in August, and shortly after he returned to England.

Another attempt was made by the Pope to secure peace, and Edward sent a commission including William de Bohun to meet the French at Avignon. They, however, met midway between Calais and St. Omar where terms were agreed and a treaty of peace signed.

In 1348/9 Edward concerned himself with securing better conditions for the wellbeing of the country, and he passed statutes for the keeping of the peace and the hire of labourers.

At the end of 1349 William de Bohun was created a knight of the Garter. The order had been instituted by King Edward III.

A large Spanish fleet was sent to attack England, in 1350, and they assembled in the harbour of Sluys in Flanders. The English fleet was at anchor off Sandwich, where the King embarked accompanied by the Black Prince, John of Gaunt, then only ten years old, and William and Humphrey de Bohun, with other Earls. The King himself was on the ship "Cog Thomas". He was in a good humour, dressed in a black velvet jacket with black beaver hat. His minstrels played and sang. The battle of L'Espagnoles-sur-Mer was then fought and though the English were greatly outnumbered they defeated and beat off the Spaniards. The combat was unique in British naval history. Not only were the chief nobility and knights present, but the King and his heir led the battle in person

In October 1350, William was made Warden of the Scottish Marches, and the King instructed him and the High Sheriff of Northumberland, who had custody of King David of Scotland, to take David back to Scotland in an endeavour to secure his throne again. The Scots were not strong enough to meet the English in open battle so they tried ambushes and other finesses to gain an advantage, but William was too expert a captain to be caught by these stratagems. Owing to David's unpopularity with his countrymen the venture was unsuccessful.

William was appointed Admiral of the Fleet in the North, and from 1351 to 1354 he was occupied with affairs in Scotland, but he came south in 1353 to join his brother Humphrey in attending the Parliament summoned by the King at Westminster.

Edward again took a force to France in 1355. The Duke of Lancaster, William de Bohun, Earl of Northampton, and Lord Walter Manny carried out negotiations with the French for a truce, and offered that King Edward himself would fight the King of France personally to save the shedding of further blood to decide their rights. If this was not acceptable the three knights would fight three French knights. Both offers were rejected and as the French could not be tempted to fight a temporary truce was arranged.

As Edward heard that the Scots were again moving, and had reached Berwick, he hastily returned to London, marshalled his forces, and proceeded north, William de Bohun accompanying him. Negotiations for a truce took place in 1356, and William was left at Carlisle in command of the forces whilst he arranged the truce with the Earl of Douglas. He was a witness at Roxburgh to the surrender by Edward Baliol of his claims to Scotland.

The King once more took an army to France in 1359, in which Humphrey and William de Bohun were present. After several successful sorties the Treaty of Bretagne was signed on the 8th May 1360, and William de Bohun was a witness. That was William's last service for his King, for shortly after his return to England he died on 16th September 1360, at the age of forty-eight, and he was buried in Walden Abbey, Essex, at the north of the presbytery. The King, whom he had served so faithfully, provided a gilt cloth for his funeral. William despite his activity in military affairs had not forgotten to be charitable and had been a benefactor to Walden and Dore Abbeys, Prittlewell Priory, and the hospital of St. Bartholomew at Gloucester. His wife had predeceased him in 1356.

Thus passed probably the most outstanding de Bohun, William, Earl of Northampton, Constable of England, and Knight of the Garter.

In the following year, on the 15th October 1361, Humphrey de Bohun, Earl of Hereford and Essex, and Knight of the Garter, died at his castle at Pleshy, unmarried and without issue. He was buried at Friars Augustine, London, before the High Altar. His will was proved by the Archibishop of Canterbury five days after his death. He desired burial without pomp, and to be attended by one Bishop and the common people. To his nephew, Humphrey, the son of William, he bequeathed a nouche of gold surrounded by large pearls with a ruby between four pearls and three diamonds, and a cross of gold in which was a piece of the true cross of our Lord. He directed that a chaplain should be sent to Jerusalem for his mother, his father, and himself, and a good loyal man was to be sent to Pomfret to offer at the tomb of Thomas, late Earl of Lancaster, 40/–d.

In 1344–5 when there was a lull in the country's military campaigns Humphrey spent some time at Caldicot Castle. There is an entry in the accounts at the Public Record Office that Henry de Churchesdon, the Earl's receiver at Brecon had sent considerable sums of money at regular intervals to the Earls Keepers of the Wardrobe, Geoffrey att Church, and Robert de Horsindon, at Caldicot Castle where the Earl was in residence.

Matthew Owen, in his "Story of Breconshire", stated that the burgesses of Brecon must have had cause to hate the memory of the ninth Humphrey de Bohun for he deprived them of their old rights and revoked grants and charities given by his ancestors. He further described him as a peevish old bachelor. It must be remembered, however, that he was only fifty-two years of age when he died, and he had spent nearly all his life from an early age in the service of his country. By his will he also gave 100 marks to Brecon Priory and £10 a year to the Friars to pray for him.

The de Bohun estates were then committed to the King's keeping until he granted them to the next heir.

Humphrey de Bohun (*Tenth*)

When William de Bohun died, in 1360, his heir was his son Humphrey (Tenth) who immediately succeeded his father as Earl of Northampton. He was born on the 25th March 1342, and was, therefore, eighteen years of age when he was created Earl. When his uncle Humphrey (Ninth) died without issue in 1361, he was the next of kin and also succeeded to the Earldoms of Hereford and Essex. He was thus one of the greatest landowners and wealthiest men in the country.

Early in 1362 whilst in his nonage he went on a pilgrimage beyond the seas, leaving Richard, Earl of Arundel, his guardian in England, Wales, and Ireland.

He was present at the confirmation of the treaty between Edward III and the King of Castile in February 1363, and on the following 5th May, having come of age, he did homage to the King for his father's and uncle's lands.

He was created Constable of England, and in 1365 he was nominated a Knight of the Garter.

Humphrey married Joan, daughter of Richard Fitzalan, Earl of

Arundel, for which he obtained Papal dispensation as they were related in the fourth degree.

In 1366 the King appointed Humphrey as his ambassador to arrange a treaty of marriage between his son Prince Lionel and the Lady Viotanta the daughter of the Lord of Milan. Humphrey successfully concluded the arrangements for the betrothal and the marriage took place in 1368.

The King sent his son John, Duke of Lancaster, with a force including Humphrey de Bohun, in 1369, to Calais to threaten the French, but the latter outnumbered the English seven to one so the King had to send for a further force under the Earl of Warwick. When they appeared at Calais the French withdrew.

In 1371, the King sent Humphrey to the continent, accompanied by the King's sixteen year old son, Thomas of Woodstock, to confer with the Duke of Bretagne. They were attacked by the Flemings on the way but defeated them, capturing the Flemish Admiral, Heer Van John Peterson. They then went on to Brest where they met the Duke.

Humphrey retired to his estates and died at Pleshy, on the 16th January 1373, age thirty-one years. His will dated 12th June 1372, shewed that he was possessed of Caldicot. He was buried in Walden Abbey at the feet of his father on the north side of the presbytery.

Matthew Owen records that Humphrey restored to the people of Brecon the rights which his uncle had taken away from them.

Humphrey's widow, Joan, had an assignment of dower on the 26th July 1372. She repaired and adorned the nave of Walden Abbey and roofed it with lead. She also rebuilt the belfry and shewed great kindness to the brethren by providing them with bread, wine, and vestments on saints days. She died in 1419 and was buried in the Abbey.

Humphrey's co-heirs were his two daughters Alianore, aged seven and Mary aged three or four.

Thomas Woodstock and Alianore

On the death of Humphrey de Bohun (Tenth) his two young daughters, Alianore and Maria, became wards of King Edward III, and he placed them in the care of his youngest son, Thomas Woodstock, in 1376, when he was twenty-one years of age. Alianore was then aged ten and Maria six. Within a few months Thomas married Alianore.

Thomas, the sixth and youngest surviving son of the King by Queen Philippa, was born at Woodstock in 1355.

At the age of six months he was appointed Guardian of the Kingdom whilst his father was absent in France.

In 1359 the marshals of his household were appointed.

Queen Philippa, who had done so many acts of piety and charity fell mortally sick in 1369, and died at Windsor, where the King and her young son Thomas were at her bedside.

Just before his death in 1377 the King gave Thomas, in support of his status, the custody of nine manors in the counties of Lincoln, Oxford, Gloucester, Essex, and Wiltshire.   He also had the third penny (£40.10.10.) of the county of Essex which was part of Humphrey de Bohun's estate, and £20 per annum from the Northampton estate of the late William de Bohun. All these were part of the de Bohun lands which were in the King's hands during the minority of the heirs. Thomas was also appointed Constable of England as long as the King had the wardship of the de Bohun lands, and he was granted 1,000 marks a year to maintain this office.

The Black Prince died of fever in 1376 and the King declared to his remaining sons, including Thomas, that Richard the son of the Black Prince was to be the heir to the throne.

Alianore was referred to as the wife of Thomas in official documents of 1377.   In the same year King Edward III died, and his sons John of Gaunt, Edmund of Langley, and Thomas of Woodstock, followed the hearse to the Royal Chapel of Westminster Abbey, where he was interred.

When Thomas was knighted on the 23rd April 1377, the wardrobe accounts shew that he received 10 ells of scarlet cloth etc.

Richard II, on his accession, confirmed Alianore's estates which included Caldicot upon Thomas, and created him Constable of England during the King's pleasure.

At the coronation of Richard on the 16th July 1377, Thomas carried the sceptre and crown, and on the same day the King created him Earl of Buckingham, girding him with a sword and granting him an annuity of £1,000 out of the exchequer, with £20 more from the issues of the County of Buckingham.   His office of Constable was continued with the additional one of General of the Forces of England at sea.

On the 28th August there was intelligence that the Spanish fleet had put into Sluys, and was to threaten the Kent coast. Thomas and his brother Edmund frustrated this plan, and later captured eight of the Spanish ships off Brest, and in April 1378, he took over the Castle of Brest.

In 1379 it was ordered that his annuity of £1,000 should be taken from alien priories.

Thomas, by virtue of his office of Constable, presided at the trial for treason against Sir John Annesley.

He was nominated as a Knight of the Garter, on 23rd April, 1380.

On the 26th October the Sheriff of Essex was ordered to pay to Thomas and his wife £40.10.10. as the fee of the Earl of Essex, and he thus became Earl.

Alianore's sister, Maria, was still unmarried, and it was the wish of Thomas that she should remain so, thus enabling him to enjoy the whole of the estates of the Earl of Hereford. He took upon himself the tutelage of his sister-in-law and had her instructed in doctrine in the hope that she would become a nun.   Thomas's brother, the Duke of Lancaster, however, foresaw the advantages of marrying his son Henry to Maria.

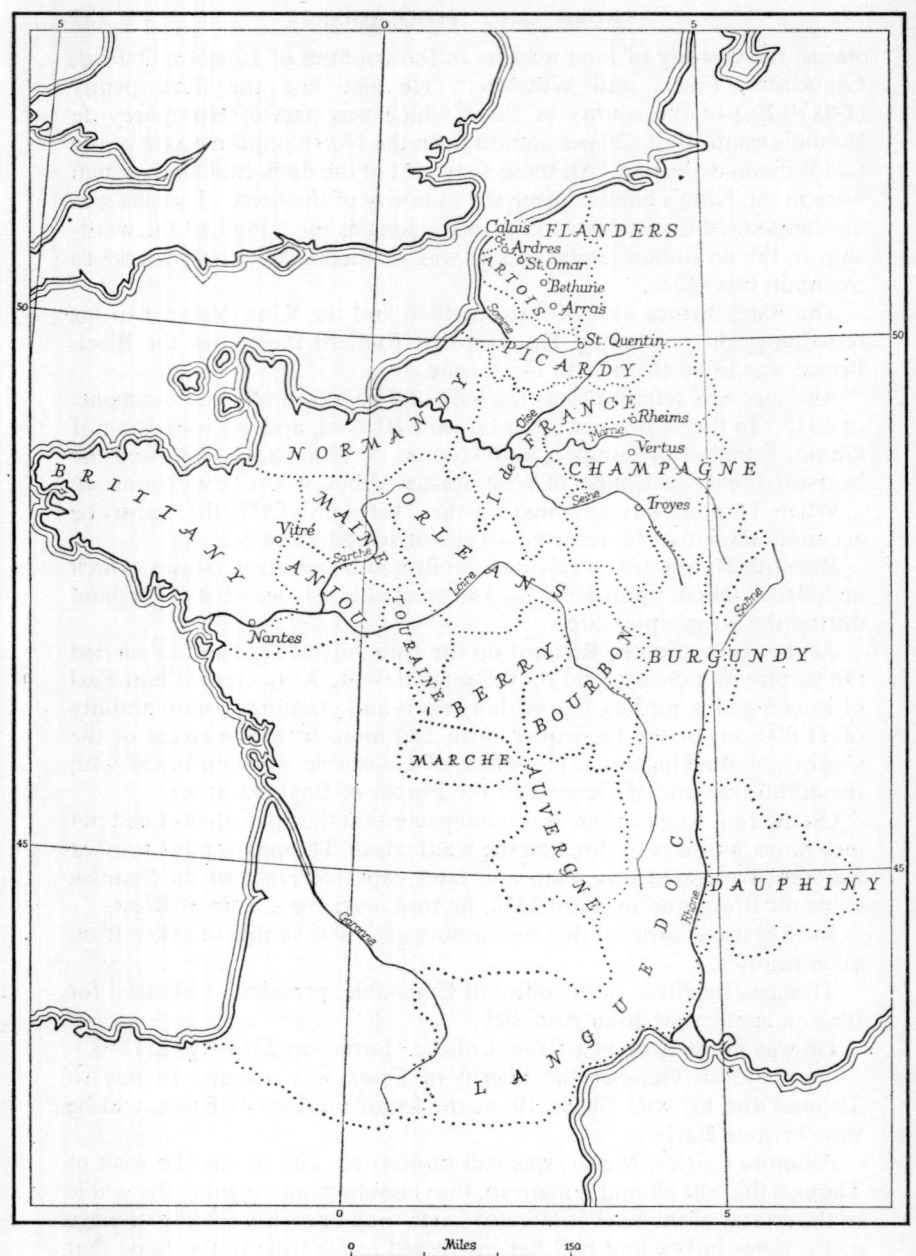

MAP OF WOODSTOCK'S CAMPAIGN IN FRANCE
drawn by Bryan Woodfield

THE WOODSTOCK COAT OF ARMS

WOODSTOCK'S BIBLE

Reproduced by permission of the British Museum

The Duke considered that with her very large estates and high birth, she was eminently suitable to be his daughter-in-law. According to Froissart he waited until Thomas was in France and then he persuaded the Lady Arundel to aid him by inviting Maria to stay with her at Arundel, where the marriage was consummated between Maria and Henry of Bolingbroke. Thomas then had to divide an inheritance which he had considered wholly his, and he never after loved the Duke of Lancaster as he had hitherto done.

In July 1380, the King appointed Thomas as the commander of an expedition to meet the request of the Duke of Brittany for assistance. He was accompanied by many barons, knights, and squires supported by a considerable force of men-at-arms and archers.

Thomas was well received by the garrison at Calais, and after staying there for two days he marched on into France. His force arrived at Ardres but the garrison, secure in their Castle, made no attempt to fight. Thomas then marched on to St. Omer, which was a handsome place, but again the French garrison remained behind the walls, so he proceeded with his advance past Bethune and Arras to Clery-sur-Somme, where he stayed for three days before continuing to St. Quintin. The inhabitants of Rheims refused to provide provisions for the English army so Thomas laid waste to many villages surrounding the town and took a large number of sheep. He then marched on to Vertus, in Champagne, where he lodged in the Abbey whilst his force destroyed the town.

They next came before Troyes where the Duke of Bergundy was quartered. Thomas summoned the Duke to bring his army out on to the open plain to do battle, but the challenge was not accepted, and Thomas again moved on without resistance. He passed a number of towns, crossed the Sarthe, and ultimately arrived at Vitre in Brittany. There he met the representatives of the Duke, who informed Thomas that they were having trouble with the citizens of Nantes. Thomas made plans to attack the town, but to his disgust the Duke of Brittany retired, so Thomas remained encamped for some weeks near the town.

The Duke of Brittany was in the meantime secretly endeavouring to secure a peace treaty with France, and when this was successfully completed Thomas, enraged and indignant, returned to England in April 1381. It had been an amazing campaign. For nine months Thomas and his army had marched unhindered through many miles of French territory.

When he reached England he found the country in the throes of the rebellions of the peasants under the leadership of Wat Tyler, and he crushed Jack Straw's rising in Essex. It was thought that he had some sympathy with the peasants, and he retired for a time to his castle in Wales. He sent word to William Somery, his reeve at Caldicot, to make preparations for his coming, and the following is the account of work done, and expense incurred, from St. Michael's day 1382, to the following St. Michael's day:

D

	£	s.	d.
2 oaks from Fryth Wood, Chepstow for making anew one outside bridge of the castle		4	6
Carrying the same		4	6
Carrying old timber from the mill		1	6
1 carpenter to make the bridge	1	3	4
Repairing 2 walls round the bridge by mason		6	0
Carrying stone for the same		2	0
Beer for the men raising the bridge			6
60 iron spikings for the gate		1	4
1 carpenter to mend gate		3	4
Doorbands with spikings		4	1
1 roofer roofing all defects of 4 towers with shingles	1	13	4
2000 shingles bought for the same		16	0
Carrying same from Newport		4	0
3000 shingle nails		10	0
300 laths		2	6
400 lath nails			10
1 carpenter to make the roof of one new stair at the door of the lord's chamber of timber		8	0
Carrying timber for same		1	6
Beer for the men helping with the stair			4
60 laths for same			5
300 lath nails for same			7½
1 Tyler to tile the same		3	4
Collecting moss for the same work		3	4
Lime for the same with carriage		3	8
7 men hired for 2 weeks to clean the houses Within the castle against the lord's coming		6	8
Pulling down ivy from Countess Tower		2	0
Mending racks and mangers in the stable near the outer gate of the castle against the lord's coming and 2 carpenters hired for 2 weeks to do the work		8	4
Carrying and collecting stone and timber for same		5	5
Spikings for the mangers			8
1 staple with hinges for stable door			6
6 locks for various houses		3	9
Roofing the said stable with straw		8	4
Collecting timber for same		1	0
Clearing a ditch to a breadth of 8 ft and a length of 40 perches between the long stable and the pond		8	0
Sum	£9	3	3½

This expenditure was incurred on the castle before Thomas Wood-stock had built the large square tower, and the entrance gate referred to was the old de Bohun entrance.

The Earl and his Countess Alianore, together with his retinue, duly made their visit to Caldicot, and whilst there Thomas decided to recon-struct parts of the castle and make additions, which are described in the chapter on the Castle.

Thomas left Caldicot in 1383 when he was appointed by the King to lead an expedition of 1,000 lancers and 2,000 archers against the Scots. The latter retired and many of the English force perished from cold and hunger. They, therefore, returned to England without accom-plishing anything.

In May 1384, Thomas accompanied his brother, the Duke of Lan-caster, to France to treat with the Earl of Flanders. At this time the King made him a grant of St. Briavels Castle for life.

Also in 1384 a Carmelite friar made a charge against the Duke of Lancaster of aspiring to the crown. Thomas greatly incensed, broke into the King's chamber, and swore bitterly that he would kill any man who should charge his brother of treason. The King was so frightened that he remained silent.

Thomas marched with the King against the Scots in 1385, and on the 6th August he was created Duke of Gloucester at Teviotdale. This was confirmed by charter of Parliament sitting in London on the 20th October, when the King invested him by girding on the sword and placing upon his head a cap and gold circlet. He then took the new Duke's homage, and ordered him to take a higher seat among the peers in Parliament. He thus had the three titles of Gloucester, Buckingham, and Essex, and was also Constable of England. He received rents of £60 per annum from the City of Gloucester, and a further £2,000 per annum was assigned to him for his services in Scotland.

The affairs of the country were mismanaged by the King and his favourite Michael de la Pole, Earl of Suffolk, who had been appointed chancellor. At the request of a deputation consisting of the Duke of Gloucester, the Earl of Arundel, and the Bishop of Ely, the King met Parliament and agreed to their petition that the Earl of Suffolk should be convicted and imprisoned at Windsor. As a result the Duke incurred the enmity of the King, who, however, soon secured the release of Suffolk.

Parliament seeing the mischief done by the extravagance of the King's officers chose fourteen lords, including the Duke of Gloucester, to administer the government.

The people were extremely partial to the Duke, whom they regarded as a valiant, wise, and discreet man.

The King now had a new favourite in de Vere, whom he had created Duke of Ireland. He prompted the King in his lavish expenditure, which he had obtained from harsh taxes. Upon advice from the Duke of

Gloucester, the Londoners marched upon the King at Windsor with a petition. Their spokesman was Simon de Sudbury, a man of sense and oratory, and he asked for wiser government and better conditions for the people. The Duke of Gloucester was present and advised his nephew to accede to the requests made to him. The King agreed to a new administration, included in which was the Duke, and a number of the evil counsellors were executed.

The King, with the connivance of the Duke of Ireland, continued to disregard the wishes of Parliament, and in November 1387, Thomas, with the Earls of Arundel and Warwick, assembled a large force to threaten the King's favourites.

The King had left London and joined the Duke of Ireland who had gathered a large force to march upon London where the Duke of Gloucester was quartered. When Thomas heard that his enemies were making for Oxford he set forth to meet them with a force equipped with the assistance of the Mayor of London. The encounter took place at Radcote Bridge, in Oxfordshire, and the Duke of Ireland was totally defeated. He forsook his troops, fled, and eventually reached Holland. Thomas was compassionate to the demoralized troops of his enemy and ordered that none be slain who did not make actual resistance.

The Duke of Gloucester then marched to London, where he was welcomed by the citizens, and he took possession of the Tower, imprisoning the King there.

The Duke remained in power for more than a year and instituted reforms for better government. He, and the Earls who sided with him, obtained a grant of £20,000 for themselves.

The alterations and improvement made by the Duke to Caldicot Castle were now completed, and it is probable that he and Alianore went there to see the splendid result. There are two stones in the foundations of the buildings added by the Duke which bear the names of "Thomas" and "Alianore."

On the 3rd June 1388, Thomas was appointed Justice of Chester.

In 1389 the King again secured control of the administration, and he removed the Duke of Gloucester and the Earl of Warwick from office. He also recalled his uncle John of Gaunt from the continent with the hope that it would curb the influence of Thomas. In the same year the Duke had the honour of composing the differences between the English and Welsh scholars at Oxford.

Parliament confirmed the grant of St. Briavels Castle and the Forest of Dean to the Duke, in 1390, and he also secured the reversions of Brustwick in Holderness, and the Castle of Oakham, with the Shrievalty of Rutland, which had at one time been part of the de Bohun estates.

The King ordered feasts and tournaments at Michaelmas, 1390, in a large square at London called Smithfield, at which the King's three uncles were present.

The Duke was restless in the following year and he set out to treat with the Master of the Teutonic Order in Prussia, but the winds were contrary and he was driven back from the coasts of Norway and Denmark, and landed at Tynemouth. He then returned to his castle at Pleshy.

He was appointed for a short time as Lieutenant of Ireland, in 1392, but he returned to London to investigate disturbances in the City of London. He interceded with the King on behalf of the citizens who had incurred the King's displeasure.

In 1393 the Dukes of Gloucester and Lancaster went to France to arrange a peace treaty, but they were only able to extend the truce.

Thomas and Alianore had a license in 1394 to found a college of priests at Pleshy, and in the same year he accompanied the King to Ireland. He did not, however, stay there long as the King sent him back to Westminster to open Parliament, and ask for a further grant of money.

The King's wife, Anne, had died, and as he was wishful to marry again, Thomas informed the King that he had a marriageable daughter, saying it would give him great pleasure if the King would choose her, but Richard considered that they were too closely related.

Many of the happening during the reigns of Edward III and Richard II are recorded in the chronicles of Jean Froissart, a French poet and historian, who was born in 1337. He came to England where Queen Philippa, the wife of Edward III was his patroness. He spent much time at the English Court, and he had a close contact with the chief characters and events of the time. He had many conversations with the Duke of Gloucester, and spent some time as a guest at Pleshy Castle. Froissart said this of the Duke: "I ensure you this Duke of Gloucester is a marvellous minded man, proud, and presumptuous. He would rule all himself, and he is so beloved by the commons that whatever he sayeth they will incline to him."

The King had decided that Isabella, the young eldest daughter of the King of France would be a suitable wife, and he sent the Earl of Rutland to make arrangements for the betrothal.

Froissart records that however much others might be pleased, it was not so with the Duke of Gloucester for he saw plainly by the marriage that peace would be established between the two kingdoms which sorely displeased him, unless it was such a peace as would redound to the honour of England. He dare not express his opinions to his brother the Duke of Lancaster as the latter was in the King's party and well satisfied with the proposed marriage.

The King of England decided to go to France to meet the French King, between Calais and St. Omer, to discuss a new peace treaty, or a long-time truce, between the two kingdoms, and orders were issued for arrangements to be made for the King's voyage and residence in

Calais. Many lords accompanied him, and the Duke and Duchess of Gloucester, with their children, were invited by the King to be in his party. The English lords were entertained in great splendour, especially the Duke of Gloucester, to soften his temper, which the French knew was against them. They were very subtle but their efforts failed, and the Duke of Burgundy said to his council: "We shall never succeed until we gain over the Duke of Gloucester. As long as he lives there will not be any peace with England for he will ever find some cause of quarrel, and renew the hatred of the people of both countries, and were it not for the amiable qualities of the King of England, in good truth, he should never have our cousin as his wife."

The Duke, however, was ultimately softened by the King promising to create his son, Humphrey, Earl of Rochester with an annual revenue of £2,000 and to present the Duke with 50,000 nobles on his return to England.

The peace terms were agreed and the marriage arrangements carried through.

The Duke was still not kindly disposed to the French, and he expressed his feelings to Sir John Lackingay, his confidential adviser, "They are so full of vanity and presumption that they can never bring to a successful issue anything they undertake. This has been apparent during the wars of my father and brother, the Prince of Wales, for they never could obtain a victory over our men. I have not forgotten my last expedition through France. We entered through Calais, and continued our march throughout the country without meeting anyone to oppose or offer us battle. Our King raises heavy taxes on the merchants who are greatly discontented, and he squanders the money, no one knows how, and thus is the kingdom of England impoverished. Things cannot long remain in this state before the people will redress them. Lackingay, all you have just heard me say consider the truth."

The Duke of Lancaster had married his mistress, Catherine Swynford, and the Duke and Duchess of Gloucester highly resented this affront to the nobility.

In 1397, being aggrieved at the restoration of Brest and Cherbourg to the Duke of Brittany, and the loss of all the conquests of Edward III, except Calais, the Duke of Gloucester retired, with his family, to Pleshy, pleading ill health. It was said that he had proposed to the Earls of Arundel and Warwick that they should overthrow the King, but they were betrayed to the King by the Earl Marshal, who was present.

The King confided in the Dukes of Lancaster and York saying "How am I to act. I am daily informed that your brother, the Duke of Gloucester, is determined to seize me." The dukes replied "Have a little patience. Our brother talks frequently of things he cannot execute."

The dukes saw, however, that friction was increasing, and, to avoid being involved by either party, they left the King's household and repaired to their own castles away from London.

The King decided to act in the absence of his uncles, and after disclosing his intention to the Earl Marshal, and issuing a proclamation to the people on the 15th July, he set forth to Pleshy to apprehend his uncle Thomas, thinking it was more advisable to destroy than be destroyed.

Froissart describes the happenings which occurred as follows: "The King came under pretence of recreation and hunting to a manor called Havering Bower, in the County of Essex, about 20 miles from Pleshy, where the Duke resided. The King then set out one afternoon from Havering, not taking all his attendants, and came to Pleshy about five o'clock. It was fine warm weather, and when he entered the castle of Pleshy they were surprised to hear, 'Here comes the King.' The Duke of Gloucester had just supped, for he was very temperate, and sat but a little while at table, either at dinner or supper. He came out to meet the King in the court of the Castle, and paid his respects to him as to his sovereign for he was a nobleman of great politeness. The Duchess and the children did the same. A table was presently set in the hall for the King, and after a short supper he said to the Duke, 'Good uncle, order your horse to be saddled; you must go with me to London, for tomorrow I am to meet the Londoners, and we shall there find my uncles of Lancaster and York without fail. I mean to take your advice on a petition they are to present to me.' The Duke, suspecting no harm, obeyed him forthwith. The King took leave of the Duchess and her children, and mounted his horse. The Duke did the same and set out from Pleshy. They took the road to Bondelay as being most level and to avoid the town of Brendwode. They rode hard as the King was in haste to reach London, and all the way talked with his uncle till they came to Stratford, on the River Thames. When the King came to this place, where an ambush was laid, he rode on before, and left his uncle behind. Then came up the Earl Marshal behind him with a great troop of men and horses, and sprung on the Duke, saying 'I arrest you by the King's order.' The Duke saw he was betrayed and called aloud to the King. The King did not turn back, but rode on fast, followed by his people."

Immediately after his apprehension the Earl Marshal conveyed Thomas to the Thames where he was set aboard a ship, prepared of purpose, and brought to the 'Princes Inn' at Calais. When the Duke found he was deprived of his attendants he was much alarmed. He asked the Earl Marshal to give him more freedom to move around, but the Earl said 'My Lord I dare not comply with your request, on pain of death.' He then saw that his death was imminent, and he called for a priest, with great calmness and resignation. He said Mass and made confession. As he was about to dine, four of the servants of the Earl Marshal cast feather beds upon him and smothered him to death.

William Rykyll, a Justice of the Common Pleas, interviewed the Duke before he died, and extracted a confession which included the following clauses:

I Thomas Woodstock, the 8th day of September, the year of my Lord and King 21 (1397), by the virtue of a commission of my Lord the King, the same year directed to William Rykyll, Justice, the which is comprehended more plainly in the foresaid commission, and foreasmuch as I knew afterwards that I had done wrong, and taken upon me more than I ought to do, I submit me to my Lord and crave his mercy and grace. Also in that time that I came armed into my Lord's presence, and into his palace. However, I did it for dread of my life. I know for certain that I did evil.

"Also that I took my Lord's letter of his messengers and opened them without his leave. I know that I did evil.

"Also that I slandered my Lord. I acknowledge that I did evil and wickedly in that I spake it unto him in slanderous-wise in audience of other folk. I meant no evil, nevertheless I acknowledge that I did evil.

"And, therefore, I beseech my liege and sovereign Lord the King that he will of his grace accept me to his mercy as I put my life and body at his will, beseeching his high Lordship that he will have compassion and pity."

On the 21st September, the 4th day of Parliament, an order was sent to the captain of Calais to produce his prisoner to take trial, to which he replied, on the 24th September, that the Duke was dead. The Duke's confession was read in Parliament, and he was declared guilty of treason, and his estates and goods forfeited.

Duchess Alianore was surprised and distressed when the news of the Duke's apprehension reached her at Pleshy. She consulted John Lackingay on the measures to pursue, and he advised her to send directly to her brothers-in-law of Lancaster and York, who might intercede with the King. The Duchess followed this advice. They replied that the King dared not act contrary to justice and reason.

The King left the Tower for Eltham, where he stayed. His actions surprised, and were resented by the Londoners. Nobody, however, dared oppose the King.

After the four men had murdered the Duke, which occurred on the 15th September according to the Calendar of Patent Rolls, they closed his eyes, and placed his naked dead body between two sheets with the head on a pillow, and covered him with furred robes. They then reported to the Earl Marshal that the Duke had been seized with apoplexy. The story was circulated publicly and some believed it, but others did not. The Earl Marshal and all the other knights put on mourning.

The news of the Duke's death was soon known throughout England and the continent. The French were joyful as the Duke had always been their opponent, but the commoners of England were very sorrowful.

The Duke's body was honourably embalmed at Calais and put in a leaden coffin with an outward one of wood, and transported by sea to England. The vessel landed at Hadleigh Castle on Thames, and thence the body was conveyed by chariot to Pleshy where it was placed in the church which the Duke had founded in honour of the Holy Trinity.

Alianore and her children were sorely grieved when the body arrived, and they had further cause of affliction when the Earl of Arundel, the uncle of the Duchess, was publicly beheaded in Cheapside in the presence of the King.

The Earl of Warwick escaped by the intercession of the Earl of Salisbury, who pleaded his great age.

The King ordered prayers for the soul of the Duke, and, on the 14th October, ordered that his body should be given to Alianore for burial at Westminster Abbey where it was interred in the Chapel of St. Edmund the King and St. Thomas of Canterbury.

The Duke possessed a copy of "Wickliffe's Bible," now in the British Museum.

The ancient historians concur in representing the Duke as an inexorable patriot. Tyrrell wrote that he was of person, very comely, majestic, virtuous, and valiant, undertaking the greatest dangers where he saw his own honour, and the public good, concerned. He was not much beloved by his own brothers, much less by most of the nobility. On the other hand he was highly beloved and honoured by the common people, because he stood up for their liberties.

After the death of the Duke the King took possession of his estates, and in accordance with custom he had the wardship of the Duke's son, Humphrey, who was under age. He placed young Humphrey and the latter's cousin, Arundel, about his person. Alianore and her daughters were placed with the Queen.

On the 18th December, 1397, the King issued a writ to Richard Whittyngton, Mayor of London, to seize all the Duke's goods and chattels to the King's use allowing the Duchess out of it goods and chattels to the amount of £180.18.0.

Alianore spent her widowhood in seclusion and died in the Minoresses Convent at Aldgate on the 3rd October 1399. In her will she desired to be buried by her husband, and made bequests to the Convent and also to the Prior and Convent of Llantony (Gloucester) and the Church and Abbey at Walden where her father Humphrey de Bohun was buried. She was buried in St. Edmund's Chapel, in Westminster Abbey, under a monument of gray marble on which was inlaid her figure in brass. Her dress is a loose plaited gown with sleeves and mittens buttoned at the sides. Over her is a canopy of three arches. In the middle one is a swan collared and gorged. In the others are the de Bohun and the Fitzwalter coats of arms.

Trokelowe wrote of Alianore that in prudence, modesty, and holiness she surpassed all the women of her day.

Shakespeare in scene II of King Richard II described the grief of Alianore in her conversation with John of Gaunt, "Thomas, my dear lord, my life, my Gloucester, is hacked down by envy's hand and murder's bloody axe."

Richard took young Humphrey, son of Woodstock, and Henry, son and heir of Henry Bolingbroke, to Ireland, where they were imprisoned in the Castle of Trim.

The King's misgovernment resulted in an insurrection in 1399, and Henry Bolingbroke, son of John of Gaunt, was summoned from exile on the continent. With an army provided by the citizens of London he marched to meet Richard at Bristol. Richard was deserted by his followers and he was forced to resign the crown and Kingdom to Henry.

Henry IV was made King of England by Parliament on 30th September 1399. On his accession he immediately recalled his son and nephew, and would have restored Humphrey to his father's honours, but Humphrey died of plague on his return, aged about seventeen years. He was buried in Walden Abbey.

Henry, in his first Parliament caused an inquisition to be made into the Duke's death, and it was found that he had been fraudulently and wickedly smothered on the King's orders by Thomas Mowbray, Duke of Norfolk. The actual murderers were Serle, Fraunceys, Rogers, and Denneys, together with Cok of the Chamber, and Hall kept the door. All the while they wept and prayed for his soul.

Anne and Edmund Stafford

After the death of Humphrey there were three surviving daughters of Thomas and Alianore. The eldest was Anne who first married Thomas, the fourth Earl of Stafford, but he died in 1393, before the marriage was consummated. She then married his brother, Edmund, the fifth Earl, by the King's special licence. He was a Knight of the Garter and did homage for Caldicot in 1402. Edmund was killed at Shrewsbury in the same year when siding with the King against insurgents. Anne finally married William Bourchier, Count of Eu.

The third daughter, Isabel, was a nun at the Minoresses Convent in Aldgate.

On the 20th June 1400, King Henry ordered the deliverance of Caldicot Castle to Joan, who was the second daughter of Thomas and Alianore, but by the 12th November, following, she had died, and the castle and manor returned to the keeping of the King until he granted the estates to Joan's sister Anne. Joan was betrothed to Gilbert Talbot, but she died before the marriage took place.

King Henry V

After the death of Edmund Stafford, his wife Anne continued to hold her mother's share of the de Bohun lands, and in 1419 she petitioned

King Henry V for a partition of the estates between herself and the King, as joint heirs. Parliament decided on the 2nd May 1421, that the partition should be made, and that Henry should choose his portion. In doing this he claimed Caldicot, the Parliamentary Roll describing it as "The Castle and Manor of Caldicot and Newton with the members, £26.13.4."

The King appointed Morgan ap Madoc as his coroner and forester at Caldicot and Newton.

There are entries in the records of the Duchy of Lancaster of expenditure on the Castle during the reigns of Henry V and Henry VI, covering such items as roofing buildings, repairing bridges, and general maintenance.

Katherine of Valois

On the 1st September 1422, Henry died, and Caldicot became a part of the jointure of his wife Katherine of Valois. The official record of this is dated 9th November 1422, and is described as "Castle and Manor of Caldicot and members in Wales to the value of £53.6.8."

Katherine, some time after Henry's death, was married secretly to Owen Tudor, a Welsh squire of her household, who had come from Anglesey, and was a descendant of a former Welsh King. They had two sons, Edmund and Jasper Tudor. Edmund married Margaret Beaufort, great grand-daughter of John of Gaunt by Catherine Swynford. It was from Edmund and Margaret that the Tudor dynasty descended.

King Henry VI

Katherine died in 1437, and her son Henry VI took possession of Caldicot Castle and Manor.

He appointed John Water, a page of his chamber, as Constable, John Lewis as Receiver, and Sir William ap Thomas as Steward. The latter had already established his reputation as a conscientious and trustworthy servant as he had been appointed steward of the lordship of Abergavenny by Lady Beauchamp, in 1421, and in 1431 the Duke of York had made him steward of Usk and Caerleon. He was also granted the Castle and Manor of Raglan. These duties of William ap Thomas were the commencement of an association between his family and Caldicot for several generations.

William was reappointed steward of Caldicot for life, on the 18th May 1440, but he died in 1445, and was buried in the Priory Church, at Abergavenny, where his effigy, with that of his wife, still remains.

Henry married Margaret of Anjou when she was sixteen years old. He had an uneasy reign with the foreboding shadows of the Earl of Warwick and the Yorkist Edward hanging over him. He lost his faculties in 1453, and Edward of York came to London, but the King recovered and took over the government again. After a period of ups and downs he was taken by Edward in 1471, and placed in the Tower, where he died. Edward had, however, been proclaimed King in 1461.

In 1443 King Henry, by letters patent under the seal of the Duchy of Lancaster, granted the Castle and lordship of Caldicot, with its members and appurtenances, to Sir John Beauchamp, whose family had had associations with the area.

In 1450 the King created his half-brothers Edmund and Jasper, Earls of Richmond and Pembroke respectively. Jasper was a staunch supporter of the Lancastrian cause, and he was granted, as part of his Earldom, a number of castles and manors in South Wales. It would appear probable that he held Caldicot from 1453 until Edward IV took the Earldom from him and granted it to William Herbert.

William Herbert

Edward IV, in the first year of his reign, made the following decision: "For his services against Henry VI we grant to William Herbert the castle, manor, town and lordship of Caldicot with all its members and appurtenances in South Wales, and the marches of the same, with all rights."

William Herbert was the son of William ap Thomas, who had been the steward of the manor of Caldicot, and he would no doubt have had a sentimental attachment to the castles and manors of South Monmouthshire with which his father had been associated. He was born in 1424, and he became a strong supporter and confidant of Edward IV. William had no surname, but the King desired him to adopt one after the English fashion. Although he apparently had humble beginnings, from his grandfather who was a master-sergeant at Usk Castle, a distinguished lineage was prepared purporting to start from Herbert, a natural son of Henry I. In Wales he was called Gwilym Ddu, William the Black, from his dark complexion.

William fought for the Lancastrians in France, and was knighted by Henry VI, in 1449. He espoused the cause of the Yorkists in 1460, and helped in their victory at Northampton.

He was present at Baynards Castle, in 1461, when Edward was proclaimed King, and at the coronation he was created Baron Herbert of Raglan. He grew steadily richer, having property in London and Bristol. with his own ships plying to and fro between England and the continent.

In 1463 the year after he had obtained Caldicot, he was created Lord Herbert of Gower, and then came into contact with Margaret Beaufort, the only child of John Beaufort, First Duke of Somerset, who had married Edmund Tudor, the son of Katherine of Valois and Owen Tudor. Margaret's son Henry, later to be King Henry VII, was born in South Wales in 1457. She was present at Raglan, Caldicot, and Pembroke Castles, but it is generally accepted that the child was born at Pembroke.

With the submission of Pembroke Castle to William Herbert the custody of young Henry passed to William, and the youngster was brought up by Lady Herbert with her own children

William was a boon companion of the King and in 1466 his son, William Junior, married Mary Woodville, the Queen's sister.

William Herbert was created Earl of Pembroke in the place of Jasper Tudor, who was steadfastly supporting the Lancastrian cause.

In 1462 Herbert was elected a Knight of the Garter and a year later he was appointed Chief Justice of North Wales. In 1468 he captured Harlech from the House of Lancaster.

A great battle took place on the 26th July 1469 between Pembroke and Warwick, at Edgecot, near Banbury.

Sir Richard Herbert the younger brother of Pembroke, performed magnificent feats of prowess, passing and repassing twice unhurt through the enemy's ranks with his pole axe.

John Clappam, a servant of the Earl of Warwick, with only 500 men, bearing the standard of the Earl crying "a Warwick a Warwick" came upon Pembroke's army suddenly. The Welshmen, thinking that Warwick had come upon them with all his force, fled, and Pembroke and his brother Richard were captured. They were conveyed to Banbury. The Earl entreated for his brother's life both for his goodly personage, and also for the noble chivalry that he had shown in the field of battle. The Earl pleaded to Sir John Conyers and Clappam: "Masters, let me die for I am old, but save my brother who is young, lusty and hardy". The plea failed and both the Earl and his brother were beheaded in the Church porch. Wordsworth in his "White Doe of Rylstone" describes the incident as follows:

John Clappam that fierce esquire
A valiant man, and a name of dread
In the ruthless wars of the White and Red
Who dragged Earl Pembroke from Banbury church
And smote off his head on the stones of the porch.

Pembroke had wished to be buried beside his father at Abergavenny, but this was disregarded and his body was taken to Tintern Abbey, of which he had had the patronage with the lordship of Chepstow.

He was only forty-five years old when he died and Sir Joseph Bradney in his history of Monmouthshire reached the conclusion that he had at least twenty children, not all, however, by his wife Anne Devereaux.

William Herbert second Earl of Pembroke
William the younger, the son and heir of the Earl of Pembroke, was only about fifteen years of age when his father died, so the estates of the earl passed into the King's hands, and it was not until the 4th October 1475, that King Edward IV granted a licence for William, Earl of Pembroke to enter freely into all manors, lordships, castles, towns, townships,

lands, fee-farms, annuities, rents, services, views of frank-pledge, courts, leets, liberties, knights' fees, advowsons, and all other possessions and hereditaments which should descend to him on the death of his father, saving to the King homage and fealty.

Prior to this, in 1471, William had received the King's license to enter freely without proof of age into the offices of Chief Justice of South Wales and Chamberlain of South Wales together with all other offices in Wales and the Marches which his father had held.

In August 1471, he had been commissioned by the King to array the King's lieges of South Wales, the Counties of Worcester, Gloucester, Hereford, and Salop, and the Marches of Wales to resist Jasper Owen and other rebels there. William fought at Tewkesbury in the same year.

William was not the dominating figure that his father had been, and he does not figure in any military action after the battle of Tewkesbury although he did send forty men-at-arms, and 200 archers, in 1475, to support the King in his attack in France.

King Edward persuaded William to exchange the Earldom of Pembroke for that of Huntingdon, and as the King wished to secure a firmer position in Wales, he created his own son Earl of Pembroke. Some of the Welsh lands were surrendered for lands in Dorset and Somerset. Caldicot seems to have reverted to the Duchy of Lancaster.

At the coronation of Richard III, in 1483, William carried the Queen's sceptre, and, thereafter, he appears to have lived a life of seclusion until his death in 1491. He had married the Queen's sister, Mary Woodville, and they had one daughter, Elizabeth, who was the heir to his estates. She married Sir Charles Somerset who later held Caldicot on lease.

Richard III made a grant of the de Bohun lands to Henry Stafford, Duke of Buckingham, in 1483, but it was not approved by Parliament, and he therefore, did not have possession of Caldicot.

Sir Walter Herbert

Walter Herbert was the younger brother of William, Earl of Huntingdon, and son of William, first Earl of Pembroke. He was very active in both national and local affairs. He was knighted by King Edward in 1474 for his services in France. Walter received his commissions from the King, and Richard III ordered him to oppose the landing of the Earl of Richmond at Haverfordwest and his subsequent advance into Wales.

Walter's marriage to Anne, the daughter of the Duke of Buckingham, may have had some influence in acquiring the favour of King Richard. The latter made him a banneret during his expedition in Scotland, in 1482, for conspicuous bravery.

He later served Henry VII, and he took an active part in Welsh affairs, being steward of a number of lordships.

The Duchy of Lancaster appointed Walter steward of Caldicot Manor in 1496, and the Castle was one of his residences. He had no children by his wife Anne, but he had several by his mistress, Jenet, the daughter of Morris Llewelyn, of Magor. Through his son Thomas the Herbert family were prominent as members of the manor community at Caldicot for over 200 years.

Sir Walter died at Raglan in 1507. He was the last of the stewards appointed directly by the Duchy of Lancaster to Caldicot. Thereafter the manor and castle were subjects of leases of an agricultural nature.

III

THE LESSEES OF THE MANOR OF CALDICOT AND
NEWTON

THE first lease of the Castle and Manor of Caldicot was granted by the Duchy of Lancaster, in 1507, to Charles Somerset, the natural son of Henry Beaufort, Duke of Somerset. He was thus a male descendant of John of Gaunt. He had married Elizabeth, the daughter of William Herbert, second Earl of Pembroke, and niece of Sir Walter Herbert, both of whom had had very close associations with Caldicot, the former as Lord of the Manor, and the latter as the steward of the Duchy of Lancaster. By his marriage he became Lord Herbert and accrued the benefit of a number of Welsh lordships. He had, when Jasper Tudor died in 1495, leased the lordship of Glamorgan.

Charles Somerset was a loyal supporter of the crown, and Henry VIII confirmed his appointment as Lord Chamberlain. At the age of fifty-three he turned soldier and saw service in France. He was duly rewarded by being created the Earl of Worcester, in 1514. His wife Elizabeth died in the same year.

He rarely visited Wales and left the burden of the administration of his Welsh lordships to his son Henry. Charles died in 1526, and he was succeeded by Henry, his only son, who thus became the second Earl of Worcester. He was prominent in national affairs, sitting at the trial of the Duke of Buckingham in 1521, and later being selected as one of the champions to uphold the credit of English chivalry at the Field of the Cloth of Gold. He was also one of the peers who sat at the trial of Anne Boleyn.

The second Earl died in 1549, and his eldest son William succeeded him. He took over the lease of Caldicot Castle and the lordship of Caldicot with Newton, and became responsible for arrears which had accumulated on the lease. In 1558 he was released from his debt in consideration of his services to the sovereigns Philip and Mary.

In 1580 Queen Elizabeth confirmed the lease to William, the third Earl, at a yearly rent of £52.13.4. He died in 1589 at the age of sixty-one years. His heir was his only son Edward, and in the Survey of Caldicot Manor of 1613 it stated that the manor was let to Edward fourth Earl of Worcester, for three lives at an annual rental of £52.13.4. He was a staunch supporter of Queen Elizabeth and was prominent at Court. He

EFFIGY OF SIR WILLIAM AP THOMAS
in Priory Church, Abergavenny

CHARLES SOMERSET

1st Earl of Worcester and First Lessee of Caldicot Manor in 1507
reproduced by permission of the Duke of Beaufort

died in 1627, and was succeeded by his son Henry, the fifth Earl. He
served as a young man in the Court of Queen Elizabeth, but he later
retired from public affairs and spent much of his time at his home at
Raglan. He was a devout catholic, and loyal to King Charles to whom
he transferred large sums of money. As a reward he was granted a
marquisate.

After the battles of Marston Moor and Naseby King Charles left his
shattered forces and stayed for a while at Raglan Castle. The Marquis
gathered forces in his castle and prepared to do battle with Cromwell's
army in 1646, but he was no match for his opponents and was ultimately
obliged to surrender. He was placed in detention in London where he
died within a few months, in December 1646.

At the death of the Marquis Cromwell acquired possession of all his
estates and the manor of Caldicot was held for the Commonwealth by
Richard Watson.

Edward, the son of the first Marquis of Worcester, was of an inven-
tive turn of mind and was engrossed in the study of the effects of steam
and water works. He was described in a commission from the King in
April 1644, as "Edward Somerset alias Plantagenet, Lord Herbert,
Baron Beaufort, of Caldicote, Grosmond, Chepstow, Raglan, and
Gower, Earl of Glamorgan." He was in Ireland when his father died,
but he left it, in 1647, for Paris where he remained in exile and poverty
until 1652 when he went to London. It was an unwise step for he was
arrested by the Parliamentarians and committed to the Tower. He was
released, on a petition to Cromwell, in 1654. On his release from the
Tower his whole interest was directed to his mechanical inventions.

Shortly after the Restoration he was again vested in the title of
Marquis of Worcester and the manors and estates taken from him by
Cromwell were granted to him, but he was in debt for such large sums
that he gained little from the return of the estates. He died in 1667.

The lease of the Manor of Caldicot granted to Edward the fourth
Earl of Worcester for three lives ceased on the death of Edward the
second Marquis and sixth Earl of Worcester, and the lease, for a period
of forty-one years, was granted to John Carye who had been one of the
Gentlemen of the Privy Chamber of King Charles I.

The steward of John Carye was Nathan Rogers.

On the death of John Carye the unexpired lease passed to his son
Edward who, in 1686, mortgaged the manor to Sir Samuel Astry for
£500.

William Wolsley who had taken the lease in reversion came into
possession when John Carye's lease expired in 1708, and he was granted
a new lease for sixty years.

Henry first Duke of Beaufort, and his wife the Duchess Mary held
sub-leases for a number of years.

A provision had been inserted in the leases of John Carye and

E

William Wolsley granting a license for the enclosure of moors, wastes, and commons, paying 6d. a year for each acre enclosed.

In 1759 a lease of the lordship of Caldicot was granted to Capel Hanbury, of Pontypool, and his assigns, for a period of nineteen years from 1768, when the lease of William Wolsley expired, at a rental of £52.13.4. per annum, and a payment of 6d. an acre a year for enclosed land, and also a payment of £400 "in the name of a fine." Francis Davis, of Chepstow, was steward.

Capel Hanbury died in 1765, and his widow Jane and son John became entitled to the benefits of the lease. A new lease was drawn up in 1773 which extended the period until 1804.

In 1784 John Hanbury died, and the rights in the lease passed to his widow Jane, who subsequently married Thomas Stoughton of Bally-horgan, County Kerry. Jane was a daughter of Morgan Lewis of St. Pierre.

A further lease for seventeen years was granted to Thomas and Jane Stoughton, in 1790, to date from 1804 when the existing lease expired. The sum of £545 was paid to the Crown for this extension of the lease.

The Duchy of Lancaster reclaimed all leases in 1802 and new leases were granted on revised terms.

Capel Hanbury, the grandson of the last Capel referred to, was the lessee in 1812, and his steward was Thomas Prothero.

Many parcels of land had been sold and a much reduced manor was let to Thomas Lewis, of St. Pierre, in 1830. His son Charles Lewis, also of St. Pierre, purchased the manor, with courts and demesne lands in 1857, and in 1885 he sold the Castle and part of the demesne lands to Joseph Richard Cobb who restored the Castle where he and his family lived for many years.

IV

THE MANOR OF CALDICOT AND NEWTON UNTIL 1421

THE positive existence of Caldicot as a community of some importance is indicated by the reference to it in Domesday Book. It came under the jurisdiction of the Sheriff of Gloucester. The Sheriff was the link between the King and his people. It was his duty to act as the steward of the King's financial interest.

In 1086, when Domesday Book was prepared, Durand was sheriff of Gloucester, and the entry stated that he had a holding at Caldicot, with three ploughs, together with fifteen semi-villeins, four serfs, and one soldier, with twelve ploughs. There was also a mill. Dewstow was a small separate holding within the see of Llandaff, but the manors of Caldicot-with-Kaerwent, and the Priory had not then been established.

The lowland country of South Monmouthshire consisted of woodland and scrub forest, with marshland at the estuaries of the larger pills, or brooks. The agricultural communities arose where clearances were made, land was tilled, and dwellings and rough agricultural buildings were erected.

All the land was granted by the King to the holders of the lordships to whom the tenant cultivators of the land were subservient in all matters.

The waste, or uncultivated land, was developed as the lord, or his officers, directed, but in the meantime it was used as rough pasture, mainly for swine, and a customary payment was made.

When the land was cleared for cultivation it was divided into strips and allocated to the lord, as demesne land, and to the tenants of the lordship, freemen, and villeins.

The first of these open fields at Caldicot were Northfield and South-field, which are now the sites of the main Council Estate and the Greenmeadow Private Estate.

In the open fields there were narrow green baulks of unploughed turf between each strip to mark the divisions of the land, and protective fences were erected at the head of each strip to prevent animals from encroaching on the ploughed area.

The three field system of cultivation was operated whereby one third of the cultivated land was sown in the spring, and one third in the autumn, and one third was in fallow.

The manorial system was, in general, marked by the Norman occupation of the country which was divided up and allocated as manors as speedily as possible to form a comprehensive national order.

Caldicot was held by the sheriffs of Gloucester until Queen Maud created Milo Fitzwalter Earl of Hereford. It was then included in his estates as a manor, and the boundaries then delineated continued for many years. The detached area of Newton (now known as Shirenewton) was included, and it consisted of the forests of Earl's Wood and Earl's Grove. These woods were intended for the use of the Earl and his tenants. All had their rights to take timber for repairs to buildings, fences, and ploughs, known as housebote, haybote, and ploughbote. They were also entitled to windfalls.

As more land was cultivated more names appeared, some embracing parts of the old fields of Northfield and Southfield. e.g. Great, or West, Field, Millfield, Churchfield, Beesditch, and Shirefield.

There were commons upon which the Earl and his tenants obtained pasture for their cattle. The largest of these was Caldicot Common Moor which was bounded by the River Severn, and extended into the adjoining lordships to the west.

Shortly after Milo Fitzwalter acquired the manor it was considered necessary to build a castle for defensive purposes against the Welsh who had not then been completely subdued, and destructive raids were possible. It was also desirable to have an administrative centre for the manor. Milo's daughter Margaret married Humphrey de Bohun, and the early de Bohuns completed the Castle. It was in these early days that separate manors were formed within the lordship. Caldicot Manor, with its demesne farm based upon the Castle continued, but land granted to the Priors of Llantony (Gloucester) became Priory Manor, and Caldicot-with-Kaerwent, later known as West End, formed a manor in the hands of knights of the Earl. The West End Manor was granted a part of Newton, and Newton itself was divided further by the formation of the Rectory and Argot Manors.

After these allocations of land were made the Caldicot Manor of the de Bohuns settled down into an orderly agricultural routine.

Certain of the Earl's tenants were freeholders whose tenancies were guaranteed as hereditary feofments. Unfree tenants had no legal rights, but followed customs by sufferance of their lord. Many of the tenants were brought into Caldicot by the Earl from the neighbouring English counties.

The customary tenants had service obligations, and had to assist the Earl in the cultivation of his demesne farm which included his allocation of strips in the open fields, and his use of the forests and wastes.

It was the practice of the Earls to grant freehold tenancies to knights in return for military service. Each knight was assessed on the basis of a knight's fief, the holder of the land undertaking to maintain for the feudal period of forty days in each year, at his own expense, one fully armed knight, with barbed horse, to perform castle guard. The holding of half a knight's fief would involve half the obligation, and shorter periods were in proportion.

The agricultural operations were closely governed by ancient customs and rules, and every tenant was thus assured of obtaining his just dues. The subsistence of the inhabitants of the manor depended upon their own labours.

The cottars, who were the poorest of the tenants, lived in rough dwellings erected on land reclaimed from waste. They paid small rents, but as they had no oxen or horses they had to give manual labour to the Earl, such as tossing hay, reaping crops and harvesting.

Boon work was also carried out by the Earl's tenants, particularly at harvest time, when not only the head of the household but the members of his family, except his wife, took part in the boons, for which they received some form of payment, either money or food. Boon work was carried out at the Castle for repairs and maintenance.

The service tenants at Caldicot and Newton were under an obligation to give the Earl Easter eggs and Christmas hens.

The Earl claimed escheated tenements, acted as ward for tenants under age, and drew profits of marriages of heiresses. No unfree tenant could convey his property to another person. He could merely surrender his holding to the Earl on the understanding that the Earl would follow custom by granting the tenement to the person intended.

The proceedings of the manor courts give instances of changes of tenancy being effected under the direction of the Earl's steward.

The Castle, as the centre of the demesne farm, had its hall, barns, stores, stable, dovecote, and fishpond, which are referred to in more detail in the chapter dealing with the works of Thomas Woodstock. The gaol and stocks were in the Castle.

All the roads and streams were the Earl's, as also were treasure trove, wrecks, and profits from the sea, royal fish, and the toll of all ships entering the Pill. The Earl's tenants at Caldicot were, however, entitled by custom to boating at the Pill upon a yearly payment.

The Inquisition Post Mortem of the lands of the seventh Humphrey de Bohun, who died in 1298, can be perused in the Public Record Office, and it contains much information on the Earl's holding of the manor of Caldicot and Newton. He held the Castle with appurtenances of the lord King. The easements were worth 6s. 8d. by the year, the garden 3/–d. and the dovecote 3/–d. There was in demesne 150 acres of arable land, and 12 acres of meadow land, 8 acres of pasture land, and 10 acres of woods. There was also the water mill, the fishpond and the fishery.

The free tenants holding knights fees were as follows:

Thomas de Huntly, John ap Adam, Leyson ap Morgan, all holding half knights fee.

Philip Martel, holding one quarter knights fee.

Ivan ap Balyn, Meurice de Redmayne, Geoffrey le Hale, Jevan ap Wronwrow Wyne, all holding one eighth knights fee.

Each knight owed suit at the Court of Caldicot from month to month.

Sir William de Valers held 20 acres of the King-in-chief by homage and fealty.

There were also fourteen other free tenants with messuages and varying holdings up to 20 acres.

There were twelve customary tenants each holding a messuage with 20 acres of land and 2 acres of marsh. Each of them owed three days ploughing per year. If they had no oxen they had to do manual work. They also had to give the Earl two hens at Christmas and twelve eggs at Easter. At reaping time they had to give three days service. Each of them, if he had a horse, had to carry three cartloads of the Earl's hay to the Castle, and those that carried hay had a meal with the Earl. They had to reap the Earl's corn, and they were permitted to keep one sheaf for their own use.

Four customary tenants had a messuage with 16 acres. They also had to give the Earl two hens for Christmas and twelve eggs at Easter. They had to plough the Earl's land and do manual work for one day per week, except Pentecost, Christmas, and Easter.

Twenty-three customary tenants held a messuage with 8 acres and gave one hen at Christmas and six eggs at Easter. They also rendered one day's work per week except on Pentecost, Christmas, and Easter.

There were twelve cottars each holding one house, and their total yearly rents only amounted to 3s. 1½d.

The total number of tenants was seventy-three, and the area included in the Earl's demesne and the various tenancies amounted to 854 acres.

The family of de Valers (later corrupted to Valleys) one of the knights above mentioned, were at West End until the male issue ceased in 1546, when the property, which included a house at West End, was sold. In the eighteenth century the house, known as Valleys House, was in ruins, and now Vallis Terrace stands on the site.

The Newton tenants are excluded from the foregoing inquisition, and are referred to in the chapter on Newton.

In considering the total extent of Caldicot the manors of West End and Priory must be included to compare with the Doomsday Book statistics.

In the reign of Edward I it was recorded in the Ministry Accounts, now to be found in the Public Record Office, that five bondmen, each holding one virgate, did work on two days a week, except in the three feast weeks, and four weeks a year were allowed in cases of sickness by old custom. It was further recorded that tenants of Caldicot used to plough the lord's land at winter and Lent, sowing with as many ploughs as they could yoke amongst them, each of them with one whole plough would plough at both sowings.

The Earl encouraged brewing and had a cauldron at the Castle which he used to hire out. A Ministry account records that the monks at Tintern paid 20s. 6d. for the hire of the cauldron from March to August, and the Earl was to receive a prise of ale from the brewing.

To keep law and order in the community, and to carry out the requirements of the lord of the manor, a number of officials were necessary. First of all was the Constable of the Castle whose duties were confined to keeping the Castle in a state of preparedness. It has been seen in the chapter on the de Bohuns that when the King had occasion to take possession of the Castle he would in the first instance, send a command to the constable to hold the Castle for the King until he received other orders. It is in the records that Thomas Woodstock appointed one John Clopton as his Constable in 1397.

The Constable had on his staff a jailor whose prison was available for wrong doers from the manor.

It was necessary to have a provisioner or keeper of the stock, and a chaplain had an honoured place to fulfil his duties at the chapel within the castle walls.

A number of artisans lived in the village and the Castle, and carried out the repair work at the Castle, the mill, and the agricultural holdings. The tenants liable for service provided the labour. If the required craftsmen were not available in the manor they were brought in from outside. Thomas Woodstock had John Jenur and William Bale, the carpenters, Roger the Sawyer, William the Smith, and Robert the mason, but he also engaged Philip Dangerfield, a smith from Chepstow.

A Steward was responsible for the administrative duties of the manor. He represented the Earl for all purposes, presided at manorial courts, audited accounts, conducted sworn inquests, and decided as to husbandry arrangements. He was assisted by a clerk of the courts, and a bailiff collected rents, carried out enforcement duties, and managed the home farm, cattle, buildings and mill.

In some instances a steward acted for more than one manor.

The connecting link between the officials of the lord of the manor and the tenants was the Reeve. He was elected from among the tenants and was, in general, a man they trusted to see that they were fairly treated whilst the lords requirements were met. The reeve directed the husbandry, regulated the labour for ploughing and harvesting, and the repairs to buildings. He had to have an intimate knowledge of the ancient customs and see that they were followed. William Somery was the reeve in 1361, when he was responsible for repairing houses and agricultural buildings, with the help of serfs, and for carrying out alterations at the Castle for the de Bohuns and Thomas Woodstock.

The woods were under the supervision of a Forester who saw to the cutting of the timber that was required and that the tenants received an equitable distribution of timber for housebote, haybote, and ploughbote.

There was a petty constable to see to the care and use of the stocks.

There were officers who dealt with the impounding of stray cattle, drainage, and supervision of the common fields.

The meetings at the Cross dealt with changes of tenancy, fines for impounded cattle, and petty transgressions in the fields.

The permanent servants at the Castle were usually drawn from the inhabitants of the manor, and received very small wages which were supplemented by clothing and board supplied by the Earl.

Up to the year 1361 the manor had advanced on sound and progressive agricultural lines, but then misfortune fell upon Caldicot. Wales, in common with parts of England, was struck by the epidemic known as the Black Death. The pestilence was traced to Caldicot, and many deaths occurred there in 1361 and 1362. In the Ministry Accounts it stated: "many of the tenants are dead and their lands are in the lord's hands."

In the following years Caldicot again suffered severely from the plague. Of the bond population of sixty-two before the plague only eleven survived in 1366, and by 1372 more had died. Very few of the tenements were farmed, and the remainder yielded no return to the lord.

Startling changes were then brought about in the manor. The castle servants were still employed on a part of the lord's demesne but work was greatly curtailed, and finally ceased.

After the time of Thomas Woodstock the manorial system broke up, the liberation of the serf was hastened, and the letting of the tenements at a full rent cancelled the services to be rendered. When the demesne land was let the need for service was removed.

Thomas Woodstock left the Castle in excellent structural condition and it continued to be the residence of a constable.

There were many changes in the holders of Caldicot Castle and Manor after the death of Thomas Woodstock, and although these did not affect the lives of the peasant community unduly the officials who were responsible for the supervision of the manor were continually changing. When Caldicot came within the orbit of the Duchy of Lancaster it settled down to a new routine.

V

THE MANOR AND THE DUCHY OF LANCASTER
1422–1857

WHEN Henry, Duke of Lancaster, died in 1361, his estate was divided between his two daughters, Maude and Blanche. Broadly the inheritance was divided into two parts, north and south of the Trent. Maude was assigned the southern portion, and Blanche the northern portion. Maude died without issue, and her estates then passed to Blanche, and thus to her husband, John of Gaunt, Earl of Lancaster, through his wife's inheritance. He was later created Duke of Lancaster in his own right. Blanche died in 1369, and the Duke, in 1371, married Constance of Castille who died in 1394. The Duke then married his mistress, Katherine Swynford, in 1396. This marriage was confirmed by the Pope, and its offspring was declared legitimate.

John of Gaunt made his will in 1398 and declared his son, Henry Bolingbroke, by his first marriage to Blanche, as his heir. The Duke died a year later.

In 1380 Henry Bolingbroke had married Maria de Bohun and had the use of the extensive estates of her de Bohun inheritance. Maria had shared her father's estate with her sister Alianore. Her portion included the earldoms of Hereford and Northampton and the lordship of Brecon. Alianore in her portion had Caldicot Manor and Castle. Appendix F shows the result of the division of the de Bohun inheritance. Thomas Woodstock, the husband of Alianore, had designs upon the whole of the de Bohun estates, hoping to consign Maria to a nunnery, but her marriage to Henry Bolingbroke frustrated this scheme.

When the Duke of Lancaster died, in 1361, his son-in-law John of Gaunt, took over a well-tried and successful administrative system for his estates, which John further improved.

Henry Bolingbroke returned from exile in France, in 1399, defeated Richard II, and was crowned King. He then, by the Duchy Charters, kept his Lancaster and Hereford inheritance separate from the Crown possessions. The original inheritance of Blanche and Maria thus provided the basis of the future extensive holding of the Duchy of Lancaster.

In 1403 Henry IV commissioned James Clifford, the Keeper of Caldicot Castle, to receive all issues from the manor after the death of Edmund, late Earl of Stafford.

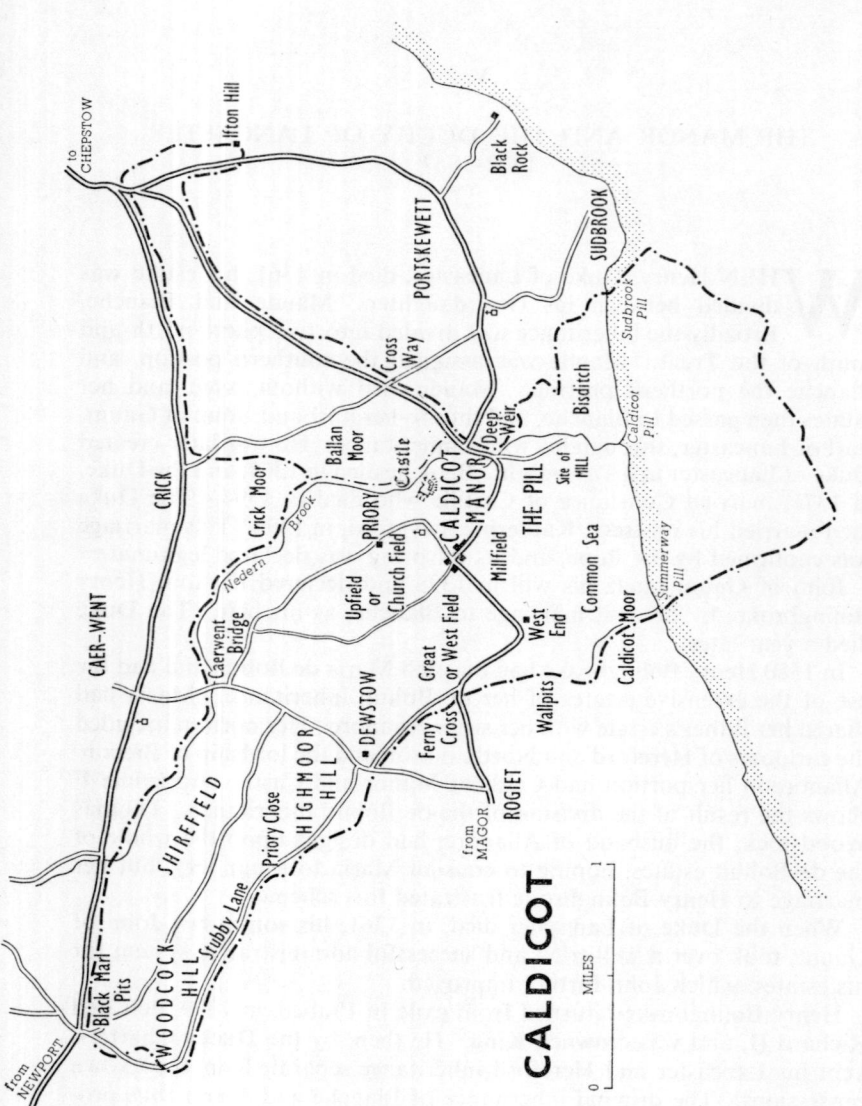

MAP OF CALDICOT
drawn by Bryan Woodfield

Henry V was the first holder of the Lancaster heritage to enter into possession of it at the same time that he ascended the throne. The union of Crown and Duchy had been firmly established in his father's lifetime. Henry was born in a chamber in the gatehouse tower of Monmouth Castle.

The officers of the Duchy were the Receiver General, the Chamberlain, the Chancellor, Chief Stewards for the North, and South areas, and the Auditors.

Henry V was not satisfied with the original division of the de Bohun inheritance. Joan, the mother of Alianore, had remained in possession of some of the de Bohun lands as dower, but when she died, in 1419, it provided an opportunity for the King to re-open the matter of the partition.

Special meetings of the Duchy Council were convened in 1420 to consider the partition, and proceedings were commenced in chancery for the lands then held by Anne, the daughter of Alianore, to be passed to the King. The latter's right to seize the estates was established, but Anne made a counter petition. A new partition was eventually made and the King's choice of his portion included Caldicot which was annexed to the Duchy lands.

When Henry V died, in 1422, his son Henry VI, who succeeded him, was less than a year old, and his regent was Humphrey, Duke of Gloucester.

Provision had to be made for the widow of Henry V, Katherine of Valois, and included in her large dower was Caldicot Castle and Manor. She appointed Sir William ap Thomas as her steward for Caldicot which he administered with other manors in South Wales. He replaced Thomas de la Hay who had acted as steward for Henry V. De la Hay was then appointed as Constable of Caldicot Castle. Morgan ap Madoc was the coroner and forester.

On the death of Katherine of Valois, in 1437, Caldicot returned to the King's hands and was included in the administration of the Duchy of Lancaster. William ap Thomas continued as steward and a number of new appointments were made. John Water, a page of the chamber, was commissioned as Constable of the Castle, and Robert Symond was appointed master forester and keeper of the woods in Caldicot and Newton. William Stradlyn, John Abrath, and Thomas Derehurst succeeded each other as receiver.

William ap Thomas, the steward of the manor, who had rendered faithful service for over twenty years, died in 1445, and was buried in St. Mary's Church at Abergavenny, where his tomb can still be seen.

During the reign of Henry VI a number of repairs to the houses and mill at Caldicot were carried out.

A grant in fee, under the seal of the Duchy was passed in 1444 bestowing Caldicot and Newton upon Sir John Beauchamp, but the manor was soon returned to the Duchy, and in 1453 it was passed in fee tail to Jasper Tudor, Earl of Pembroke. He held it until his lands were forfeited to the King in 1461, when Edward IV granted them to William Herbert, the son of Sir William ap Thomas who had been steward of Caldicot Manor. William was later created Earl of Pembroke, by Edward IV, and he held Caldicot until his death in battle in 1469. The King then held the castle and manor until the Earl's son was of age. Young William then acquired his father's estates. When he died in 1491 Caldicot again reverted to the Duchy. In 1496 we find Sir Walter Herbert, the brother of the last named William Herbert holding the appointment of Steward of Caldicot Castle and Manor under the Duchy. John Parker was also appointed receiver and bailiff of liberties in Caldicot and Newton and master forester there during the King's pleasure.

This procedure continued, with the Castle inhabited, until Sir Walter Herbert, the last of the Duchy stewards, died in 1507. The manor of Caldicot, with the Castle, then became the subject of a lease drawn up by the Duchy of Lancaster with Charles Somerset, in the following terms.

"The King devised at farm to Charles Somerset, Kt., Lord Herbert his castle and lordship of Caldecote with Newton, parcel of the Duchy of Lancaster, in the Marches of Wales with all rents, services, farms, mills, meadows, feedings and pastures, perquisites of court, and with toll, custom, and other casual profits and commodities whatsoever belonging or pertaining to the lordships and castle of Caldecote with Newton; tallages, great sessions, wards, marriages, reliefs, escheats, advowsons of churches of chapels and charities when they occur, utterly excepted and reserved to the aforesaid lord King, To have and hold all the premises, except the pre-excepted, to the aforesaid Charles and his assigns, from the feast of St. Michael the Archangel next to come after the date of the presents to the end of the term of 9 years then next following and fully completed. Rendering therefore annually to the lord King and his heirs for all the premises £52-10 stg., namely of the ancient farm £52-3-4, besides an annual increase of 4s. 8d. at the feasts of Easter and St. Michael the Archangel by equal portions. And the same farmer at his own costs and expenses will sustain and maintain all repairs of the water mill of Caldecote, also tiling of houses within the castle there, during the term aforesaid. And at the end of the term shall hand back both that mill and the roofs or tilings aforesaid well and competently repaired. Provided always that the aforesaid Charles shall have annually from his farm aforesaid an allowance of 105s. 4d. on and for the exercise of the offices above written, whereof for the office of bailiff of Caldecote and Newton 40s., and for the office of Clerk of the Court there 13s. 4d., and for the office of master forester, 52s., as is due and accustomed of old for the fees and wages in the same offices.

In testimony given at London, 25th July, year 1, Henry VIII."

Charles Somerset was created Earl of Worcester in 1514, and the lease of Caldicot Manor continued in the hands of his family until 1667 when it passed to John Carye, and then through several hands, referred to in the chapter on the Lessees, until all that remained of the manor was sold by the Duchy of Lancaster to Charles Edward Lewis, of St. Pierre, in 1857.

The obligations referred to in the first lease to repair the houses in the Castle soon lapsed, and by the middle of the sixteenth century the Castle was in a ruinous condition, parts of it being used for accommodating cattle and agricultural supplies.

In the rental of the manor holdings at the time of Queen Elizabeth in 1574–5 there were thirty free tenants paying by the year 112s. 4¾d., ½lb. of pepper, ½lb. of cummin, and one red rose. There were sixty rentals by copy of court rolls totalling £20.10s. 1½d., and two tenants at the will of the lord of the manor paying 2s. 0d. The renting of the demesne lands rendered £15.10.6., and escheated lands 14s.

There were also the following rents:

	£	s.	d.
Caldicot Mill, with appurtenances and land,	5	6	8
Customary tolls from tenants of the Queen for use of Bisditch meadow,		4	0
A custom called chence (boating at the Pill)	1	6	8
Making in all a total of £49.6.4¼., and the pepper, cummin and rose.			

There was in addition the total rentals of £10.2.11½., from the Newton Tenancies.

To ensure that their estates were properly administered the Duchy appointed commissioners in 1557 to survey the possessions of the Crown, and they were authorized to consider whether rents could be improved. The more frequent the surveys the less chance there was for irregularities to arise and continue. Many surveys were undertaken in the second half of the sixteenth century. A very complete survey was made of Caldicot Manor in 1613, and certain tenants who took part in that survey recalled that their fathers had assisted in the survey of 1576, and in other surveys prior to that. The surveys were completed in a formal Court of Survey by a jury presided over by the steward or by an official surveyor appointed for the purpose.

Many of the provisions of the 1613 Survey are set out in Appendix 'B', but there was also a schedule of all the holdings of land. The parcels and situations referred to are as follows: Creeke Field, Bisditch, the Slade, the Brockwells, Northfield, Newmeades, Lowerfield, Sherfield, West Field, Smyth Moore, the Warthe, Well Moore, the Hooles,

Southfield, Longcroft, Lower Southfield, Cattbrane, Churchfield, Webbs Lease, Rushmeare, the Hangingland, and the Rodge. The name Rushmeare would indicate that in the past rushes would be grown there for the roofing of the buildings in the manor.

The jurors set down in the 1613 survey, when defining the boundaries, that the three other manors in Caldicot of Westend, the Priory and Dewstow, were so intermingled that they could not separate them. Although this is primarily an account of Caldicot Manor and its holders reference has been made to the other manors in another chapter.

In 1608 a survey was made of the forests of Earlswood in the Newton part of the manor of Caldicot and Newton, and the total number of trees was found to be 11,652, with a value of £911.14.0. Newton had also developed as a separate village community. It had from the time of the early de Bohuns had its own church, built by the lord of the manor, and named St. Thomas a'Becket. The 1613 survey also revealed that there were freehold and copyhold tenants, and the number of cottage dwellings was increasing as encroachments of the waste took place. There were also three water mills, the Curbehind and Lady Mills on Mounton Brook, and another mill on the Troggy Brook.

In 1584 the third Earl of Worcester, who then held the lease of Caldicot and Newton Manor, addressed a plea to the Duchy of Lancaster claiming that, under his lease, he was entitled to the custody, herbage, and windfalls of the Earls Woods, which contained 600 to 700 acres. He claimed that John Griffith, Francis Alderford, William Basse, Yeorworth Smith, Philip Hopkin, John Hopkin, Hugh Perce, Thomas ap John, William Thomas David, David Morgan, George David, John David, Lewis Griffith, William Roffen, and Thomas Kemys, tenants of the manor, had made spoil in the wood, and cut down many timber trees. By courtesy they might and may have three thousand loads of wood lying upon the ground, which they never took, but still cut down great timber trees without any controlment and the same converted to their own use.

John Griffith stated that he was the customary tenant of a messuage with meadow and pasture within the manor of Caldicot, and he was, therefore, entitled to cut down the trees for necessary repairs. He had felled certain oaks for the repair of his messuage as it was lawful for him to do. The other tenants also submitted that they had only taken timber to which they were entitled.

A pamphlet issued in 1607 gave an account of serious flooding in twenty-six parishes bordering the River Severn from Mathern to Rumney. Caldicot was one of the sufferers of the "Woeful news out of Monmouthshire". There was immense loss of human life as well as of horses, cattle, and sheep, and the writer of the pamphlet expressed the opinion that "while the Clergy doth nothing but look for livings, and the Gentry esteem more of their hawks, hounds and other their vainer pleasures than the godly discharging of their offices wherein the Lord hath set them." The writer however added—"more would have perished for want of food and extremity of cold had not the right Honourable the Lord Herbert, son and heir to the Earl of Worcester, and Sir Walter Montague, who dwelt near to the aforesaid places, sent out boats to relieve the distressed. The Lord Herbert himself going unto such houses as he could."

Although John Cary's lease of the manor did not commence until the death of Edward, Marquis of Worcester, in 1667, he had submitted a petition to King Charles I, in 1639, stating: "the manor of Caldicot is in lease for two lives yet to come, and is of no benefit at all to your Majesty, save in the rent, and that there are belonging to the said manor large wastes and commons out of which there may some improvement be raised to your Majesty with charge. This humble suit is unto your Majesty, that you will be pleased to grant me a lease of the said manor for 41 years in reversion of the present estate, and also to grant a lease for 41 years of such improvements as shall be made at the charge of the petitioner out of the wastes and commons of the said manor, under the rent of 6d. the acre."

The King referred this petition to the Chancellor of the Duchy of Lancaster who drew the King's attention to the multitude of commoners claiming interest in the commons and waste, but the Chancellor added that if the petitioner could increase the King's revenue it would be a very good service and would deserve the lease.

The auditors to the Duchy referred the Chancellor to the lease granted by King James I to the Earls of Worcester, for three lives, at a rent of £52.13.4. per annum, saying: "there are certain moors or commons of large extent, but I have not any survey which doth manifest how many acres they contain, neither the goodness or validity of the land, and I conceive that there can be no improvement of rent made thereof during the terms of their lives in being. There is, out of the rent of £52.13.4d. allowed sums for the payment for the offices of bailiff, clerk of the court, and master forester, which several fees upon granting a lease in reversion I conceive may well be abated."

In 1640 the King granted the petition and instructed the Attorney to the Duchy to prepare a Bill for his Majesty's signature.

Before John Cary could carry out his plans the country became embroiled in the Civil War, and it was not until 1667 that Cary's forty-one year lease commenced. He had thus established the enclosure of parts of the commons and wastes with legal authority and a similar provision for the payment of 6d. per acre for enclosures was included in subsequent leases.

The manor of Caldicot and Newton, after the usurpation by Oliver Cromwell, was one of the Crown manors of which a return was made in 1652.

The holdings were then as follows:

	No. of tenants	
By Copy of court roll	79	
Lands under demise or grant	16	95

The total yearly rents were as follows:

	£	s.	d.
Quit Rent & Royalties	32	18	2
Copyholds	22	10	6
Leases	106	11	4
		£162	0 0

The Water Mills were occupied by

William Blethin, Llandegelly, Newton.
Robert Rosser, Curbehinds, Newton.
Roger Rowland, Caldicot.

The decayed castle and certain parcels of land had been leased by the Earl of Worcester to Katherin Kemis, a daughter-in-law by her first marriage of Francis Herbert who held many tenancies set out in the 1613 survey. The Kemis, or Kemeys, family accumulated much land at Caldicot over the succeeding years.

Another holder of land by copyhold in this survey was Charles Van whose family later made many purchases of land in Caldicot and further reference is later made to this.

Parliament replaced the Earl of Worcester as lord of the manor in 1653, by Richard Watson.

On the restoration of King Charles II the manor was returned to the Duchy of Lancaster, and there was a succession of leases on terms which ensured the proper agricultural development of the manor.

In the year 1770 King George III authorized the Chancellor of the Duchy of Lancaster to nominate William Foord to make a survey of the manor of Caldicot and Newton and ascertain what the rent payments and other profits should be, and what tolls, fines, heriots, reliefs, deodands, waifs, estrays, amerciaments and other casual profits and emoluments, were due and payable. The survey was to take a view of the manor including the messuages, lands, tenements, mills, woods, rivers, fishing, with the watercourses, hedges, pales, ditches, and fences thereto, also all incroachments made upon the wastes.

William Foord carried out his task with care and efficiency, and his report and map provide an enlightening glimpse of life in Caldicot at that time.

The persons occupying office were the steward, clerk of the Court, master forester, and keeper of the gaol.

The following were the farms of the manor:

	a.	r.	p.
Castle Farm	68	2	26
Webleaze (adjoining Castle Farm)	72	0	3
Broad Leazes (Farthinghill)	42	2	26
Lord's Mead (near Rodge)	40	0	24
Stoophill (part Millfield)	33	2	16
	257	0	15
Incroachments	14	3	18
	271	3	33

The moors and wastes were as follows:

	a.	r.	p.	a.	r.	p.
Westward Moor	653	3	16			
Ifton Moor	202	2	18			
Little Moor	15	1	36			
Benacre Moor	15	2	0			
Common Sea	99	0	0			
Ballan Moor	8	3	11			
Simers Hill	13	3	20			
Black Marl Pits	16	2	24			
				1025	1	5
Earlswood	521	0	0			
Coombwood	16	0	8			
Mynyddbach	12	1	0			
				549	1	8
				1574	2	13
Less incroachments				133	2	25
				1440	3	28

The number of tenants involved in the incroachment was forty-five.

The number of freehold customary and copyhold tenants paying quit rents and chief rents at Shire Newton was thirty-two.

There was in Shire Newton, belonging to his Majesty, two water mills, one used as a paper mill having a dwelling house and nine acres of rough ground, and the other was used as a corn or grist mill.

William Foord expressed the view that the wastes and commons in Caldicot and Newton were more than sufficient for the commoners' rights and, therefore, he recommended that at least 100 acres of the best parts be inclosed for the benefit of his Majesty or his lessee.

F

The number of freehold, customary, and copyhold tenancies in the manor of Caldicot was as follows:

In the Parish of Caerwent	10
In the Parish of Caldicot	60
	—
	70

To which should be added the thirty-two at Newton previously referred to.

Ancient custom prescribed that if a customary or cophyhold tenant died, his best live beast became due to the lord of the manor, and if there was no live beast a heriot of 5/– should be paid. William Foord recommended that in all cases the cash alternative should be adopted.

Reference was also made to royalties in respect of wrecks, waifs, estrays, goods and chattels of felons and fugitives, and other amercements, but these were small and Foord valued them at £5 per annum.

There was a yearly rental of £2.2.0. paid by lease for an exclusive fishery, on the sea coast at Caldicot, called Denny Sands.

John Hanbury held the lease of the manor from the Duchy of Lancaster at this time, and the receiver for the crown estates in the lordship was Thomas Davis.

The deponent after its preparation by William Foord was sworn and signed, at Chepstow, on the 30th May 1772.

After William Foord's survey the Duchy commenced a process of selling off areas of land from the manor. Morgan Lewis, of St. Pierre, in 1763, purchased 55 acres of copyhold land, and this was enfranchised in 1853. Many other sales were effected.

25 acres were subject to encroachment by fifteen small-holders and they were purchased from the Duchy in 1843 and 1844.

In 1852 the South Wales Railway Company purchased 7 acres 2 roods 13 perches for their new railway track.

The remainder of the land was sold in 1857. Charles Edward Lewis of St. Pierre, purchased 166 acres, including the Castle and the title of the manor. Francis Clark acquired 6 acres at Caerwents Brook, and Edward Freke Lewis bought the following:

	a.	r.	p.	a.	r.	p.
Caerwents Brook	17	3	13			
Lords Mead & Rodge	67	3	33			
Whitehall	6	0	5			
Caerwents Brook			24			
				91	3	35

A small area of 1r. 16p. at Deepweir was sold to Richard Williams, and 29p. of garden ground near the Church to Mary Ann Bayam.

The ownership of land at Caldicot by the Duchy of Lancaster then ceased.

The tenure of land had altered over the years. In Norman times all lands in England were held to have been granted by the sovereign and were held of him in consideration of certain services rendered by the holders. The tenements were freehold and villeinage. During the medieval period of villeinage there were in Caldicot, in addition to the freeholder, semi vergators, gafolmen, quarterers, semi quarterers, cottars, and customary tenants, mostly paying low rents, but rendering of services gradually ceased, and the holdings were freehold, leasehold, and copyhold. Copyhold titles were attested by a copy of a court roll, witnessed by the lord's steward. An act of Parliament was passed in the reign of Charles II abolishing villeinage, but retaining copyhold. Finally, in 1850, Parliament established a law with a view to gradually abolishing copyhold by facilitating enfranchisement.

VI

THE CASTLE

UTHORITATIVE writers in the past have been at variance in their
suppositions of the dates of the building of the early stages of the
castle. It did not exist when Domesday Book was prepared in
1086, but by 1216, when King John ordered it to be seized, the Keep
together with the curtain walls and three other towers had been
completed.

The agricultural operations in Caldicot Manor had been greatly
extended by the time Milo Fitzwalter was granted Caldicot as a part of
the estate of the Earldom of Hereford, and it was necessary to have an
administrative centre. The Welsh were hostile, and could constitute
a threat to the Caldicot lands so that it appeared wise to site a fortress
in such a position that it would dominate the Earl's lands and the
important sea approach, from the River Severn at Caldicot Pill. Thus
the Keep came to be built, possibly by Milo Fitzwalter. It has only been
called the Keep in recent years. In the earlier days it was known as the
High Tower or the Dungeon Tower.

The finest masonry is to be found in the Keep. It is built of a local
stone and is set upon a rock base. Against its foundation walls earth
was banked up to form a mound surrounded by a moat. Above the top
of the mound was the entrance door which was approached by a move-
able ladder, or set of wooden steps. Entrance was to the middle floor.
Just inside to the left of the entrance door there is a small flight of steps
in the thickness of the wall which leads down to a large circular basement room surrounded by a stone seat. From this basement a trefoil
headed doorway leads to a still lower vaulted dungeon, underneath the
supplemental tower which is built to the westward outside the main
wall of the Keep. This added tower is of solid masonry above the dungeon which is about 11 feet long by 7 feet wide, and could only be
reached by a ladder.

In the entrance room above the basement, was a large fireplace and a
recess in the thickness of the wall in which there was, and still is, a well
descending for 40 feet. This room was probably the living quarters of
the guard.

On the right hand of the entrance door is another flight of winding

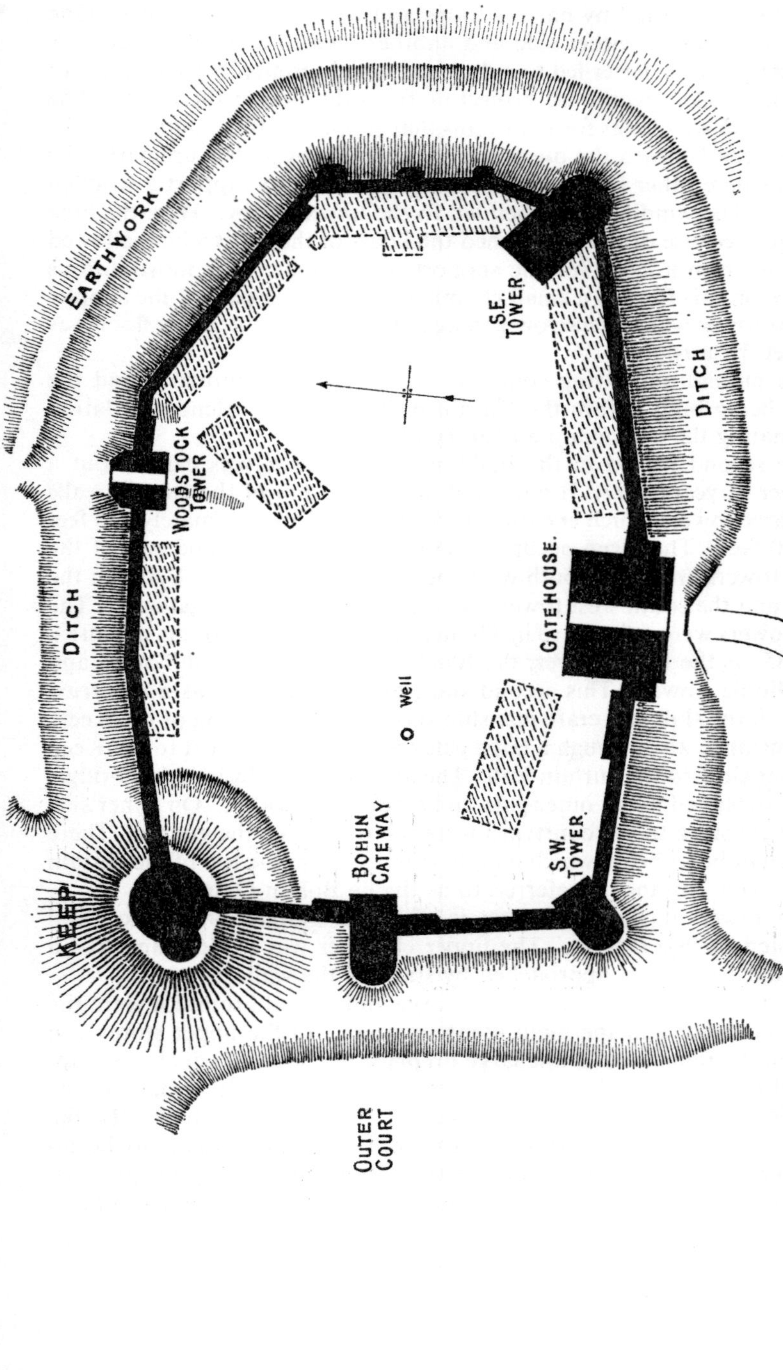

EARTHWORK.

DITCH

DITCH

S.E.
TOWER.

WOODSTOCK
TOWER

GATEHOUSE.

Well

KEEP

BOHUN
GATEWAY

S.W.
TOWER.

OUTER
COURT

PLAN OF CALDICOT CASTLE

stairs in the thickness of the wall which lead to the upper storeys. The room above the entrance room has the remains of a large fireplace. This apartment is lighted by narrow loops and has recessed windows. One has stone seats on either side and another formed a small oratory. A passage from the latter led to a doorway which originally gave access to a small wooden penthouse projecting from the side of the tower. The corbels and wall holes for the beams that supported these outside works can be seen beneath the doorway. A set of holes higher up marks the places where other beams came through the wall to support a wooden gallery. The winding stair then led to the upper storey. Here the area is larger because of the diminished thickness of the walls which allowed room to form a ledge for the support of the floor. The most curious feature on this floor is a small chamber in the upper part of the supplemental tower where a narrow passage branches from it. This floor was covered by a roof.

The mound and string course of the Keep are continuous and the Keep being built before the curtain walls, stood in splendid isolation dominating the surrounding countryside.

The second period in the building of the Castle was carried out a number of years later. It consisted of the erection of the curtain walls and three towers which enclosed a court-yard of approximately 320 feet by 250 feet. The Keep occupies the north-west corner and two of the other towers are at the south west and south east corners. Between the Keep and the south west tower was the original entrance gateway. The four towers were referred to in Thomas Woodstock's accounts of works, in 1385, as the High Tower, the Black Tower, the Painted Tower, and the Middle Tower. This second stage of construction was not carried out with the skill and craftsmanship shown in the building of the Keep. The entrance was through a large gateway in the tower next to the Keep and was close to the curtain wall. The approach was by a timber bridge. It was defended by an outer gate and a portcullis within. On either side of the entrance to the courtyard were the rooms for the guards. There were chambers above, which had their access from the top of the curtain walls. This entrance is referred to as the de Bohun Gate.

The tower at the south-west is of more simple construction and consisted of two storeys. The upper chamber was vaulted and had a fireplace, and it was approached by stairs in the wall.

The tower at the south-east was large and in and around it were the lord's chamber and the main living quarters. In the upper storey can be seen the remains of a fine large fireplace the hood of which was supported on bold corbels. Further reference to this tower is made in the description of the works carried out by Thomas Woodstock. To the east of the tower is a breach in the wall, and there seems to be no positive record of how it was made. Beyond this breach are two small octagonal turrets, both of which contained shafts and served as

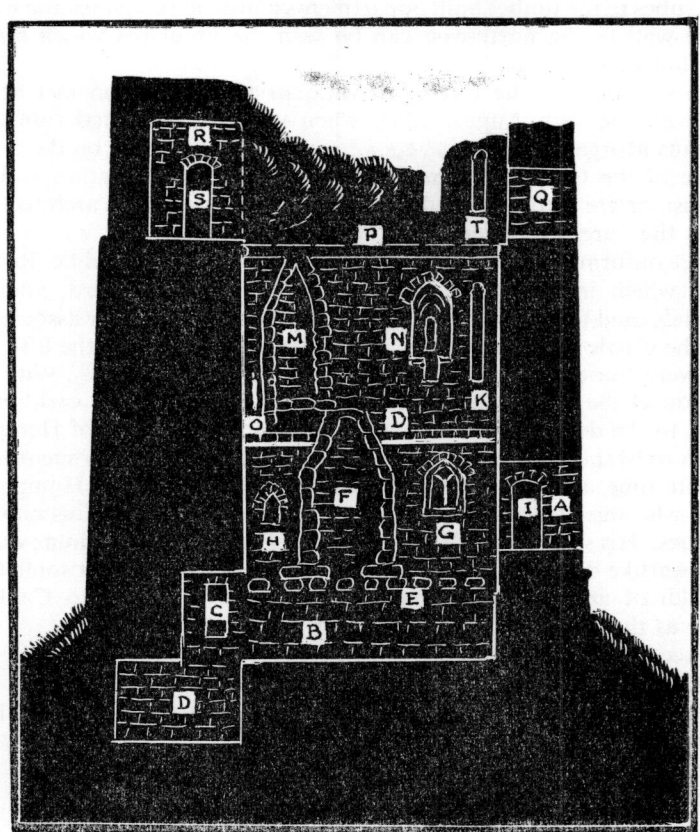

A	Entrance doorway	L	Row of corbels
B	Basement storey	M	Fireplace
C	Trefoil headed doorway	N	Looped window
D	Lower dungeon	O	Loophole
E	Corbels	P	Ledge formed by diminished thickness
F	Fireplace		
G	Looped recess	Q	Recess with window
H	Loophole	R	Large recess in supplemental tower
I	Entrance to winding stair		
K	Trefoil headed entrance doorway	S	Entrance to passage in above
		T	Entrance from stair

SECTION OF THE KEEP OR NORTH WEST TOWER
drawing by Caerleon Antiquarian Society, 1854

garderobes to the timber built appartments constructed against the walls. In the wall to the north-east can be seen the fireplaces which served these timber buildings.

The members of the Caerleon Antiquarian Association met at the Castle on the 18th August 1853, when it was a neglected ruin, and Octavius Morgan, M.P., F.R.S., F.S.A., read to them a paper on the architecture of the Castle. He made a very detailed examination and his conclusions are recommended to any reader desiring more architectural details than are here given.

More information has now been discovered in the Public Record Office which indicates the structures within the courtyard, and the materials used for repairs. The early de Bohuns had a closer association with the Castle in its early days, and up to, and including, the fifth earl they were buried at one of the Llantony religious houses. With the addition of the Castle and manor of Pleshy, as part of the earldom of Essex, to the de Bohun estates as a result of the marriage of Henry de Bohun to Maud de Manderville, the earls and their families spent most of their time at Pleshy, until the time of the unmarried Humphrey, ninth, who was at Brecon and Caldicot for periods between his military activities. His son, the tenth and last of the Humphrey de Bohuns was of a less warlike disposition than his predecessors, and he spent some time at Caldicot and Brecon, carrying out extensive repairs to Caldicot Castle as the following accounts show:

Account rendered by William Somery, Reeve of the Castle and Manor, to Earl Humphrey de Bohun, in 1361:

Reeds bought for roofing houses. Roofing two granges and a byre with the help of serfs.
Mending broken door of a grange.
Mending the castle bridge, almost ruined.
Mending the roof of the granary within the castle.

Accounts of the Earl Humphrey (Tenth), in 1369, were for the following work:

Masons, carpenters, tilers and plumbers hired to repair the towers, chambers, chapel and various places within the castle.
36,000 shingles bought at Kairlion and 1 boat hired to convey them to Caldicots Pill. 18,000 of these shingles were taken from the Pill to the Castle by tenants of the lord as boonwork.
One carpenter hired to repair and mend many defects of 4 towers.
One plumber hired to repair and mend all defects in the circuit of the Great tower, and Countess tower and the lords new chamber with one wardrobe.
One carpenter hired to make the whole carpentry of the great chamber annexed to the lords chamber, and cutting down the timber in the lord's woods.

Carriage of trestles from Bristol.

Mason and men hired to make cement and repair the walls of the said chamber.

One man with his horse hired to convey sand.

Expenses of John Oxle and the reeve going and working in Newport, Kaerlion and Striguil for 12 days buying the materials required.

One rope bought for pulling stone.

In 1371, William Somery, the reeve of the Earl, Humphrey (Tenth), carried out further work as follows:

One man hired for choosing and cutting down 19 oaks in Wentwood.

Various men with their oxen and wagons hired for carrying the said oaks from Wentwood to the castle.

Carpenter hired to make a bridge for the castle.

Men and materials for repairing the roof of the chapel and the granary.

One carpenter hired to make stable mangers.

One carpenter hired to make and put on a long joist to carry the solar of the lord's chamber, together with three posts put underneath the joist; and earthing up the said solar.

Repairing and making one latrine under the door of the great tower.

The tenth and last Humphrey died in 1373, and his two young daughters, who were his heirs, were taken into the care of King Edward III. He appointed his youngest son Thomas Woodstock as the guardian of Alianore, the elder daughter, and they were eventually married. Thomas then began to show some interest in Caldicot Castle, which was included in the inheritance of Alianore, and in 1382 he decided to pay a visit to Caldicot. He instructed William Somery to this effect, and the reeve made strenuous efforts to make the castle presentable for the visit by carrying our extensive renovations.

Thomas Woodstock duly made his visit to Caldicot and decided to carry out major alterations. His instructions provided for the demolition of the existing wall between the south-west and south-east towers, the erection of a new wall with an elaborate new entrance gateway, the building of a new postern gate, a Great Hall with domestic offices, and a general improvement of the remaining internal structures.

William Somery had now been appointed the Earl's steward, and his first account, in 1383, was for the rebuilding of the wall between the south-west and south-east towers, as follows:

Paid for various building in the Castle of Caldecote for making of one new stone wall between the lord's chamber and the tower called Culverhousetour, as in breaking stones in the quarry, carrying from there to the Castle, burning lime, digging and carrying sand, buying and seeking sea coal for burning the said lime, buying timber, trimming and clearing foundations, hiring of carpenters for repairing defects in the houses with timber, buying 3 carthorses, and tools of iron, making scaffolding, and doing various other works in the castle. This was followed, in 1385, by the following work:

Account of William Somery, steward of the Lord Duke of Gloucester from the feast of St. Michael 9 Richard II (1385) to the morrow of St. Michael 10 Richard II.

Paid to Robert Mason for the reward granted to him for making one new wall between the dovecote and the great tower besides the £66.13.4. allowed to him by consideration of the lord's council because he made the said wall thicker by one foot and higher ½ foot more than is contained in the indenture and agreement.

One piece of new wall of the thickness of 5½ foot and height 30 feet between the tower called Black Tower and the painted Tower with lances, crests, and battlements sufficient.

One new stone bridge breadth 4 feet made towards the tower called Black Tower, by agreement with the lord William Castellan, Knight.

Paid to the said Robert Mason for the repair of a new tower where before was a dovecot, height with the battlements of the said tower 50 feet and thickness 6 feet with one portcullis and one vault for drawing the said portcullis, and with 3 chambers and stone windows, and 3 fireplaces and 3 latrines to be made in the said chamber.

Carpenters paid for making a gate of the castle, and a staircase towards the lord's great chamber. One new latrine on the wall of the castle.

Trestle tables, trestles, mangers and stalls and other necessaries.

Iron work for the said gate.

Materials for tilers to roof various houses of the castle.

William the glazier for glazing 2 windows in the chapel, 2 windows in the lord's great chamber, and 1 window in the lesser chamber.

The following were materials purchased for the work:

1 webbe of lead bought at Bristol for the work of the said castle together with carriage to the castle.

Tin bought for soldering the gutters and for having in stock.

Another webbe of lead bought.

1 fattemele of lead bought for fixing doorbands and ironwork of windows of the castle.

350 spikenails. 700 boardnails 400 shinglenails

900 hatchnails 1000 lathnails 200 boardnails

200 shinglenails 100 hatchnails 200 lathnails

Paid Gregory Tyler, tiling anew one latrine in the new work of the castle and mending other tiled houses in the castle.

Paid to the same Gregory inspecting and mending the other shingled houses in the castle with the lord's shingles.

Paid to the said Gregory putting lead on the walls round the Middle-tower.

Carriage of 4 waggonloads of sand to put under the said lead.
1 quarter of quicklime. Heating unburnt lime for the use of the castle, together with carriage.
Certain boy carrying the said sand to the said wall for one day.
The work was continued into the following year as follows:
Adam Geffrey, Surveyor of the workmen working in the Castle at Caldicot, 10 Richard II, (Dec. 1386).
12 oaks cut down in the lord's forest. Stripping and sawing the said timber.
Payments to John the carpenter, William Moreheld, carpenter, William Balle, carpenter, Jenur the carpenter, Roger the sawyer.
Boards bought at Newport for making embrasures, doors, windows and other necessaries. Latches bought.
Great boards bought for making trestle tables, presses, mangers, etc.
Paid Philip Dangerville, smith of Strigul, for door-bands, hooks nails and iron roves for making the new gate in the Castle.
Hiring 2 men for clinching the new gate in the Castle. 3 padlocks bought.
Ochre bought for colouring the said gate.
2 iron bars with staples for shutting the new gate. 3 great locks for the gate.
Paid William Smith of Caldicot for doorbands, latches and catches in the new tower.
200 shingles bought at Newport also mangers and racks, and broad boards for louvres.
Account of William Somery steward of the Duke, 10 Richard (1386).
New Tower where before there was a dovecote. Height with the battlements 50' and thickness 6' with 1 portcullis (Part paid last year).
Timber bought at Strigul from John Clothurbox and 144 lbs of iron bought for making bars, hooks and catches on the windows of the said tower.
Roofing on 1 stable of the lord, with straw and stakes.
Workmen for daubing the roof and walls of one new house at the end of the staircase of the Hall in the preceding year.
One trough for the fishpond made of the lord's timber.
Breaking the wall in the hall near the chapel for making an arch so that men being in the hall can see the divine office in the chapel by the lords order.
Making the arch, repairing windows and corbels in the said chamber.
Daubing the said chamber with burnt lime.
Carrying away rubble from the said walls and mud put out of one chamber near the cellar.
Vaulting one small chamber in the new tower.
Machicolating the said tower with limestone and in making 2 walls

in the kitchen whereof one for the hearth of the kitchen digging and carrying clay for the same.

10 locks with as many keys, one for the door of the Wardrobe, one for the door under the lords chamber, one for the door called norssery, one for the door to the cellar, one for the storehouse, one for the door of the high tower, one for the door of the painted tower, 2 for the doors of the black tower and one for the coffer for putting books in.

Making a palisade in the castle between the gate and the lord's chamber.

Lead brought at Bristol for the work of the said castle, for soldering the gutters and for having in stock.

Lead bought for fixing doorbands and ironwork of windows.

Bought spikenails (350) 700 boardnails, 400 shingle nails, 900 hatchnails and 1000 lathnails.

New latrine built and tiled and mending other tiled houses in the castle.

Putting lead on the walls round the Middle Tower.

Account of William Somery, steward of the Lord Duke of Gloucester, Earl of Essex and Buckinghamshire 11th year of Richard II (1387).

Spikenails for doors of the new Tower. 500 boardnails for doors and windows of said Tower.

Hatchnails, iron bought for bars, hooks, doorbands, catches, latches for 12 doors, and 1 portcullis and 6 windows in said Tower.

Lead for fixing hooks, catches, on walls of said Tower.

Man hired to cut down 25 great oaks in the Earls wood,

Carrying the same from the wood to the Castle for the new Tower, men coming with their oxen on boonwork.

Carriage of 14 great trees from Chepstow.

Raising great timber to the new Tower. 33 boards bought at Newport and Bristol. Expenses of John Carpenter going to Bristol to buy the boards. Hire of men to carry out rubble from the new Tower.

Robert Mason for making one wall containing in length 120 feet, and height agreeing with the height of the wall on the east side of the gate of the castle, and so in height from the said wall of the said gate level to the top of the tower in which the Lord's great chamber is. Wall to be 7 feet thick.

The wall is assigned for 1 larder next to the said gate of castle 16 ft. One kitchen, 22 ft. The Dresser, 10 ft. Pantry and Buttery 20 ft. Hall 50 ft. 1 chamber 12 ft, which contain in whole with 10 ft of old wall, 130 feet. In which wall he will make 2 windows for kitchen, 3 or 4 windows in Hall and other windows sufficient for chamber, as well for the lower as the upper chamber and for the larder. 2 drains for larder and kitchen for waste disposal. He will make one window within the said wall for the Lords rampart walk, going from his great chamber to the new chamber. One fireplace and one latrine for new chamber. One staircase from the new chamber for going to the battlements of said wall.

Iron for bars for 1 great window and 3 lesser windows.

1 carpenter to cover with shingles the defects of one tower called Countess Tower.

1 roofer to roof over the lord's stable and to repair all defects of said stable.

One reaping stick, for reaping, collecting and carrying same.

One new doorband for door of stable and fixing crossbars to the door of same. Carpenter for repairing this door.

4 boards bought from William Phillips to make one gate in the new Tower.

There are two stones in the foundations of the new work bearing the names "Thomas" and "Alianore", which can still be seen.

The details of these accounts bring to life the picture of the Castle with all its internal structures and massive external walls and towers, well maintained, providing the grandest of administrative centres and a home for its noble owners and their serving men.

Queen Katherine, when she was widowed by King Henry V, was granted as part of her jointure the Castle and manor of Caldicot, and she found the Castle had been badly neglected after the death of Thomas Woodstock. She, therefore, instructed her bailiff, John Gour, to carry out the necessary repair works.

The first account was in 1424, and included the following items:

Repair of various towers within the castle.

Pulling down old shingles of the whole roof of the tower called the Dungeon, and mending and repairing the timber of the roof. Laying boards on the gutters under the lead sheets. Covering the aforesaid tower with slatstones and quicklime. Mending the lead sheets of the gutters.

Men coming with oxen and wagons and carrying 18 wagon loads of rough stones from the Queen's quarry to the castle for the repair of the tower called Litelhalle, and making anew all the battlement of the tower. Pargetting all the walls of the same.

Collecting twigs for binding the roof of the courthouse called Long-house.

Tiling the chapel house of the manor.

The following year the Queen carried out further repairs as follows: Repair of various little towers and other houses within the castle.

Men coming with oxen and wagons with 16 loads of rough stone from the Queen's quarry for burning quicklime therefrom, also a further 11 loads of stones.

30 men coming on boon work bringing 13 wagon loads of flat stones from the quarry and laying at various towers and gutters.

Bread, beer and relish provided for the men.

A boatload of sea coal from England by the Severn to Caldicot Pill.

Scouring and clearing the kiln at the castle.

Taking the lime from the kiln to within the castle.

Mending and tiling the new hall.

Scouring rubbish and clearing the floor of the new chamber above the gate of the castle.

Digging and making a ditch round a house of the precinct of the castle called the Courthouse for keeping out beasts destroying the roof.

Cresting of all crenellations of the whole stone wall round the old hall with freestones, and for cresting of the stone wall from the old hall to the end of three chambers annexed thereto at the north side.

Covering the roofs of three little towers on the east side of the aforesaid three chambers with flat stones, and making and laying all gutters.

New roofing of the tower called Thomas with flat stones. Laying and roofing steps at the ascent of the same tower.

Roofing of certain stone steps at the entrance to the chambers and garrets above the gate at the entrance to the castle.

Making a new door of freestone at the entrance of the aforesaid chambers and garrets.

The final account of John Gour, the Queen's bailiff and collector, for the year 1427, included the following:

Taking away the whole old timber of the Painted Tower which was rotten and in a ruinous state.

Costs of various tenants on boonwork drawing and carrying timber from Earlswood into the castle for the new woodwork in the tower.

Various men with their oxen and wagons carrying 31 loads of stone from Trinitycliff to the castle.

Collecting and putting together stones round the precincts of the castle and town of the same.

22 wagonloads of limestone for quicklime.

Seacoal bought at Bristol for burning the lime, carried by water to Caldicot.

John Mason making and mending the stonework of the Painted Tower. Making new chimney and cresting the walls.

3 hooks bought for the hanging of the door of the tower.

Joan Harberd carrying the old shingles from the precincts of the castle to the chapel house to serve for the Lady's minister.

When Sir John Beauchamp held the Castle and manor in 1443 he had the following work done at the Castle:

Mending of certain tower called Thomas Tower.

One pair of stocks made for the prison of the castle.

Mending and repairing a penfold.

6000 stone tiles bought at Lydney and taken by water.

Other timber bought from the cellarer of Tintern Abbey to be made into shingles.

King Henry VI carried out further repairs to the towers and dungeon in 1434, and later in 1498 it is recorded that Henry VII employed sawyers, carpenters, tilers and plumbers at the Castle.

It does not appear that there was any more expenditure on maintenance, and the Castle gradually deteriorated in condition.

In 1507 the Castle and manor of Caldicot was a parcel of the Duchy of Lancaster, and it was then demised on lease to Charles Somerset, Lord Herbert, as an agricultural holding. Whereas the manor flourished the Castle ceased to be living quarters and rapidly became a ruin.

Surveys made by the local inhabitants in the latter half of the sixteenth century refer to an old ancient castle that is ruinous and decayed.

Most of the shell remains, and it is not difficult, to mentally reconstruct the appearance and life in the Castle when it was the centre of activity in the manor.

Although the dominance of the Castle over the village had ceased the inhabitants continued to have an affection for the empty shell. It was usual for celebrations to wend their way to the Castle, and reports in the local press of the second half of the nineteenth century reveal that the Church, the Chapel, the Friendly Societies and other organizations held fetes and sports in the courtyard. This use was curtailed when Mr. J. R. Cobb purchased the Castle in 1885 and by restoration and additions he adapted it to his requirements as a private residence.

VII

THE MILL

THE Mill at Caldicot was an integral part of the agricultural operations of the community. The tenants of the Lord of the Manor, through their service obligations, ground their master's corn and in return were permitted to grind their own grain. The Mill accounts in the Public Record Office shew considerable profit from whole corn, meal, malt, and mill dust, all of which were sold or added to the stores of the manor. There was a granary within the walls of the Castle.

The existence of the Mill was recorded in Domesday Book, in 1086, and although there is no further reference to it in the time of the early holders of the manor, items of account appeared regularly when the Kings had a closer association with it.

The account of William Somery, the Reeve, in 1361, included the following item:

In roofing the Mill with help of serfs 10/-. Mill wheels—carpenter 2/-. In binding the said wheels with irons bought, and with stipend of the smith—6/6. In two bills for the millstones made anew with steel bought for the same—2/2. In mending the roof of the granary within the castle with nails bought for the same 10d.

Earl Humphrey (Tenth) carried out repairs to the Mill and granary from 1361 to 1366.

Thomas Woodstock, Anne Stafford and Henry V also incurred expenditure during the time they held the manor.

In the Duchy of Lancaster accounts for 1436, when King Henry VI held the Castle, the following item appeared:

John Baker, the bailiff at Caldicot, seeks allowance of one little boat bought for the use of cleaning the river belonging to the lord's Mill there on the north side of the Castle, price of the boat 13s. 4d. Item for a millstone bought for the use of the same mill, price 13s. 4d. Item in carrying the same 20d. Item in piercing the same 20d. Item for making the eynkes of the same, 8d. Item in making the spindle, 8d. Item in making the bill, 12d. Item for making the cog and rung, 12d. Item in cleaning the river belonging to the Mill 6/8d. Hay, 20d.

When the manor became an agricultural holding, and the subject of long leases by the Duchy of Lancaster from 1507, the Mill was let as a separate holding.

Queen Elizabeth leased the Mill to William Moryes in 1584, and he took action in the Court of the Duchy of Lancaster against eight farmers because they took their grain to other mills and he had to pay the whole of the rent from his own purse. He asked for a writ ordering the defendants to send their grain to the Queen's Mill. In the survey of 1613 Henry Vaughan, a relative of the Herberts by marriage, had the tenancy of the Mill with 11 acres of land for a rent of 7s. 4d.

In the survey of the manor in 1650 Roger Rowlands was recorded as the tenant of the Corn Mill, but when William Ford made his survey in 1771 it states on his map on the site where the Tin Stamping Works now stands, by the railway crossing at Caldicot Pill, that the "Corn Mill was here formerly."

VIII

THE CROSS AND THE COURTS

THE lives of the tenants within the manor were governed by customs. These customs are set out in the Survey of 1613 and had been in operation since time immemorial probably operating when the Normans were first responsible for the government of the manor. One such custom was that "their Court ought always to be kept at the Cross in Caldicot or near thereunto." There is still an area called the Cross, but the ancient structure which had stood for centuries was removed in the latter part of the eighteenth century and a sundial was erected in its place. In 1869 the Parish Vestry Meeting gave permission to a Mr. Hollis to remove the old steps and sundial from their position outside the White Hart Inn. This Mr. Hollis did and there is no indication of what he did with them.

The Cross originally consisted of a base of stone steps rising in the form of a pyramid to a shaft headed by a cross, but in 1643 the puritans succeeded in obtaining an order for the destruction of all crosses. Committees of Magistrates were formed in every county to carry out this work and they appeared satisfied to remove the heads only, so any bases and shafts remained. The lower steps served as seats when the courts and manor meetings were held.

There was a wide open area around the Cross where the villagers assembled to air their grievances, and to hold the obligatory Court monthly on a Monday. The details of the proceedure are set out in Appendix B.

The relationship of landlord and tenant was governed by the customs of the manor, and the findings of the court were based upon precedent. The steward of the lord of the manor was responsible for convening the meetings in the open at the Cross. He also arranged for the selection and presence of the jury chosen from the tenants. The bailiff assisted in the holding of the court, serving notices, and collecting fines. The court dealt with methods of cultivation, misdemeanours, and the problems and changes which arose in the relationship of landlord and tenant.

There were many acts of wrongdoing, and even the vicar of Caldicot was not above suspicion. In the Patent Rolls of 1334 it states that the ship Le Mariote sailing from Bordeaux to Bristol with a cargo of wine was wrecked near Goldcliff. When the cargo was claimed it was found that, among others, the prior of Goldcliff, the vicar of Nash and John the vicar of Caldicot had helped themselves to it.

Courts were held at Caldicot in the name of Queen Katherine. In the Monmouthshire County Records a case is referred to between William Bayons, complainant, and John Senare and Joan Peylewyn, defendants, which stated that the final concord of the Court held at Caldicot on 29th June 1434, before Morgan ap Madoc, deputy of Sir William ap Thomas, steward. The jury consisted of Richard Herberd, Hollapp Jenkyn, Alexander Stanshaw, William Valleys, and other faithful men of the Queen. The case related to a free cottage with curtilage, called Vantoteshall, and the consideration decided upon was "a sore sparrow-hawke."

The following are further examples of cases held at the Court at Caldicot:

Court of the lord King held on Monday, 16th March, in the 15th year of King Henry VI (1437) before Morgan ap Madoc, deputy of William ap Thomas, Kt., then steward there. . . ' Fine 3s. 4d.

John Hawkin is convicted that he occupied and stole one Ridingcloth, price 8d. of the chattels of Richard Smythe of Kayrewent, against his will and the peace of the lord., therefore he is fined.
Fine 5s.

Henry Gorgevele gives to the lord of fine 5s. to have entry into one cottage with courtyard adjacent, late of Robert Coniers, to hold to him, Alice his wife and Joan daughter of the same, for the term of their lives, or of the one living longer according to the custom of the manor, by the rent and services therefore formerly due and accustomed. And so he has freedom thereof and does fealty.
16d.

The Bailiff presents one black heifer, price 12d., also one black heifer, price 4d., coming to the lord as strays at the feast of the Annunciation of Blessed Mary last year preceding.
And because no one claimed them, therefore they remained forfeit to the lord, because they are of a full year's age.

To take levy from Thomas ap Howell to answer to the lord because on 10th May, 15 Henry VI, within the lord's demesne at Caldicot he made trespass, armed battery, and shed blood on Thomas Taylour contrary to peace.

William Gogh, 6d. and John Conier, 6d., in mercy because they brewed beer and broke the assize.
Chattels forfeit

The bailiff presents 1 plok of old timber coming to the lord from wreck of the sea and forfeit to the lord and sold for 4d.

Court held on May 2nd, in the 34th year of the reign of our Lady Queen Elizabeth (1593) having deputed Roger Seyes to be steward.

Lewis Harbert, and other, who failed to make suit of Court according to the custome of the manor accordingly fined sixpence.

Edward Morgan, gent., and eleven others, who as jury present on oath that Thomas Lewis who held freely of this manor is dead and that Henry Lewis is his heir, the lord having a relief of 8s. 10d.

Court of Robert Sydeny Knight held 7th May in the 43rd year of our Lady Queen Elizabeth (1602).

To this Court came William Edwards alias Jones and surrendered in the hands of the lord one messuage, one barn, 20 acres of land, lying within the aforesaid manor and with means and bounds defined from antiquity.

Court of 10th May 1674.

To this Court came John Edwards and surrendered in hand one cottage and garden with appurts. in Caldicot to the use of Phebe Field, spinster, for ever.

In the early Chancery Proceedings between 1538–44, David Atkins was the complainant against William Bowen, concerning waste of a mill in Shirenewton, formerly of William Parker.

In the Star Chamber Proceedings, during the reign of Queen Elizabeth, William David, of Penhow, was the complainant against James Morgan, High Constable of Caldicot, with his petty constables, alleging conspiracy in the corrupt purchase of a mare in Chepstow market and corrupt accusation of stealing the mare at the Assizes. Assault by William Morgan upon complainant on his way to the Assizes leaving complainant for dead in an alehouse at Penhow on his way back from the Assizes.

One of the last memorable occasions at the old Cross was on the 21st October 1741, when John Wesley, on his way from Newport to Bristol via the ferry from Black Rock, stopped at Caldicot. The following is an extract from his journal: "About one I came to Caldicot and preached to a small attentive congregation of people on 'Blessed are they which do hunger and thirst after rightousness for they shall be filled.' " He reached Bristol between seven and eight p.m. When he addressed his Caldicot congregation he stood on the steps of the Cross.

IX

THE CHURCH AND THE BELLS

THE village Church of St. Mary, the Virgin, was, in the first instance, closely connected with the Priors of Llantony Secunda, in Gloucester, and the manor they had established in Caldicot. When Milo Fitzwalter, as sheriff of Gloucester, had founded the Priory in Gloucester, in 1137, he stated in his charter that he made a gift of two parts of the tithe in all things at Caldicot to the canons of Llantony on the day and hour when that church was dedicated. This gift formed a substantial endowment to the Priory, and the prior lost no time in commencing agricultural operations, and building the church.

A charter of King John referred to a gift by Henry de Bohun to the church of Caldicot, between the years 1199 and 1216, so it can be assumed that the building of the church commenced on the Priory land during this period.

The Norwich Taxation shews that in 1254 Caldicot was impropriated to Llantony.

The first vicar to gain mention was John, who, in 1334, was found to have taken part, with others, in removing wine from the ship *Le Mariote* when it was wrecked at Goldcliff.

There was a close connection in the medieval period between the lords of the Castle, the Priory, and the church. The parish priest reigned within the walls of his church, and there he said Mass attended on Sundays by the greater part of the villagers. The peasant, as he stood or knelt on the floor at the church, could not understand the Latin service, but most priests and confessors exploited a fear of hell.

The nave of the church was the "village hall" for most communal purposes, and in the fifteenth century it was common for church ales to be provided and consumed in the church or the churchyard, payment being made and the proceeds used for the maintenance of the building.

The pattern of life at the church changed with the dissolution of Llantony (Gloucester) Priory by Henry VIII.

Two commissioners, Dr. John Vaughan, and Dr. Adam Becanshaw, visited Newport, in 1536, but it is not known after their conclusions what happened to the priors.

In 1534 the Papal authority over the church was set aside, and

although King Henry assumed the title of supreme head of the church
he desired little change in the dogmas and rites. In 1551, however, a
new confession of faith was embodied in forty-two articles.

Richard Johns was vicar of Caldicot, in 1535, evidently appointed
by the King who then held the Priory Manor, and had the advowson in
h is hands. The King sold his Caldicot interests to Richard Seaborne in

CALDICOT CHURCH
drawing by Thos. T. Birbeck

1557 and they remained with his family until 1603 when Edward Kemeys
became the owner of the estate, and the advowson remained with members of his family until the nineteenth century.

Charles I, in an endeavour to form a permanent navy levied a rate,
known as Ship Money, in 1636, and the amounts apportioned to
Caldicot were £16.15.2. upon the parish, and £1.4.0. upon Howel
Adams, who was vicar from 1636 to 1638.

When the Commonwealth attained power in 1649, the Vicar of Caldicot was Nathaniel Collington, B.A., who had been installed by Nicholas Kemeys, a staunch Royalist. Collington was, therefore, deprived of his living, and a Puritan, Hopkin Rogers, was appointed. When Charles II gained the throne Hopkin Rogers was in turn deprived, and Nathaniel Collington was restored. He resigned, however, in 1664, and John Williams, B.A., was appointed by Lady Kemeys.

In 1662 the Act of Uniformity was passed which required every beneficed clergyman to declare his full assent to everything contained in the book of Common Prayer, and all who refused to observe the rites and subscribe to the doctrine were excluded from communion. It was at this time that the nonconformists took a more prominent place in the community.

The advowson of the church remained under the patronage of the Kemeys family until 1838 when the Rev. Henry Sayce, then the vicar of Caldicot, purchased it for £390. He in turn sold it, in 1840, to General Sir Edmund Keynton Williams, who, a year later, saw his son Edmund Turberville Williams, B.A., of Exeter College, Oxford, installed in the living. The latter was a worthy servant to the parish until he retired in 1885. The Rev. E. T. Williams lived for a few years at Mount Ballan, until 1853, when he purchased Caldicot Hall, or Great House, from Henry Wise, and in 1862 he was responsible for the building of the present Caldicot Vicarage. He also increased the number of church bells.

The church registers only exist from the year 1717, when the death was recorded of Morgan Lewis, the vicar of Caldicot.

The vestry minutes are not very extensive but include the following items:

1808 Wine for 3 Sundays—9/-d.

1812 New iron chest—£6.12.6d.

1835 Paid Claridge, clockmaker, of Chepstow 3/-d. for mending clock and bass viol.

1823 Paid Edward Wise £2 for attending to the clock.

1839 Paid Mary Pollard £1 per year for cleaning surplices.

1846 Inventory of Church furniture by the Churchwardens, Thomas Rowlands and Walter Edwards:

    1 Surplice, 1 white damask communion cloth.

    1 White Maniple, 2 white corporals, 1 Plain Linen Cloth.

    1 Folio Prayer Book, 1 Bible, 1 Quarto Prayer Book.

    1 Quarto Communion and offices.

    1 Octavo   do.

    1 Bier, 2 chalices, 1 Patton, 1 Alms Dish.

1858 It was agreed to instal the church clock in the tower.

1856 Henry Wise, who had been a churchwarden from 1809 to 1840, died.

The churchwardens were generally farmers, but the innkeepers were also prominent. Henry Prior, of the White Hart, served from 1836 to 1867, and Thomas Hicks, of the Tippling Philosopher, also held office.

The census of Places of Worship taken in 1851 gave the following information of the church:

Net income from endowment   £180 per annum.
Sitting accommodation   200 with room for many more.
Average congregation—morning 100—afternoon 60
Sunday School   „   50   „   30
This was certified by Rev. E. T. Williams, Vicar.

The church comprises a nave with a north aisle, chancel, and a central tower. It has a specious south porch with low stone benches at each side. Over the inner door is a niche containing a statue of the Virgin Mary and Child. To the right are small doors connected by a flight of steps to give access to an upper storey in the porch.

Above the outer door set into the inside wall is a much worn carving of the Virgin and Child, which was brought from Llantony Abbey.

The font at one time was just inside the south door, but is now placed near the west door.

The hand-made silver mountings on the churchwarden's staves, and other silver work in the church, was wrought by Omar Ramsden.

In 1860 the church choir presented a brass chandelier to the church.

There are finely carved capitals of the pillars supporting the arcade in the nave.

There is a priest's door in the south wall of the Sanctuary.

Extensive restoration of the church was carried out at the instigation of the Rev. E. T. Williams in 1858.

The only reminder of the Herbert family, so prominent in Caldicot for hundreds of years, is the flat stone in the floor of the north aisle which marks the place where the body of Susan Herbert lies. She died on the 1st November 1629, and was the wife of Francis Herbert who founded Herbert's Charity which has been of great value to the parish.

The association of the villagers with the church was very close in the nineteenth century and there were many happy gatherings. In 1859 the Harvest Festival was held in the open in the castle ruins, and in 1867 a choral festival was enjoyed in the church followed by a luncheon in a large tent in the castle courtyard.

In the early 1870's it was felt that there was a need for a church at Highmoor Hill and the parishioners made great efforts to raise the money to erect a suitable building. In 1873 and 1874 a number of concerts were arranged and special collections were made in the church.

In 1874 the foundation stone was laid and building proceeded. The church was completed with the help of many people. It was of gothic type with six windows with side lancets and a seventh large window in

INTERIOR OF CALDICOT CHURCH
From a drawing in the National Library of Wales

the west wall with a bell cot for one bell above it, and overall a stone cross, the gift of Jones Bros., Masons, of Chepstow. An old pulpit was removed from Llanfrechfa Church and renovated, and an old reading desk was given by Tintern Parva. St. Pierre Church gave an altar table, and the vicar of Bath provided a Bible, prayer book, and an alms dish. A fund for the glass required was raised by Miss English, of Caldicot. The land for the church was given by the Rev. E. T. Williams, the vicar of Caldicot. The sand needed for the construction was given by Mr. Dowle, of Ifton, and the stone was dressed and neatly put together by Moses Squibbs, who was also the assistant overseer of the parish. The church was built to seat 100.

On Whit Tuesday, 1876, the opening ceremony took place. It was a mission church primarily for the needs of the people in the Highmoor Hill area, sometimes called Highmass Hill.

The Church Bells
There are now eight bells in Caldicot Church. The oldest is No. 8 and is probably by a founder named William Warwick, of Bristol, in about the year 1450. It is similar to the No. 7 bell at Yatton, Somerset, cast in 1451, as the Yatton Parish accounts prove. The lettering is large and very gracefully formed, with an elaborate cross and medallion. The inscription is as follows: + In HO O NORƎ SANƆTA MARINƎ

The E's in Honore and Marine and the C in Sancta are reversed, and "Marine" is the founder's error for "Mariae". The lettering and stops are two inches high.

The No. 7 bell is inscribed "LAUDATE DEUM IN SIMBALLIS SONORIS, 1627." It was possibly cast by John Palmer who had a foundry at Gloucester from 1621 to 1638.

Bell No. 6 was installed in 1699 by Mary Kemeys whose family had acquired the old Priory Manor, and had the advowson of the church. The bell was made by Evan Evans of Chepstow.

No. 4 bell was installed by the churchwardens, William Foord and Samuel Musgrove, in 1858, from the foundry of G. Mears of Whitechapel.

Bell No. 3 inscribed "LAUDATE DEUM CYMBALLIS" (and bell No. 5 inscribed "In HONOREM DEI") were presented by the Rev. E. Turbeville Williams, the vicar of the parish in 1882. They were cast at the foundry of Llewellins and James, at Bristol.

Bells No. 1 and 2 are inscribed "LAUDATE DOMINUM" and "EXALTABO TE DEUS," and were also presented by the Rev. E. Turberville Williams, in 1883, and were cast by Llewellins and James.

Bells 6 and 7 were recast by G. Mears, of Whitechapel, in 1858.

All the bells were rehung and mounted in iron stocks in an iron frame by Gillett and Johnson, of Croydon, in 1911.

In the will of John Bryme, Clerk, dated 27th February 1525, and proved 21st March 1525, it stated: "I will that my executors shall provide or cause to be provided at my cost and charge one other bell to the three bells that be now in the parish Church of our Lady at Calecot in the diocese of Llandaff to the effect and purpose to make four bells all in acconcorde and ringing as shortly after my decease as conveniently maybe."

It would appear that the number of bells was reduced from four to one before No. 7 was installed in 1627.

The following are the sizes of the bells:

No.	Date	Size	Weight		
			Cwts.	qurs.	lbs
1	1883	27"	4	3	12
2	,,	28"	4	3	14
3	1882	31"	5	3	10
4	1858	34"	6	2	11
5	1882	34"	6	0	17
6	1699	37"	9	0	7
7	1627	41"	10	1	18
8	1451		13	0	6

In 1876 the bell ringers had formed an association and rang at Bath. The ingers were also proficient with hand bells and entertained at many local functions in the nineteenth century.

X

THE NONCONFORMISTS

THE influence of the Puritans was continued after the restoration of the monarchy by the dissenters or nonconformists.
After the passing of the Act of Uniformity, in 1662, many clergymen were unable to accept the principles laid down, and small bodies of people met, generally in private houses, to worship in the manner their consciences dictated.

The episcopal returns prepared for the diocese of Llandaff, from 1665 to 1676, recorded that Hopkin Rogers, of Caldicot, and Robert Jones, of Shirenewton, were Heads or Teachers, and the meetings were held in their houses.

Hopkin Rogers, described as a gentleman, served on a jury for the manor of Caldicot in 1665. In the time of the Commonwealth he was appointed vicar of Caldicot by Cromwell, but he was deprived of the living when the monarchy was restored. He then led his followers, as dissenters, from his house.

The notes against the Deanery return state that the nonconformists numbered persons of good estate such as country gentlemen, and those who were in arms in Cromwell's rebellion, together with their servants, including many of the meaner sort of people and their wives and children. They were composed mainly of three sects, Independents, Anabaptists, and Quakers.

Later returns of the Llandaff Diocese recorded the following meeting places in Caldicot:
1799, Protestants meeting in a dwelling house.
1807, the Wesleyan Chapel.
1812, Baptists meeting in a dwelling house.
1830, Bible Christians meeting in a dwelling house.

The foundation stone for the Bible Christian Chapel in Chepstow Road, was laid in 1865, and the service following was held in the Wesleyan Chapel which had been placed at their disposal.

The first Wesleyan Chapel, referred to above, was on the site of the present new shopping centre near the Cross.

A return was made in respect of the Wesleyan Chapel for the 1851

97

census in which it stated that the chapel was erected before 1810, and had 110 free sittings and seventy other sittings.

There was a morning service only, at which an average of 150 persons attended. There was no Sunday School then, but one soon followed.

The chapel was quite small, and for the anniversary in 1867 the tea meeting was held at the White Hart Inn when 200 were present.

In 1877 the Anniversary Public Tea took place in a tent in the castle grounds.

A new chapel was built, and it was registered for worship on the 10th October 1895, but it was not until the 15th August 1898, that it was registered for marriages. The application was signed by the trustee, Richard Hubert Hill, whose family was prominent for many years in the life of the parish.

The old chapel was used for a number of purposes after 1895, and was finally a part of a commercial garage until it was demolished to make way for the new shopping centre.

XI

THE CHARITIES

I T is appropriate that a member of the Herbert family, who had added
much to the life of the Caldicot community, should establish the
most important charity of the parish. Francis Herbert, gentleman,
by his last will and testament gave and bequeathed sixty pounds towards
purchasing lands to the absolute use and only relief and maintenance of
the poor of the parish for ever.

Francis Herbert died in 1628, and he appointed Henry Vaughan,
who had married Herbert's sister Mary, and his brother Richard
Herbert, of South Brook, as executors. Before the negotiations for the
land were completed Henry Vaughan died, and his son, Hugh, was
appointed in his stead. The main parcels of land purchased were 4 acres
stretching from the present Herbert Road to the new motorway, and the
old allotments in Sandy Lane of about 1½ acres.

Susan, the wife of Francis, is buried in Caldicot Church and a large
slab indicates the place of burial.

The Charity Commissioners granted the trustees approval to the sale
of the two parcels of land to the Chepstow Rural District Council for
post-war development for approximately £10,000 which provides an
annual income of about £500 for disbursement to the poor.

Francis Herbert was the great-great-grandson of Sir Walter Herbert,
one of the last residents in the Castle.

Another small charity was founded by Catherine Kemeys by indenture dated 19th January 1680, whereby she conveyed to Mary Kemeys
and Charles Price, as trustees, a barn and orchard and 1½ acres of land
in the parish of Ifton for the education of poor children so as to read the
Bible and to write a legible hand. The land is on the left hand side of the
road from Ferney Cross to Ifton and is now held by the Monmouthshire
County Council as the education authority.

Catherine Kemeys was firstly the widow of Hugh Herbert, the son of
Francis Herbert. She secondly married William Kemeys, of Kemeys.

XII

THE POOR AND THE OVERSEERS

For centuries the parish priest had been responsible for the relief of the poor within his parish and he collected alms for that purpose. The poor were principally of two classes, the sick and infirm, who were unable to work; and the idle and sturdy who did not choose to do so.

The attitude towards these two classes is typified in the following epigram written by Robert Crowley, about the year 1550:

> I heard two beggars that under a hedge sate,
> Who did with long talk their matters debate.
> They had both sore legs most loathsome to see,
> All raw from the foot, well most to the knee,
> "My leg," quoth the one, "I thank God is fair,"
> "So is mine," quoth the other in a cold air,
> "For then it looketh raw and as red as any blood,
> "I would not have it healed for any world's good,
> No man would pity me but for my sore leg,
> Wherefore if I were whole I might in vain beg,
> I should be constrained to labour and sweat,
> And perhaps sometime with scourges be beat."

To regularize the giving of relief to the needy Queen Elizabeth enacted the poor law statutes which provided for the appointment, in every parish, of overseers of the poor whose chief duties were, firstly to levy rates for the performance of their duties relating to the poor, impotent, old, and blind; and secondly to provide work for such as were able to work, but could find no employment.

Justices of the Peace were empowered to appoint three or four overseers from the householders in the parish, and they had to work in conjunction with churchwardens. They were empowered to build poorhouses at the expense of the parish for the reception of the impotent poor.

In later legislation the duty of appointing the overseers was transferred to the parishioners, who at their annual parish meeting at Easter elected some of their number to act throughout the following year.

This proceedure was carried out at Caldicot. The Vestry minutes, from 1836, record the appointment of Overseers of the Poor annually. They were a good cross section of the villagers. The publicans appointed included Henry Prior, of the White Hart, and John Joseph of the Tippling Philosopher. Edward Reece, the shoemaker, and George Hollis, the grocer, also served but the greater number were farmers.

Four cottages had been provided, near the Cross, to be occupied by the aged and infirm poor.

After the passing of the Poor Law Amendment Act, of 1834, Boards of Guardians were established for five divisions of the county based upon the market towns of Abergavenny, Chepstow, Monmouth, Newport, and Pontypool.

Caldicot was included in the Chepstow Union. Shortly after its formation, in 1836, the Chepstow Board borrowed money and commenced the building of a Workhouse which was ready by 1838, and was known in recent years as Regent House.

In 1844 the Vestry meeting decided to sell the Caldicot poor houses and remove the families to the new Chepstow workhouse, but there was some delay, and in 1845, the overseers, churchwardens, and constable were empowered to evict the tenants. We find, however, that the houses were still occupied in 1848 when it was decided not to sell them, and so the position remained until 1856, and then Mr. Price, the Guardian for the parish, was asked to request the Chepstow Board to sell the poor houses without delay. The Board consented to this and the premises were put up for auction at the White Hart Inn, with a reserve of £100.

In 1809 there were twenty-seven ratepayers, and a rate of 1/9d. in the pound produced the £60 the parish required for their expenses. The following are typical items of expenditure:

Postage of a letter	1/–
Fees of Parish Clerk	£5.10.0d.
Day's sawing	7/–
Hauling Bricks	10/6d.
Catching Moles	£21 for 2½ years

By 1850 the population of the parish was growing as a result of the work on the new railway, and the South Wales Railway Company was asked to contribute to the rates. The amount that the voluntary overseers was empowered to collect had greatly increased and the Vestry, at their meeting in 1851, agreed that a paid Assistant Overseer be appointed to collect the rates. It transpired that this was a more difficult task than anticipated. Mr. Day was first appointed at £12 per annum, but a week later he was disqualified. S. Musgrove was then appointed, but he failed to give sureties. The post was then advertised and Mr. Hollis, the grocer, was given the position at £13 per annum. We find, however, in 1856, that the assistant overseer had not taken up his duties so Mr. W. Price was appointed at £14 per annum. He held

the post for less than a year when Mr. Thomas Wise held the office.
He resigned in 1860, and it was decided that no further appointment be
made, but in 1866 it was decided to advertise again for an Assistant
Overseer. Although James Adams was appointed at £21 per annum he
failed to produce securities, so Robert Squibbs was appointed. The
office was then held for over 100 years by the Squibbs family. Moses
succeeded his father, Robert, and Ernest, the son of Moses followed.
Eventually Ronald succeeded his father, Ernest, but this is beyond the
period primarily covered by this book.

XIII

THE VILLAGE CONSTABLE

THE village constable played an important part in the life of the community. His office existed from the time when the administration of the manor was formulated. He was first an officer of the manor responsible for maintaining law and order, and it was his duty to keep the stocks and other corrective appliances in usable condition. He also assisted with the collection of rates, fines, and fees. It was a compulsory office without official payment.

In the latter part of the sixteenth century Parliament entrusted to the constables, and not the churchwardens, supervision over beggars, the lodging of the impotent poor, and the apprenticing of children. After the Elizabethan statutes, appointing the churchwardens and the overseers as the Poor Law authorities, the constable continued for another century as the premier officer in the administration of the Vagrant Acts. He also dealt with the supervision of alehouses.

The constable was authorized not only to apprehend a person who had committed a felony, but if he saw a minor offence committed he could place the offender in custody, or in the stocks, until he could bring him before a magistrate. His staff of office was sometimes affixed to his door.

Originally an officer of the manor he was never expressly transferred to the parish for appointment. Down to Victorian times he was appointed at the Court Leet for an area that was not always identical with a whole parish.

The petty constables were appointed by the Justices and had, under penalty, to execute their warrants, and obey their order.

Within the county the principle division was the Hundred, an administrative unit of unknown origin, which served as a convenient local subdivision for most county purposes. One such division was the Caldicot Hundred which included not only Caldicot and Newton, but many of the small parishes surrounding them. The Justices were appointed for these divisions, and they worked in conjunction with the Court Leet.

In 1634 four Justices of the Peace for the Caldicot Hundred, Edward Morgan, David Morgan, Nicholas More, and Richard Kemys, made the following report to the Justices of Assizes and Gaol Delivery for the County of Monmouth,

We, his Majesty's Justices of the Peace, whose names are subscribed within our division being within the hundred of Caldicot, according to his Majesty's instructions, tending for relieving the poor, the placing of poor children to be apprentices, the punishing of rogues and vagabonds, and the legal suppressing of disorderly alehouse keepers as well licensed as unlicensed, have at our sundry meetings taken such course that all our poor are competently provided for and fully relieved, no compliants being any way made to the contrary, and have placed nineteen poor children to be apprentices.

And upon perusal of the several presentments of the Petty Constables at our sundry meetings we find the number of five and twenty rogues and vagabonds there punished and sent to the place of their birth, and such constables as we found remiss and negligent in their office we have inflicted such penalties and punishments on them that the law required, and legally punished the abuses and disorders of Alehouses within our district, and reduced them to an indifferent number as was required at our hands, and to the uttermost of our powers have been careful in the performance of all the rest of our instructions.

This meeting was held at Penhow, and another meeting of the Court Leet within the Hundred of Caldicot was held in 1826 when separate petty constables were appointed to "the Parish of Caldicot" and "Caldicot Lower End," and at Newton to "Shirenewton Village", and "Shirenewton Parish End."

A Hayward was also appointed at this leet for Caldicot, whose duty it was to take charge of fences, enclosures, commons, and waste, and he was also authorized to impound cattle when necessary.

It was found in the nineteenth century that the appointments of overseers, surveyors, and petty constables were made at the Vestry Meeting, and any deviation in the appointments by the Justices was deemed as an arbitrary exercise of power. The Vestry minutes for Caldicot bear this out. At their annual meeting they invariably elected from their number, the overseers, surveyors, and constables, in addition to their churchwardens, and they called upon the constable to assist them in the performance of their duties. In 1845, Thomas Adams, the local butcher, was a petty constable and the meeting agreed that he should accompany the churchwardens and the overseers to evict the tenants from the poor houses which were to be sold. In later years lists of as many as eight men were approved for liability to serve as constable.

In 1857 the police under the justices was superseded by Robert Peel's new police, and the Monmouthshire County force was formed in that year with Major Herbert as the first Chief Constable of the County.

XIV

MILITARY SERVICE

ALTHOUGH the men of Caldicot were primarily men of the plough the change to military service was always near to them. In the medieval period the de Bohuns, as holders of the manor, and to whom the tenants were under obligations, raised the forces for fighting against their enemies from the men in their manors. The men of the Marches made redoubtable soldiers, and were present with the de Bohuns in the wars against the Scots and the French. Humphrey and William de Bohun, with their men, were particularly prominent at the battle of Crecy and it can be taken for granted that men from Caldicot were present in these actions.

In 1648 Sir Nicholas Kemeys, of Llanvair Discoed, who owned the manor that had once been the Priory Manor of Caldicot, raised a force of 160 men to take and defend Chepstow Castle against Cromwell's forces.

Caldicot was represented in the Royal Monmouthshire Militia which was created in 1660. It was embodied for duty during the Seven Years' War from 1760–63; the American War from 1778–83; the Napoleonic and the Crimean Wars.

The Lord Lieutenant was responsible for the raising and upkeep of the militia, and he usually appointed prominent local landowners as the officers. In a commission dated 15th November 1715, John Morgan, of Tredegar, the Lord Lieutenant of Monmouthshire, appointed Thomas Lewis, of St. Pierre to be captain of the militia for the Hundred of Caldicot. The hostilities with the French in the year 1756 caused a reorganization of the militia for before that little had been done to render it efficient.

On the 20th July 1807, Lt. Col. Thomas Molyneux inspected the Chepstow and Caldicot Volunteer Infantry at Chepstow, and he was very pleased with their appearance. The bad weather, however, prevented the men from going through the whole of their evolutions "for which they were so distinguished."

A new Militia Act was passed in 1807 which authorized the raising of 1353 men in Monmouthshire. Each parish was allotted a quota.

The parish constable prepared a list of the men of military age in his

105

parish. These were presented to the Lord Lieutenant who selected the number required.

There were many changes in the formation and title of the Monmouthshire Militia until it became a part of the South Wales Borderers.

XV

THE ROADS

THE routing of the roads, tracks, and paths remained very much the same in Caldicot from the time the manor was developed until the nineteenth century. The earliest track would be that used by the Romans from Caldicot Pill to Caerwent. The main road later was from Chepstow to Deepweir, and from thence to the Cross which was the focal point of the gatherings of the villagers. A road to the east of the Cross served the Church and the Priory manor, whilst a road to the west passed through the West End manor to Ferny Cross and on to Magor and Newport. Another road from Ferny Cross served Dewstow passing on to Caerwent bridge and over the Neddern to Caerwent. This road is referred to in a grant made in the thirteenth century as, "the Royal way from Caldicot to Dewstow."

In medieval times the lord of the manor, through his officers, ensured that the roads were kept in useable condition because he was directly concerned in their use for the agricultural operations of his demesne land. With the decay of the manor the upkeep of the roads became the direct responsibility of the local inhabitants and the standard of the road works, and the attention given to them, varied considerably from parish to parish. A person journeying through a number of parishes often had obstacles and very uneven surfaces to overcome.

Capel Hanbury, of Pontypool, who leased Caldicot manor from the Duchy of Lancaster, was one of the first men to use a carriage in Monmouthshire, and in 1804 Charles Heath wrote that Hanbury took nine hours to travel twenty-one miles to Monmouth with the help of labourers to open gates, pull down hedges and make new ways.

The local inhabitants were satisfied if there were tracks, however rough, to meet their needs, and they continued so in Monmouthshire until the Turnpike Acts proved the means of providing a network of superior roads between the market towns.

The deplorable state of the roads in the county was referred to in the House of Commons when Valentine Morris, of Piercefield, was examined regarding the application for a new Turnpike Act, in 1754. When asked, "what roads are there in Monmouthshire?" he replied, "none."

This evoked the further question, "how do you travel?" His answer was, "in ditches."

One of the most important appointments at the annual parish meeting was that of surveyor. He was responsible for the repair and maintenance of the roads, right-of-ways, bridges, and ditches. He called upon the residents to carry out the necessary works, and supervised his labour force supplied mainly by the farmers.

In the parochial minutes of 1816 it is recorded that the surveyor placed a new bridge over Neddern brook to Crick, at a cost of £2.10.0., and it was agreed to ask Caerwent parish to share the expense. A year earlier the surveyor saw to the casting of the reens at the Common Sea and Benacre.

In 1853 James Sharp, of Little Dewstow, was the surveyor, and he conferred with the Caerwent surveyor regarding the repair of Deepweir bridge.

Mr. Dowle was the surveyor in 1860 and he was instructed by the parish meeting to take possession of all waste land adjoining the highways.

The minutes aired a complaint in 1871 that there was insufficient access to the Neddern at Deepweir bridge for carts hauling water.

The Turnpike Act of 1758 brought great benefit to Caldicot. It provided for the repair of the road from Magor to Chepstow Bridge. Caldicot was a part of the No. 1 District established by the Act, and the Rev. Edward Davies, the rector of Portskewett, was appointed the unpaid surveyor of the reconditioned road from Magor to Deepweir. This was an additional appointment to that of the parochial surveyor who could be called upon by the turnpike trustees to share his labour force. Parish surveyors were, in general unwilling to co-operate, and in some cases were compelled to do so.

Gates and toll bars were erected and the turnpike trustees levied tolls for the use of the road. The collector issued a ticket entitling the holder to return through the same gate, or through any other gate within seven miles, during the same day. Exemptions were granted to farmers and labourers taking agricultural carts. There was no toll house at Caldicot, but there was one at Portskewett.

In 1865 a Highway Board was established to take over the roads of a number of parishes, including Caldicot, based upon Chepstow which was the nearest market town. The Board appointed its own surveyor, and this office was abolished in the constituent parishes to be replaced in each parish by an unpaid way warden who was more of a watch dog than an executive officer. The first way warden for Caldicot was Henry Jones, of Court House. He was replaced in 1867 by Mr. Dowle who was asked by the parish meeting to question the Highway Board about the best method of contracting for road repairs.

In 1872 the turnpikes were abolished and their functions transferred to the Highway Boards.

XVI

THE RAILWAYS AND WORKS

The Effect of Railway Developments

THE railway line which connected Gloucester with Milford Haven, passing through Caldicot, was constructed by the South Wales Railway Company. The Great Western Railway Company had already initiated a service from London to Gloucester. The Great Western Railway Company by agreement provided the South Wales Railway Company with locomotives and rolling stock, and on the 18th June 1850, the line from Chepstow West Station to Swansea opened, and Caldicot heard the unaccustomed roar and rattle of a train service for the first time. The population of Caldicot had not varied very much through its period as an agricultural community and in the census of 1841, before the advent of the railway, it revealed a population of 625. Succeeding censuses which were taken at ten yearly intervals, shewed an increase as the railway activities progressed. The first indication in the registration records of the presence of railway workers, was in 1851 when the birth of a child, to Samuel Reeves, a railway worker, was registered. The 1851 census shewed that William Davis, a railway policeman from Bridgend was registered in a cottage at Caldicot Pill.

As the workers who had been working on the railway construction, and lodging in Caldicot, left the district on the completion of the line it resulted in a decrease in the population in 1861, when the census recorded 579 inhabitants.

The representatives of the parish at the Vestry Meeting were not slow to take advantage of the railway for an additional source of income, for in 1850 they resolved to rate the South Wales Railway.

The next advance was the making of the Severn Tunnel. In 1872 an Act of Parliament was obtained for its construction, and in 1880 work commenced. The census taken in 1881 indicated a large increase in the population to 1401. Many railway workers were settling in the parish and the number of houses had increased from 130 in 1841 to 256 in 1881.

At Caldicot Pill there had only been Pill Farmhouse and one cottage, but houses now began to spring up rather haphazardly at Beesditch which had one time been an open field, but had later been enclosed by

109

an Inclosure Act, and much of the land figured in the sale of the estate of Henry Wise in 1857.

With the completion of the Severn Tunnel in the parish of Port-skewett, and Severn Tunnel Junction in the parish of Rogiet, there were two lines of track passing through Caldicot, the Severn Tunnel line being underground for most of the way.

There was a greater upheaval in the adjoining parishes of Portskewett and Rogiet with Ifton.

At Portskewett the population rose from 244 in 1871 to 1190 in 1891 and in the same period the village of Sudbrook was constructed bringing the number of houses from 48 to 184.

Rogiet and Ifton where there were only twelve houses in 1861 in-creased to forty-six houses in 1901 and the population progressed from about sixty in 1861 to 194 in 1901.

Although the main works were in the adjoining parishes many of the railway workers who were settling in the area appeared to prefer Caldicot in which to live, and the number of houses increased from 120 to 259 by 1901, completely altering the agricultural character of the parish. According to Bradney the rateable value of Caldicot rose from £1,829 in 1815 to £9,591 in 1891, so that the increase in population did not come without compensating financial advantages.

The railway development resulted in an increase in licensed premises. The Pill Inn was opened with W. Nicholas the licensee and the West of England Hotel had a short existence whilst workers required temporary accommodation.

Works at the Pill

At the same time as the railway was being constructed efforts were being made to establish an industrial undertaking on the site which for hun-dreds of years had been occupied by the Corn Mill of the lords of the Manor. The land was in the possession of Henry Wise in 1853 when he conveyed it to his brother-in-law Henry Pride. The site was of about four and a half acres in extent and there was a cottage upon it.

Henry Hughes purchased the site from Henry Pride in 1860 and he also entered into agreement with the South Wales Railway for a siding. This was the start of a very chequered career for the new works which were to be established. Hughes built an iron and wire works, installing plant and machinery and erecting terraces of houses for his employees.

The parish registers show, in 1863, that a child was born to John Hopkins, a wiredrawer, and deaths of wire workers were recorded in 1872.

In 1870 Henry Hughes conveyed the Caldicot Iron and Wire Works to Messrs. Bevan, Richards, and Crosswell, and they, in 1876, conveyed their rights in the company to Theophilus Bevan. Three years later the works were converted to the Caldicot Tinplate Company, and the workers were then described in the parish registers as tinmen.

There was a further change in 1886 when the Caldicot Tinplate Company ceased and was replaced by the Severn Tinplate Company.

In 1898 business reached a very low ebb. A receiver was appointed and work was abandoned. In 1905 the disused works were sold to the Dowlais Estate agents, Messrs. Edwards Brothers, and it was not until 1909 that they found a purchaser, willing to restart the works, in William Thomas Jones. He and his family have retained their interest in the undertaking of tin stamping. Although this book is not dealing with events after the nineteenth century it may interest readers to know that in 1919 the management was reformed as the Caldicot Tin Stamping Works Ltd., and later, in 1938 as Caldicot Works Ltd., when the printing and lacquering of tin was carried out, and has been so most successfully ever since.

XVII

THE SCHOOL

THE education of the children, such as it was, during the period with which we are concerned was mainly in the hands of the Church.

In 1666 the Bishop of Llandaff admitted William Thomas, literate, as schoolmaster to teach boys at Caldicot, and on the 19th January 1680, Catherine Kemeys, by indenture, founded a charity for the education of poor children so as to read the Bible and to write a legible hand. The legacy was not substantial and the terms placed limitations, but it ensured a regular form of education.

In 1807 children attended at the house of Mr. John Knight for tuition, and a widow, Mrs. Plaice, also kept a private school. A master was paid £3 per annum in 1816–19 to educate five children.

The Charity Report, in 1837, stated that there was no school-house in Caldicot, but an old schoolmistress taught five children to read in her cottage with a few others paid for by subscription.

The scholars attended at the church in 1841, when the census revealed that Isaac Spencer, who lived near the Cross, was the schoolmaster.

It was felt amongst the local clergymen and laymen that better facilities for education should be provided at Caldicot, and preliminary discussions terminated at a meeting at Mount Ballan, the residence of the vicar of Caldicot, on the 18th April 1845. The following were present: Rev. Lewis, Portskewett, Rev. Williams, Crick, Rev. Steele, Caerwent, and Henry Wise, Captain Jones, Messrs. Rowlands, Hodgson, and Bate of Caldicot. Captain King was the chairman. Details were discussed and a decision was made a year later to build a school in Church Road, Caldicot, upon land provided by Henry Wise. Until the completion of the new school the children continued to be taught at the church.

In 1847 the new school was completed at a cost of £115.2.0. and the following subscribers met most of this cost, together with £22.6.10. for additional expenditure: The Vicars of Caldicot, Portskewett, and Caerwent, the Duke of Beaufort, Henry Wise, the National Society, James Proctor, the Bishop of Llandaff, and the Diocesan Board of

Education. The balance was met by the proceeds of jumble sales. It provided accommodation for about forty pupils.

The school was the centre for many social evenings. In 1869 Mr. Alfred Cooper, the headmaster, received great credit for the performance by the senior boys of a play: "Whittington and his Cat." A drum and fife band had been trained by Mr. Cooper as a supporting item. An annual winter concert was also held, and, in 1877, 250 people were present. The bellringers gave selections on the hand bells.

With the growth of the population of the parish the school accommodation had to be increased and, in 1864, the village was all abustle for the official reopening which was followed by a march to a tent in the castle grounds for a cold meal.

XVIII

THE INNS AND SOCIETIES

ALEHOUSES have existed from time immemorial and catered for pilgrims and travellers as well as the local inhabitants. Ale had been unchallenged as the native drink of English men, women, and children at every meal. It was a weak brew and did not keep for long.

The de Bohuns brewed their own ale at the Castle, and hired out a cauldron to anyone requiring it. The borrower usually gave the Earl a prise of ale from the brewing. Visitors to the Castle assuaged their thirst from the Earl's ale, and he was liberal in supplying his tenants with drinks. When Thomas Woodstock was carrying out his building operations at the Castle it is recorded in his accounts that ale was provided for the tenants he called from the manor to help him.

In some parishes men and women drank ale in the church or churchyard, the proceeds going to the upkeep of the fabric, but in 1603 this practice was forbidden.

In 1437 two men were fined at the Caldicot Manor court because they brewed beer and broke the assize.

An early reference to an inn in the manor of Caldicot is in the 1613 survey, where, in defining the boundary, it mentions "from the Crick bridge to the house of William Jones, being the ale house there."

The early nineteenth century saw the introduction of Friendly Societies into the community life of Caldicot. They were invariably linked with an inn. The poorer classes became increasingly desirous of making provision for sickness and funeral expenses. When the Boards of Guardians displaced the overseers, in 1834, in the duty of looking after the poor, the personal interest in the parishioners was lessened, and there was a dread among the poor and aged of a "pauper's funeral." Hence the desire to join the societies and make the weekly payments required. Their meetings at the inns generally resulted in convivial evenings.

The most popular inn seems to have been the White Hart which had facilities for the entertainment of a large number of patrons. It existed in 1758, and when the friendly societies were formed it was the natural place for the headquarters of the earlier ones. The Caldicot Benefit

Friendly Society was formed in 1820 at the White Hart with 242 members, and this was followed in 1822 when the Society of Tradesmen and others met in the same inn. The ladies, not to be outdone, formed their society, the Caldicot Female Benefit Society, at the White Hart, in 1837. In the same year the Old Tippling Philosopher Friendly Society was launched in the inn bearing the same name.

The Caldicot Benefit Friendly Society seems to have been the strongest and most enduring of the societies. It lasted for over forty years and probably with other such societies it lost members to the newly formed

OLD WHITE HART AT THE CROSS
drawing by Thos. T. Birbeck

Oddfellows in 1865. The Friendly Society during its existence provided many pleasant and well supported events for its members and the public in general. Their anniversary was celebrated by a parade through the village, a church service, and a convivial evening at the White Hart. The Female Benefit Society also had their annual gathering when they had tea at the White Hart, dancing, and entertainment. In 1859 the men's society had 231 members and the ladies had seventy-six members, which encompassed a large proportion of the population of the village.

Local benefit clubs were gradually displaced by branches of larger orders and societies. The Ancient Order of Foresters, based upon the White Hart, was established in 1889. The first anniversary was celebrated in August 1890, by the brethren meeting at the inn in full regalia and then parading to the church for service. They then marched through the castle grounds to Portskewett and Sudbrook, and back to the White Hart for dinner. In the evening they held rustic sports in the field adjoining the Castle.

The Caldicot Castle Lodge of Oddfellows was founded in 1865. The *Chepstow Mercury* records that the society, at their first anniversary celebration at the Tippling Philosopher toasted their order in the following terms:

> May Oddfellows thrive, Like bees in a hive
> And ne'er sting each other
> May the Tippling Lodge grow, Like peas in a row
> And always grow together.

The quiet village of Caldicot awoke from its drowsiness when the Oddfellows celebrated their anniversary each August until the end of the century. The members first of all assembled at their clubroom at the Tippling Philosopher and then marched to the church headed by a band. Amongst the bands they engaged were the Shirenewton Silver Band (1871), the Lydney Brass Band (1885), and the Royal Monmouthshire Engineers (1878). A fete was then held in the Castle with music, dancing, and sports, terminating with fireworks. Landlord Hicks provided a sumptuous repast at the Tippling, and after a day of good cheer and innocent mirth the members returned to their homes well satisfied with their anniversary.

Henry Prior was mine host of the White Hart from 1841 to 1875, and he was very prominent in local affairs. He was a churchwarden for a number of years and a regular attender at the Vestry meetings. When the number present exceeded the capacity of the Vestry, Henry escorted them to the White Hart, where there was a clubroom used for meetings and village auction sales. When he died, in 1875, he was succeeded by Edward Knight, from Church Farm, who had married Elizabeth, the daughter of Prior.

The Old Tippling Philosopher was not far behind the White Hart in popularity. It was known to exist in 1801, and as the railway workers entered the district its patrons increased. John Joseph and his daughter's husband, Thomas Hicks, held the license from 1857 to near the close of the century. Its unusual name has drawn attention to it for very many years. In 1878 W. H. Greene called at the Inn and endeavoured to solve the meaning of the name, but despite cross-examining old inhabitants he was unable to elucidate the mystery. A sad aspect of its use was when men were killed at work in the Severn Tunnel the inquests were held at the Tippling.

An early inn about which there is little trace was the Ship Inn, under license to William Grail, in 1808.

The Cross Inn appears in the records in 1831 from which date it was in the Hollis family for a number of years.

The great influx of railway workers in the second half of the nine-teenth century resulted in a number of licensed premises being opened.

The Malt House, in Chepstow Road, near the Cross, was held by John Jones, as licensee from 1852 to 1861.

The Albion, in Newport Road, now known as Albion House, was licensed for a short while, about 1862, by Mr. Long, whose family held the property for many years.

The Beesditch area developed at the same time as the work on the railway, and later of Severn Tunnel. It is rather a haphazard group of dwellings, but it has quite a substantial inn, known as Pill Inn.

In 1841 William Nicholas of the Pill, was described in the census as "coal merchant and victualler."

An establishment with the more imposing title of The West of England Hotel was licensed in 1864, but with the reduction in the number of railway workers the license ceased.

The Castle Inn was held first by John Evans in 1873, and it is still flourishing.

In opposition to those who received their inspiration from strong drink Richard Adams, of West End, in 1875, held a meeting at his new room to institute a Lodge of Good Templars. Sixty to seventy people were present. Before that, however, in 1859, a Temperance Picnic was held in the Castle. Trains from all parts brought visitors including a large concourse of Irish. It was said that some 3,500 people were present.

XIX

NEWTON

NEWTON, also known as Shirenewton, derived its name from Sheriff's New Town. It was not a settlement when Domesday Book was prepared in 1086, but it was added to the Caldicot lands of the early sheriffs of Gloucester between the time of Durand, who was Sheriff in 1086, to the time his nephew Milo Fitzwalter was sheriff in 1127. It was a part of the manor of Caldicot and Newton which was bestowed upon Milo when Queen Maud created him Earl of Hereford in 1141, and it was after him that the wooded area became known as Earl's Wood and Earl's Grove. It would presumably have been added to the Caldicot Manor, which had been an inhabited settlement for a considerable time, to provide the timber necessary to build the new, and maintain the old, structures of this developing area.

The forest workers in due course built homes in Newton, and by the time of the third Humphrey de Bohun, who had inherited the estates through his marriage to Milo's daughter, a village was growing up.

The church was built by the fifth Humphrey de Bohun, known as the Good Earl, soon after he became the holder of the manor, on the death of his father, in 1220. He not only built the church, which he named St. Thomas a'Becket, but he endowed it. By deed, with his seal, dated 1262, he stated that he granted "to God of the Church of St. Thomas a'Becket, the Rectory by him built" together with a part of the village adjoining the church, and land being 60 acres of arable, meadow and wood, and a part of Earl's Wood. The land was in divers fields and places, the main portions being now known as "the Churches," and "Parson's Grove."

The Rectory Manor was held by the successive incumbents during their term of service at the church, and as the forests were cleared, and encroachments evidently took place, the area of land attached to the manor had increased to 181 acres in 1806. Apart from the 30 acres known as Church Hayes the land was composed of unenclosed allotments mostly in the area of Parson's Grove, Earlswood Chapel, and the Tump. The Earlswood land was included in the enclosure award of 1853 and the tenants held their land by copyhold.

The church is on high ground and is now conspicuous for miles

118

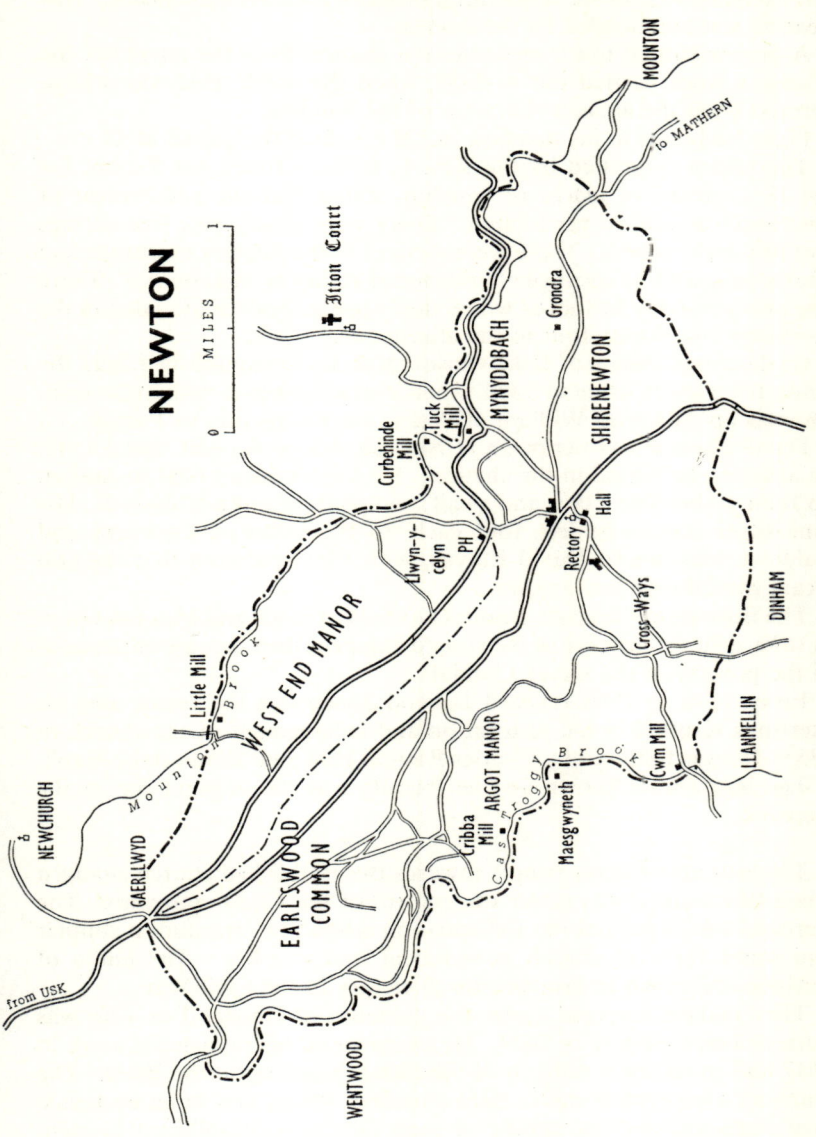

MAP OF NEWTON
drawn by Bryan Woodfield

I

around, but at the time of its erection it stood in a clearing made by the earl's tenants to provide agricultural produce for their subsistence. This clearing was surrounded by the woods.

A fine embattled tower separates the chancel from the nave, but the extensive work carried out in 1853, when the north aisle was added, detracts from the ancient character of the building.

Pope Nicholas, in his taxation in 1291, valued the parish at £8.

The return submitted by the Rev. E. Inwood Jones, the Rector, for the 1851 census of places of worship, stated that the endowment of the church was £310 per annum. There were ninety-nine free sittings and fifty-eight others. There were services in the Sunday mornings and afternoons, with an average attendance of eighty at each service. There was also a Sunday School at which thirty-seven children attended in the mornings and twenty-four in the afternoons.

Of the clergy, Adam of Usk, whose chronicles were published, held the living for a short while to 1399, when he exchanged it with his cousin, Thomas ap Adam ap William of Weloc, for the rectory of Panteg.

David Paynod was the priest at Newton, and in his will, dated 1542, he asked to be buried in the chancel. He left his russet coat to Jankyn ap John, to his wife a cow and a calf, two platters and a tablecloth. His nine silver spoons he left, four each, to the vicars of Caerwent and Caldicot, and one to David Etkyns, with the stipulation that the two vicars should sing for his soul.

The Bishops of Llandaff, Francis Godwin in 1603, and Morgan Owen in 1640, held the benefice of Newton to augment their income on account of the poverty of the see of Llandaff.

From 1848 to 1856 Edward Inwood Jones was the rector and his exertions resulted in the restoration and enlargement of the church in 1853. He was followed by Charles Rankin Hall, and James Ashe Gabb.

The house now known as Cae Pwcella was the original site of the Rectory.

*   *   *

The attitude of many people towards the established church changed when the country was under the control of the Commonwealth. The Puritans who followed the Reformation wished to introduce a simpler and purer form of church government and worship. The union of Puritans did much to give Cromwell victory in the Civil War.

The Quakers emerged under the guidance of George Fox who was born in Leicestershire in 1624. He commenced his ministerial work in 1647 and preached a religion of toleration based upon the Bible. The Quakers were against oaths, paid ministers, tithes, and other ecclesiastical demands, and the raising of their hats as a compliment to men. They patiently submitted to the wrongs inflicted on them and led blameless lives with integrity. Their doctrine of non-resistance was cruelly exploited by their persecutors.

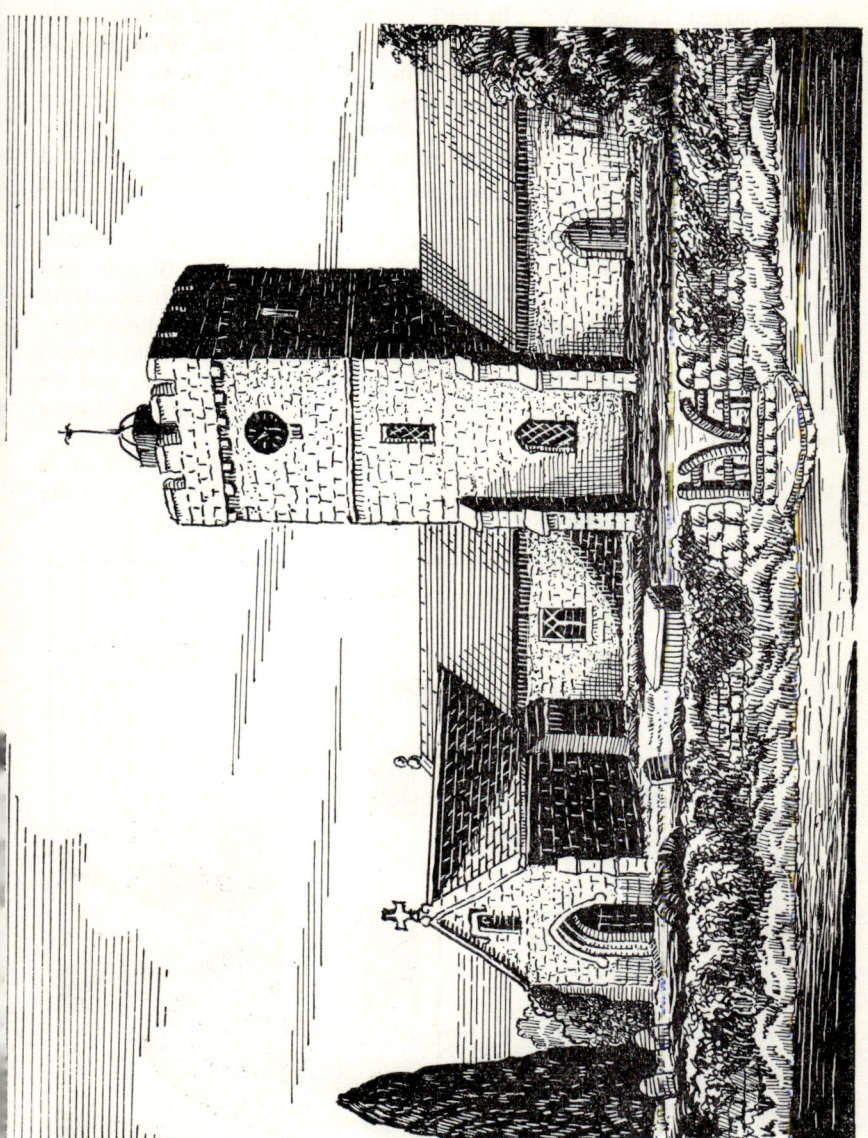

Shirenewton Church
drawing by Thos. T. Birbeck

Fox passed through Wales in 1657, but before this some of his friends had established meetings there. Elizabeth Holme and Alice Birkett lodged for a while, in 1658, at the house of Walter Watkins in Shirenewton where they conducted a meeting. That night the villagers caused an uproar about the house, and the following day the two women were taken before the justices, but were found innocent. Walter Watkins and his wife were later sent to Usk gaol for the non-payment of tithes valued at 20s. by a priest.

Francis Gawler, an early supporter of George Fox in South Wales, also visited Shirenewton with Elizabeth Holme and Alice Birkett, and they were taken from their meeting there before three justices—John Nicholas, William Blethyn and Robert Jones. They ably defended their cause and proved that they had broken no law. After Gawler had quoted from the scriptures Justice Jones said: "You are in the right, and we were mistaken." The three friends were then taken to an ale-house nearby and liberated.

In 1692 the meetings were held in Shirenewton in the house of Patrick Waters. In about 1730 a meeting house was built in the centre of the village at a cost of £204.18.8.

EARLSWOOD CHAPEL
drawing by Thos. T. Birbeck

In 1753 William Brown of Philadelphia, on his tour of Wales, visited Shirenewton where he stayed at the house of Seth Waters. He then preached to a few friends of low estate, had dinner at an inn, and drove on to Pontypool.

The meeting house at Shirenewton was closed in 1823.

The Quakers also had a small burial ground, enclosed by a stone wall, on the road from the village to Cross Hands. The plate on the gate bears the inscription "Friends Burial Ground 1700." The remains of simple gravestones still stand. Hannah Jones, of Dinham was one who was buried there in 1774.

The meetings of the Quakers were held continuously in Shirenewton from 1658 to 1823.

As the support for the Quakers declined in Shirenewton the Method ists became established.

The census of places of worship taken in 1851 enumerated a number of premises throughout the parish. The earliest was the Wesleyan Chapel, near the Brook, at Earlswood. It was erected in 1799, and had free sittings for 150 people with free space or standing room for another 250. They had an afternoon service with an average attendance of 100. There was a children's service on Sunday mornings at which about thirty attended.

There was a Wesleyan Chapel in the village erected about 1825, with free sittings for eighty. They met for Sunday evening service only. In 1876 a Wesleyan Sabbath School was started in the village barn with the consent of the farmer.

A chapel has been active at Gaerllwyd since 1842. It was known as Mount Zion, and was opened as a Welsh Calvinistic Methodist. Its capacity in 1851 was 100 free sittings. The meeting was, and still is, on Sunday afternoons when an average of sixty attended. The children met on Sunday mornings. On the 31st March 1851, the chapel commenced a day school on their premises. The chapel was transferred to the Presbyterians, and later the Baptists took it over.

The Bible Christians erected a chapel at Mynyddbach in 1850 with free sittings for forty. They met three times on Sunday, but the average attendances were rather low; eight in the morning; eighteen in the afternoon; and four in the evening. It was later taken over by the Methodists.

The Bible Christians had started meeting about 1840 when they gathered in a private house known as Fisher's Place. An average of thirty people attended the services on Sunday evenings.

Another Methodist Chapel was built on the Shirenewton to Wentwood road in 1860 and named "Hope."

*   *   *

There was a small manor of Argoed which comprised mainly the Argoed Farms and Cribba Mill. It was also referred to as the manor or lordship of Butlershold, Hentsfoothold, and Parkershold. It was held by free tenants who rendered military service. In 1574 Walkyn ap Howell held Butlershold by military service and suit of court with all his tenants. Thomas Reynolds and his heirs and Thomas William Edmonde both held the remaining thirds on similar terms.

The land between the Usk Road and the Mounton Brook was largely held with the manor of Caldicot West End, and was sometimes called Gamage's land after the first holder of the manor in the early fourteenth century.

Apart from the land held by these manors the remainder of Shirenewton, Mynyddbach, the Grondra, the Cwm, and Earlswood was a part of the manor of Caldicot and Newton. Details of Newton as it was on the death of the lord of the manor, the seventh Humphrey de Bohun, Earl of Hereford, in 1298, is recorded in the inquisition of his estates in the keeping of the Public Record Office. The earl had in demesne two messuages, 60 acres of arable land, 3 acres of pasture, 20 acres of wood, and one water mill, together with rights in the Earl's Wood.

There were forty-seven free tenants holding in all 350 acres. One customary tenant held 16 acres, and five customary tenants held 9 acres each. The tenant with the largest holding had to work for the earl for eight days in the autumn, and give him one hen and twelve eggs. The other customary tenants had to hoe for one and a half days and give the earl a hen and some eggs.

There were also fifteen Welshmen who were free tenants of smallholdings from 1 to 25 acres in extent, and they owed no suit to the lord of the manor.

The total of the land under cultivation was 597 acres.

The Newton lands passed into the possession of the Duchy of Lancaster at the same time as Caldicot did, in the fifteenth century, and was included in the leases made by the Duchy.

In the reign of Queen Elizabeth the rentals reveal in 1574–5 that there were thirty-three free tenants and twenty-five copyhold tenants at Newton.

In 1613 the boundaries of Newton were set out in a survey authorized by the Duchy and were as follows: 'the boundary begins at Gaerllwyd to Blackwell, to Thomas Jones Barn, to a little common called Duckless, to Curbyhyndes Mill, to Lady Mill, to the Pulpit, to the house of John West, to Broadcroft, to Dynham's Well in Westmead, to a line called Crossway, to the Garretts, to the Crooked Bridge, along Troggy Brook to Willam Harris Mill, and then to the Gaerllwyd aforesaid.''

What is now an expanse of open country overlooking the River Severn, was in 1608 the densely timbered Earl's Wood, containing 11,652 trees, many of them described as "great trees."

When William Foord made his survey on behalf of the Duchy in

1770 most of the trees had been felled and sold, leaving the land as open common and waste, the areas being as follows:

	a.	r.	p.
Earlswood	521	0	0
Coombewood	16	0	8
Mynyddbach	12	1	0
	549	1	8

Foord reported that upon the moors and wastes several cottages had been built and land enclosed, for which the occupiers paid an acknowledgement. There were forty-five such enclosures covering a total area of 133a. 2r. 25p.

The Duchy of Lancaster availed themselves of their power to sell their holdings by disposing of their land and buildings in the Newton Manor in the eighteenth and early nineteenth centuries. By the time the enclosure awards had been made, the Duchy owned no land in the manor.

The enclosure awards, relating to the open fields, commons and wastes, were made in 1853 and 1858.

With the conversion of copyholds to freeholds the influence of the manors finally ceased.

C. E. Lewis of St. Pierre became lord of the manor when he purchased the remainder of the land, and the privileges relating to the Caldicot and Newton manor, from the Duchy of Lancaster in 1857, and he sold the Newton portion of the manor to Charles O. Liddell in 1900.

*   *   *

The road system in Newton took shape as the forests were worked, and the hamlets developed. The tracks in Earlswood commenced from a central point at the junction now called Cock-a-Roosting. Most of these can still be found. The main feeders to the outside villages and towns were, the road over Earlswood to Gaerllwyd and Usk; the road from Shirenewton Village to Crick, and the road from Shirenewton to Mounton and Chepstow. Crossway was also a junction of lanes from Caerwent, Dinham, the Argoed, the Cwm and Shirenewton Village. This main network of roads and lanes still exists.

The eighteenth century saw the emergence of the Turnpike roads in the district.

The Turnpike Act of 1758 dealt with roads within the compass of Chepstow town. The preamble contained a long list of roads which were in so bad, ruinous, and founderous condition, and in many places so narrow, that it was very dangerous and difficult for horses, coaches, carts, and carriages to pass. The act divided the roads into seven districts, the second being the New Passage District which included a road through Crick and Shirenewton to Devauden Green where it joined the Chepstow-Abergavenny road.

The New Passage Trustees met for the first time, at Black Rock, where there was a large hotel, on the 22nd May 1758.

In 1770 there was an act to continue and enlarge the act of 1758 by adding to the Usk District a road from Four Ash Gate, by Pontyclyvon, by the Alms Houses of Coed Cunnor, by Trevella, over Earlswood, to Shirenewton Church.

In 1832 representatives of the Chepstow Turnpike Trust met trustees of the Abergavenny and Usk district and decided to make a new road from Chepstow to Abergavenny as an alternative to the difficult and extremely hilly road via St. Arvans, Devauden, Star Pitch, and Llansoy to Usk and Abergavenny. The cost of £5,400 for making the new road was to be met by £2,600 in subscriptions and £2,800 on loan from the exchequer.

The description of the route to be taken was as follows: "From the present turnpike road at Piercefield Lodge, towards the lower turnpike road leading from Usk to Monmouth at Gwernesney. The branch to be called the Shirenewton Branch, and should commence at Piercefield Gate and terminate at Gwernesney Church."

The making of the road was left to John Proctor and David Carruthers, of the Grondra, and William Hollis, of Shirenewton. The road was completed and opened in 1835, and tollhouses were sited at Shirenewton and Gwernesney, the gates being let for £264 and £254 respectively. At the beginning of 1873 the trust was wound up and taken over by the Chepstow Highway Board who later transferred it to the County Council.

*   *   *

The mills were provided as the growth of Newton, as an organized agricultural community, required them. There were two natural situations for mills: the Mounton Brook and the Cas Troggy Brook. There were many mills sited in the valleys through which these brooks ran, but the only ones, with which this account is concerned, are those which commenced as part of the original Caldicot and Newton Manor and the manors later formed from it. These are the grist mill and the fulling mill on the Mounton Brook, and the Cwm and Cribba grist mills on the Castroggy Brook.

It has not been possible to trace the date of their erection, but there is no reference to the mills in the description of the lands held by the seventh Humphrey de Bohun when he died in 1298. When, however, the surveys of the manor were made by the officers of the Duchy of Lancaster in 1574–5 two mills were established. In the survey of 1613 it stated that there were two water grist mills and one fulling mill at Newton.

One of the water grist mills was on the Troggy Brook and would appear to have been Lower Coombe Mill which was held by William Blethin when the 1613 survey was made. It was also referred to by William Foord in his survey of 1770. In 1831 it was held by John Roberts and described as a "water corn grist mill, outbuildings, fold, yard and premises." By 1890 it had ceased to work.

The water grist mill on the Mounton Brook was described variously as White Mill, Curbehind Mill and Goodbehind Mill.

In the list of rentals in 1574–5, and 1577–8, when Queen Elizabeth was on the throne, Edmund Morgan paid a yearly rent of 20s. for one grain mill called Curbehindes Mill. In 1730 it had been converted to a paper mill when it was leased to Christopher and Samuel Howell, papermen, of Shirenewton. The lease included waste land, a mill and kiln, together with implements and tools, and was for thirty-one years at £7 per annum. In 1769 John Hanbury, who was lessee of the whole manor of Caldicot and Newton, subleased to William Knowles, a Chepstow brickmaker, waste land and a water mill and paper mill late of Isaac Howell, deceased. Knowles and his son worked the paper mill until 1805. They were followed by John Reece, and James Jones and his partners, until the mill stopped working by 1849.

In a draft conveyance in the Monmouthshire County Archives the property is referred to as, "all that mill used as a paper mill, having two vats with the storerooms, dyeing houses, and other outbuildings, being at a place called Mynyddbach, within the lordship of Newton."

The fulling or tuck mill was situated a short distance down Mounton Brook from Curbehind Mill. It was of early origin and was referred to in 1567 when Robert Atkyns rented it from the third Earl of Worcester, who was then the lessee of the manor of Caldicot and Newton. In the list of tenants in 1574–5 a rent of 40s. per annum was paid by John Thomas for the fulling mill.

A perambulation of the manor of Chepstow, prior to 1830, refers to the paper mills at Pandy, in the parish of Itton, and continues, "from thence we kept the left hand brook up to Hollis Mill, then to the Dyers Mill (both in Itton), and then to the Tuck Mill belonging to William Curre, and along the same brook to Curbehind Mill, commonly called the White Mill, in the lordship of Caldicot and Newton."

When the survey was made in the late 1870's for the first ordnance map both the Tuck Mill and Curbehinde Mill were in ruins.

Little Mill was farther up the Mounton Brook from Curbehinde, and was upon land that was part of the Caldicot West End Manor, sometimes known as "Gamage's land." It was a paper mill in 1754, owned by William Fry. It passed through a number of hands until 1835 when it was worked by Thomas Ellis and William Hollis. It appears to have been last worked in 1837.

The Cribba water grist mill, also of longstanding, was not referred to in the surveys of either the Newton or Rectory manors. It must be assumed, therefore, to have been a part of the smaller Argoed Manor, based mainly upon the Argoed farms. The documents of sales in the County Record Office would confirm this. In 1665 Peter Rogers of Cribba Mill served upon a jury, and William Foord marked the mill upon his 1770 survey map, but not as a part of the Newton lands. Successive members of the Bladon family held, and worked, the mill throughout the whole of the nineteenth century.

*   *   *

The first census of the population of Newton was made by Henry Compton, Bishop of London, in 1675 and the families were made up of fifty-three conformists, twenty papists, and seven nonconformists.

The first official census was made in 1801, and from then until 1851 the parish was divided into two parts, the Parish and the Village. The 1801 census enumerated 519 persons and this gradually increased to 933 in 1851. This was the period of relative prosperity brought about in the parish by the introduction of the Mounton Valley Paper Mills.

Thomas Hollis of Mounton, who died in 1787, did much to establish the paper making industry at Mounton, and he married Susan Evans, of Shirenewton. He was followed by five generations named William, and the third William Hollis married the daughter of the Rev. J. A. Gabb, the rector of Shirenewton. Hollis was sheriff of Monmouthshire, in 1831, before moving to Shirenewton where he took up residence at the Court, or the Hall as it is now called. He rebuilt and enlarged the premises and set up a large establishment there.

The 1851 census showed the diverse nature of the occupants of the parish. As with Caldicot the community was almost self supporting with its various craftsmen and the essential labour. There were all types of agricultural, building, and forestry workers, domestic workers, shops for the needs of the villagers, and even a straw bonnet maker. There were thirty men employed directly in the paper mills. There were professional men, and men of no occupation other than being "of the gentry" and employing others.

The encroachments and enclosure of commons and waste resulted in the Earlswood area being ultimately divided up into a number of scattered small holdings. By the end of the nineteenth century, and the beginning of the twentieth century, the land had been mainly gathered into the hands of two people. William Edward Curre had about 1,370 acres, the largest units being the farms of Llwyn Kellin, Lower House, the Rhewl, and the Grondra, whilst C. O. Liddell had an estate of about 820 acres based upon Shirenewton Hall, which included Great House Farm, the Argoeds and the Cwm.

As the Newton parts of the Caldicot manors had been administered firstly from Caldicot, and later by the Duchy of Lancaster, there was no manor house in Newton. The rectory manor was, however, administered from the rectory by the incumbent.

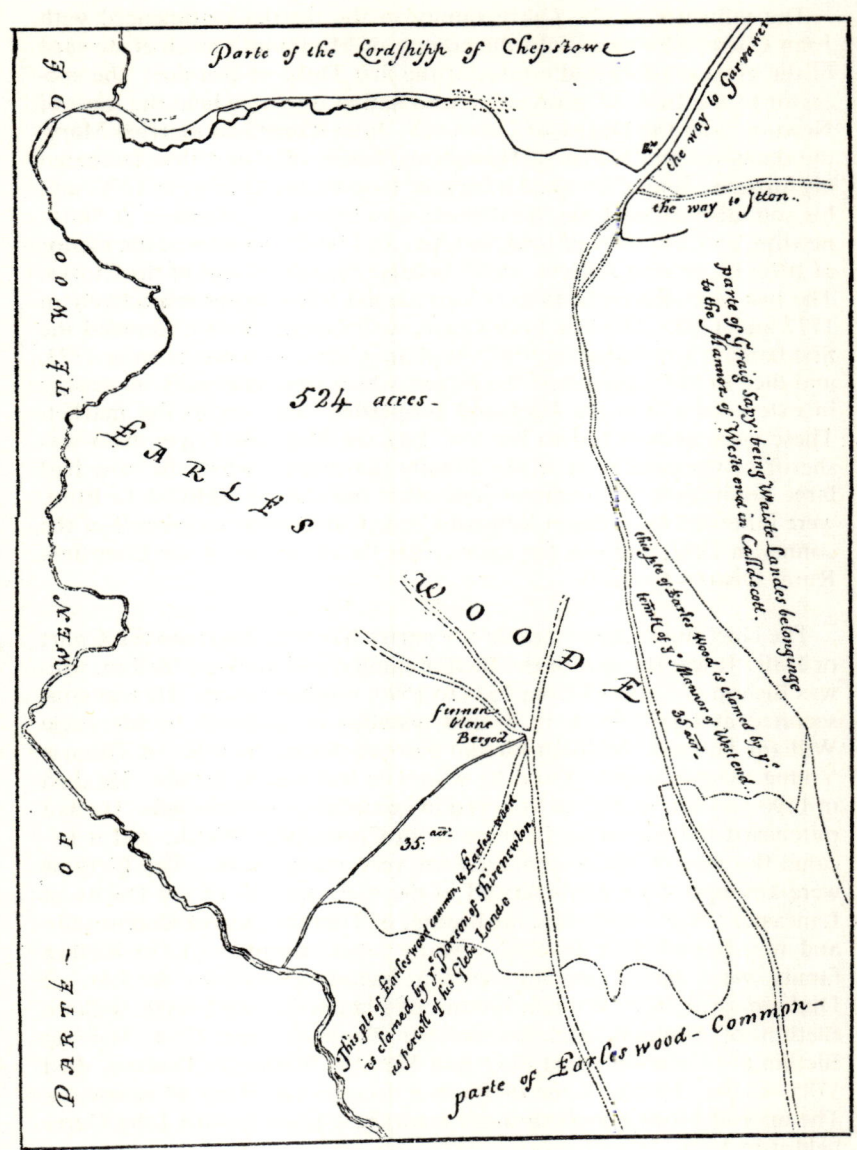

MAP OF EARLSWOOD
drawn by Bryan Woodfield

The influence of the Curre family in the district commenced with John Curre, who came into the county of Monmouth as chief steward of the great manors and estates of the first Duke of Beaufort, the successor to the Earls of Worcester, who had at one time held the lease of Newton from the Duchy of Lancaster. John Curre had married Mary, the daughter and coheir of Humphrey Turberville, and thus increased his fortune. John Curre had a lease of Rogerstone Grange in 1670, and his son, also called John, lived there, and leased the mansion at Shirenewton, and 200 acres of land, in 1701. In 1749 he purchased the manor of Itton from John Jeffreys, and it became the family seat of the Curres. The two next descendants were also named John, dying respectively in 1777 and 1798. The last John Curre, with George Smith, founded the first bank in Chepstow, in 1787. William Curre, who was born in 1773, and died in 1855, then held the estates which were gradually increasing in extent as additional land and properties came on to the market. These were bequeathed to his son, Edward Matthew Curre, who was sheriff of the county in 1859. Finally the estates, which by now had large holdings in Shirenewton and other parishes in addition to Itton, were inherited by William Edward Carne Curre, who was sheriff of the county in 1892, and was for many years the chairman of the Chepstow Rural District Council.

*   *   *

The chief house and estate in the parish has been Shirenewton Court or Hall. It was the seat of the Blethin family, and William Blethin, who was Bishop of Llandaff from 1575 to 1590, was born there. He was consecrated at Lambeth in 1575, and installed at Llandaff by his uncle William Thomas. William Blethin married Anne, the niece of Thomas Young, Archibshop of York, by whom he had a large family. He died in 1590 and was buried at Mathern in accordance with his will. He had purchased the manor of Dinham from Christopher Welsh, and it became the seat of his descendants for very many years. The Blethins were amongst the tenants named in the early surveys of the Duchy of Lancaster. William Blethin, the brother of Timothy, was of Shirenewton and was buried there in 1742. Many other members of the Blethin family were buried at Shirenewton including William Blethin, of Dinham, died 1676, William Blethin of Llanmellin, died 1700, William Blethin of Dinham, and his brother Thomas, died 1714, William Blethin of Llanmellin, died 1742, and Timothy Blethin, of Dinham, died 1785. After this the name of Blethin disappeared from Shirenewton. The mansion then passed through a number of hands until John Curre held it in 1701.

William Hollis, the paper maker, who had married the daughter of the rector, purchased the property and built the present house on the site of the old house of the Blethins. He left the Court in 1848.

In 1880 the estate was purchased by Edward Joseph Lowe, of

SHIRENEWTON HALL
drawing by Thos. T. Birbeck

This proposed observatory was not subsequently
built by E. J. Lowe

(*Sketch in Chepstow Museum*)

Nottingham, who renamed the house "Hall." In 1887 Mr. Lowe reported an extraordinary snowstorm at Shirenewton with the fall of snowflakes up to 4 in. long. One which he caught on glass was 3½ in. long, 2½ in. broad, and 1½ in. thick. After Mr. Lowe's death in 1900 the Hall Estate was acquired by Mr. Charles Oswald Liddell. The latter also purchased from the St. Pierre Estate the title to the lordship of the manor of Newton.

The only other house of any great significance in Newton was the Grondra. According to Sir Joseph Bradney the name meant the round homestead, so-called from the round hillock on which it stood. It was standing in 1492, and in 1552–3 it was held by Walter and John Hughes. They sold the Grondra to William Kemeys whose grandson later disposed of it. The family of Jones then settled there. Robert Jones, of the Grondra, died in 1693, aged eighty-three years, and his grandson Robert, who was sheriff in 1728, held and lived in the house until his death in 1730. In his will he left to his uncle Samuel Jones, of Salisbury, near Magor, his freehold and copyhold lands. He also left £5 to the poor of Shirenewton. Nathaniel Jones, the brother of Robert, owned the Argoed, at Earlswood, where he died in 1734. The Grondra was later purchased by the Chepstow banker, John Proctor, who was living at Dewstow. He permitted his daughter Sarah and her husband David Carruthers to reside at the Grondra, and in his old age he lived with them until he died at the age of eighty-three in 1837.

David Carruthers had served in the Peninsular War and was very active in the life of the parish. He died in 1859, and was succeeded by his son James Proctor Carruthers. It was reported in the Chepstow Weekly Advertiser in 1860 that the young squire of the Grondra gave a repast to a very large number of his friends and neighbours. He unfortunately died at the age of forty-six as a result of an accident when he fell from his cart. His son James Carruthers succeeded him and lived in the Grondra until he sold it to Edward Curre, of Itton Court.

*　　　*　　　*

Several benefactors have founded charities for Shirenewton. None of them produced large sums, but they displayed a desire to aid the poor of the parish.

The Rev. William Dyer, the rector of Shirenewton, who died in 1816, left £70 to be invested to provide articles of clothing for the poor on St. Thomas's Day.

Timothy Blethin, who died in 1735, left 8 acres and other land to produce an income for twelve poor widows to receive 2/6d. per annum.

The Rev. Charles Ranken Hall, rector until he died in 1884, left 12/6d. per quarter for the relief of poor and deserving cases.

Major A. E. L. Lowe provided £1.10.0. per annum for the following purposes:

10/– to the bellringers on the Sovereign's birthday.

5/– to the parish clerk for maintaining the founder's gravestone.

15/– for Christmas dole to six poor aged people of Shirenewton.

The Poors Allotment, for the benefit of the parish, is 5 acres in extent.

*   *   *

The school at Mynyddbach emanated from a grant of land from the Duchy of Lancaster for a term of ninety-nine years, dating from 1829, on which was to be built a school for the education of the poor. The trustees were the Rev. J. A. Gabb, the rector, William Curre, of Itton Court, William Hollis, the papermaker, and David Carruthers, of the Grondra. This school was provided and maintained by private contributions until it was taken over by the newly elected school board in 1876, and later the County Council.

The 1851 census revealed that there were, at the school, a schoolmaster, a schoolmistress, and an assistant.

Later another school was built at Earlswood.

The Chepstow Weekly Advertiser referred to Earlswood Board School in 1878 when a tea and singsong was held with eighty-six persons present.

*   *   *

The village inns have had a long and well loved place in the local communities. The lives of the parishioners revolved around the church and the tavern, and, although there is no record of it, it is highly probable that there were premises in Shirenewton, in the middle ages, licensed by the lord of the manor to brew ale.

Over the years there have been many licensed premises in Shirenewton, most of modest character. One of the earliest was the Five Bells which John Jones held on a ninety-nine year lease from 1767, and it was open to the end of the period with which we are concerned. It was in the centre of the village under the shadow of the church, and in 1873 it was the headquarters of the Shirenewton Benefit Society, and the Shirenewton Female Benefit Society.

The name of Benjamin is very prominent in the licensees of the various inns. There was a Robert Benjamin at the Five Bells in 1891.

The Tan House, on the fringe of the village, probably derived its name from the fact that G. Thomas, a tanner, lived there in 1713. John Benjamin held a license for Tan House in 1851, and it continued as a licensed premises throughout the nineteenth century.

Upper House, the last house in the village on the road to Earlswood, was licensed in 1847, appeared on the 1881 ordnance map, and was included as a public house in the 1901 sale of the Shirenewton Hall Estate. A Benjamin was also licensee of these premises.

The King's Head was a well patronized inn in the village on the road to Crick. Lewis Richards held the license from 1822 to 1826, and it was in this public house that the Shirenewton New Friendly Society and the United Friendly Society were founded in 1823.

The first friendly society established in the village was the Shire-newton Society of Tradesmen and Others which was founded in 1807.

There have been three inns which derived their names from trades, the Carpenters' Arms, the Butchers' Arms, and the Engineers' Arms.

The Carpenters' Arms is situated on the Chepstow to Usk road, very near to the site of the old Tuck Mill. It was licensed in 1860 and is still in business. There was a severe fire there in 1880.

Christopher Benjamin was the landlord of the Butchers' Arms in 1851 and the license lapsed in 1876. The *Chepstow Weekly Advertiser* recorded in 1869 that Zacharia Martin had left the Butchers' Arms and taken the road to Earlswood when he saw Michael Jones ahead. Martin said to his companion: "I have a great mind to go and give that fellow a hiding." This he did and duly found himself before the justices who sentenced him to fourteen days hard labour.

The Engineers' Arms had rather a short existence when William Burroughs held a license from 1861–76.

The Tredegar Arms was, and still is, in the centre of the village. Thomas Jeremy held the license from 1861–80.

The last to be mentioned is the Cross Hands Inn on the junction of the Chepstow-Usk Road, and the Shirenewton-Devauden Road. It existed in 1839 when an auction sale was advertised to take place there. It had facilities for entertainment, and in the 1860's it was a favourite meeting place for the local Friendly Society. It was at the Cross Hands that the Agricultural Labourers' Union first appeared in the district when they held a sparsely attended meeting.

Friendly Societies were very strong in Shirenewton, a large pro-portion of the families being members. In the 1860's the Shirenewton Friendly Society had their annual anniversary dinners at the Cross Hands. Their celebrations often provided entertainment for the whole parish. Before dinner they had a church parade and this was headed in 1863 by a Drum and Fife Band which had just been formed at Shire-newton. In 1879 Whitsun week was the time for celebrating the anniver-saries of the societies. On Monday the New Friendly and Benefit Society, of 103 members, met in the vicar's new room, and then had dinner at the Five Bells. On Tuesday the Female Society met at the club-room at Upper House, and on Wednesday the Hand of Sympathy Lodge of the Philanthropic Society with eighteen members, met at Upper House. In 1885 the dinner for the New Friendly Society and United Society was provided by Mr. Jeremy, of Tan House. On Whit-Monday, 1890, the Friendly Societies had a parade and church service followed by a dinner at the Five Bells. The celebrations concluded with rustic sports at which 800 people were present. Music was provided by Tintern Works Band.

In the 1870's the Loyal Grondra Lodge of Oddfellows had their headquarters at the Five Bells, and in 1873 Mr. J. P. Carruthers, of the Grondra, was chairman at the annual dinner.

Between 1888–95 the Cross Hands became well known over a wider area when Bill Benjamin, a pugilist of great repute, held the license. He was born in 1825 and when a youth worked for David Carruthers, of the Grondra, who taught him the rudiments of boxing. After being successful in local bouts Benjamin's ambition led him to thoughts of being champion of England. A false rumour was spread in 1858 that he was to fight Tom Sayers, the champion of England, on Caldicot Moor, and a large crowd assembled there to no purpose. The *Chepstow Weekly Advertiser* suggested that he should confine his pugnacious habits to the wilds of Shirenewton.

In January 1858, Benjamin's ambition was realized and Harry Broome, who had been tutoring him, matched him to fight Tom Sayers, who had held the champion's belt for two years, for £200 a side. Benjamin was 5 ft. 11 in. tall and a stalwart figure. The fight took place at Strood. Benjamin, however, had never met a fighter of the calibre of Sayers and after three rounds in six minutes he cried: "Hold, enough" retiring rather ignominiously. The *Chepstow Weekly Advertiser* expressed the hope that Broome would cease to pay his discreditable visits to Shirenewton and that he would not find backers for his unlawful pursuits.

Benjamin was a quiet inoffensive man who lived with his mother in the village, but he was not deterred by the advice of the *Advertiser*, and in April 1859, a further contest between him and Sayers took place at Aldershot before a miscellaneous crowd of roughs and patrons of the "noble art." Benjamin had attributed his first defeat to Tom Sayers "hitting him in the stomach without telling him." Sayers took the fight easy at first, but in the fourth round Bill caught him with a "hot 'un." This put Sayers on his mettle and he set about his opponent administering severe punishment. The fight ended with a win for Sayers in the eleventh round. The *Advertiser* summed up: "The disgusting exhibition lasted only 22 minutes. We hope this misguided young man will now return to his agricultural pursuits, and that we will hear no more of these disgraceful proceedings." Benjamin, however, afterwards fought Dick Shôn Shâms, the champion of Wales, and beat him in three rounds. Bill was a tall goodlooking man, and he spent nearly all his life in Shirenewton. He died on the 29th January 1906, at the age of eighty-one, and at his funeral at Shirenewton a large crowd was present.

In 1860 another prizefighter from Shirenewton named Henry Evans fought Lake of Newport for a purse of £25 a side. They evaded the vigilance of the police and fought at Grange Court. Evans was trained and handled by Bill Benjamin. Much money was wagered on the fight which went for twenty-three rounds. Evans' hands were then so mutilated by the bare fisted slugging that he had to retire and was adjudged the loser.

There may have been licensed premises at varying times in other parts of the manor, but there is no positive record of them.

* * *

The population of Newton reached a peak of 933 in 1851, inhabiting 199 dwellings, but, thereafter, there was a gradual decline, and by 1901 the population was 779 and the number of dwellings 177. During this period Caldicot, which was smaller than Newton in 1851, having 661 persons in 133 dwellings, grew rapidly to 1,196 persons in 259 dwellings in 1901. With the break up of the manor of Caldicot and Newton and the cessation of the interest of the Duchy of Lancaster all the ties between the two parts of the manor were severed.

A great feature in the life of Shirenewton during the second half of the nineteenth century was the annual Floral and Horticultural Shows held in the park of Shirenewton Hall from 1858 onwards. A band was generally in attendance and nearly all the villagers were present.

The villagers were otherwise occupied in 1859 when a gentleman of Shirenewton went off to be married and left three casks of beer for the villagers. A number of men and children became abominably intoxicated, staggering about and lying on the ground. It was all most unseemly!

It is apparent from accounts in the *Chepstow Weekly Advertiser* for the second half of the nineteenth century that the people of Newton were ready to take advantage of any opportunity to enjoy themselves. They had the annual fetes and sports of their local organizations, but they displayed their loyalty to the crown in 1885 by celebrating the twenty-first birthday of the Prince of Wales by hoisting flags in the village and lighting a bonfire on Mynders Hill accompanied by lusty cheers for the Prince.

In 1886 they celebrated Queen Victoria's birthday by ringing the church bells and displaying flags. A year later they paid their respects to the Queen on her Diamond Jubilee. The church tower was decorated with flags. Banners and festoons of flowers and evergreens spanned the road. Each house was decorated to display loyalty to the Queen. Then there was a service of thanksgiving at the church, followed by a march to Shirenewton Hall Park where there was tea for the children and sports.

In 1884 it was rather amusing to find the Gospel Temperance Meeting at the Five Bells Inn.

The ties of Newton with Caldicot were severed by the sale of the Duchy of Lancaster lands of the Manor of Caldicot and Newton, and Shirenewton became a self-contained local government unit with its own parish council and representation upon the Chepstow Rural District Council. A Parish Meeting was held at Mynyddbach School on the 4th December, 1894, to elect nine members to serve upon the newly constituted Shirenewton Parish Council and upon taking a poll the following were elected:—T. Anstey, E. C. Curre, A. L. Lowe,

W. Price, M. Quinton, T. Richards, J. A. Reeves, J. Williams and J. Williams (Argoed). The Parish Council duly met for the first time on the 20th December, 1894, at the school, when Mr. Lowe was appointed chairman and Mr. Curre the vice-chairman. The office of clerk fell to Thomas Williams.

XX

THE OTHER MANORS

Manor of Caldicote-by-Kayrwent(West End)

THE manor of Caldicote-by-Kayrwent, later called West End, was originally a part of Milo Fitzwalter's lordship, but in about the year 1250 a part of the original manor of Caldicot was handed to Peter who was succeeded by his son Reginald. The latter also had a messuage and 65 acres of land at St. Brides Netherwent. Reginald died in 1286, and his holding passed into the hands of King Edward I. In 1308 John, the son of Reginald, was granted several manors including Talgarth as well as Caldicot-by-Kayrewent.

In 1310 the escheater of King Edward II defined the manor of Caldecote, which John de Sapy held for the term of his life by Commission of the King, of which John, the son of Reginald, by his deed enfeoffed the lord King. There was in the manor a capital messuage with garden, and arable tenements in demesne of 51 acres, which were rented to tenants of the manor. There was also 16 acres of meadow. There were eleven tenants, and sixty-two villeins and cottars. The pleas and requisites of court were valued at $\frac{1}{2}$ mark per annum. The lord of the manor and his tenants also had rights over a part of Earl's Wood, which portion was located between what is now known as the Usk Road, and the Mounton Brook. The sum of the whole extent of the manor was said to be £22.9.2$\frac{3}{4}$. by the year. This manor was nearly comparable in size and value with the manor of the de Bohuns.

In 1311, at the instance of Queen Isabella, the grant was enlarged and confirmed subject to the rendering of the usual services.

A license was granted to John Sapy, in 1348, to grant the reversion of the manor to Katherine, the wife of his son Thomas.

In 1381 John Sapy was ordered by the King to surrender the manor to Gilbert Gamage who had paid a license to the King of 10 marks. Gilbert Gamage had married Lettice, the daughter of Sir William Seymour of Penhow. His great-great-grandfather, Godfrey de Gamage, came to England with William the Conqueror.

The manor was successively held by William, John, Morgan, Sir Thomas, and Robert Gamage. Then in 1583, the manor of West End,

CALDICOT HALL OR GREAT HOUSE
drawing by Thos. T. Birbeck

as it was then known, passed to Margaret, the daughter of Robert Gamage, and she married Thomas Lewis, of Van.

The manor remained in the Lewis family until Edward Lewis died in 1674, owing much money. His trustees sold some of his land, including Caldicot, to pay his debts.

In 1675 Charles Van owned much of West End and his family held it for three generations, until 1778.

Henry Wise, who built Great House (later called Caldicot Hall), near the church, was acquiring as much land as he could in 1778, and he purchased the Van lands. His son Henry, junior, inherited the property to which he added his own purchases. When he died in 1857 his large estate, of about 700 acres, was divided up into lots and sold by auction.

Priory Manor

Caldicot became associated with the Priors of Llantony during the reigns of the Empress Maud and King Stephen. The monks were then oppressed and pillaged by the natives in the Brecon mountains and in their distress they appealed for aid to the Bishop of Hereford. He prevailed upon Milo Fitzwalter to grant land at Gloucester for the erection of a priory. The church was dedicated to St. Mary, the Virgin, and in 1136 it was consecrated by the Bishops of Worcester and Hereford. The priory was name Llantony Secunda.

Milo also endowed the priory by granting to it two parts of the tithes of Caldicot, and in the thirteenth century the de Bohuns granted further parcels of land. The new Llantony grew in opulence and splendour, and substantial development was carried out at Caldicot by forming Priory Manor with its home farm based upon what is now Church Farm. Some of the land was let to tenants thus securing a source of income. A part of the land consisted of strips in the open fields.

The County Archives contain a document, dated 1407, whereby the Prior of Llantony granted a cottage the rent for which was a pound of Cummin at Michaelmas.

Richard Hempsted was prior of Llantony at the time of the dissolution. He subscribed to the supremacy in 1534 with twenty-two others, and in 1539 they signed the surrender. Thereafter he obtained a pension of £100 per annum.

The Act of Parliament in 1536 formally suppressed all monasteries with a clear yearly value under £200 and vested them in King Henry VIII.

King Henry then seized the Priory Manor at Caldicot and he appointed Clement Dace as his bailiff and farmer. The following are the details of collections made in 1540:

Assize Rents 6d.

Rents of Customary Tenants payable at the terms of the Annunciation of Blessed Mary Virgin, and St.

Michael Archangel equally as by a certain rental made
thereof by the Auditor.   106.7d.
Farm of the Rectory with all houses situated within the
site and all manner of tithes, offerings, revenues, and
emoluments pertaining to the said Rectory.   £16.
Portions of Tithe—namely tithe hay in Beesdich,
Wolpittes, Newmeade, Caerwents meade and the
Moors.   16.10d.
Perquisites of Court   5. 0d.

Sum Total of Receipts   £22. 8.11d.

Payments—for the Church   20s. 0d.
Annual Pension
     Paid to the Vicar of the Parish Church of Caldicot
     in augmentation of his salary.   10s. 0d.
Fees stipends and expenses of the steward and in fees
of the accounter and bailiff   20s. 0d.
Stipend of Clerk of Auditor   2s. 0d.
Expenses of steward journeying to Caldicot for holding
the courts there this year   9s. 2d.

Total   31s. 2d.

The balance was paid by the accounter to Arthur Porter, the King's
Receiver.

In 1557, during the reign of Philip and Mary, it was decided to sell
the Priory Manor. The value arrived at was the total of the yearly rents
and perquisites at thirty years purchase making a grand total of
£174.5.6. This sum included the advowson of the vicarage of Caldicot
at one year's purchase.

The purchaser was Richard Seyborne.

The Priory lands eventually passed to John Seyborne, who in 1603
sold his interest to Edward Kemeys.

Edward, by will, bequeathed his property at Caldicot to Nicholas
the second son of his brother Rhys. Nicholas was a loyal supporter of
King Charles against the Roundheads. He was knighted at Westminster in 1641 and was created a baronet in 1642. In May 1648, Sir
Nicholas and some other gentlemen of the county obtained possession
of Chepstow Castle and they regarrisoned it, for the King, with 160
men. On the 10th May Cromwell marched against the Castle in person,
but he had no cannon, and as Sir Nicholas refused to surrender Cromwell marched on leaving Colonel Ewer to proceed with the siege. He
was subsequently supplied with guns and made a determined assault
upon the Castle. Colonel Ewer's report to Parliament recounts:

we raysed the battlements with our short guns and made their guns unuseful to them. We also played with our shorter pieces into the castle, one shot fell into the governor's chamber, which caused him to remove his lodgings to the other end of the Castle. We then prepared our batteries and this morning finished them. About 12 of the clock we made a hole in the wall. The soldiers in the castle perceiving that we were like to make a breach, cried that they would yield the castle. Squire Lewis came upon the wall and spoke to some gentlemen of the county telling them that he was willing to yield to mercy. I went into the drawbridge and spoke with them. I answered that I would give no other terms than that they should submit unto mercy which they swore they would not do. The soldiers deserted Sir Nicholas Kemeys and came running out of the breach. My soldiers seeing them run out, ran in at the same place, and possessed themselves of the castle, and killed Sir Nicholas Kemeys.

CHURCH OF PRIORY FARM, CALDICOT
drawing by Thos. T. Birbeck

This happened on the 25th May 1649. A document in the County Archives indicates that Sir Charles Kemeys, the son of Sir Nicholas, later held the property that was once the Priory Manor. The lands remained with the Kemeys family until the end of the eighteenth century when they came into the hands of the Wise family. In 1857 Henry Wise's estate, which he had enlarged by a number of purchases, including large parts of the West End and Priory Manors, was put up for auction at the Beaufort Hotel, Chepstow, in 104 lots. The latter covered 600 to 700 acres of land, and included much of the lands which at one time were open fields and common pastures. The following farms were included in the sale: West End, Lower House, Pill House, Church Farm, and Brockwells. Henry Wise, who was the son of Henry Wise of Great House, was very prominent in the life of the parish. He was a Churchwarden from 1809 to 1840, was benevolent to the parish, and on his death at the age of 82 he was buried in Caldicot Church.

The Manor of Dewstow

The name Dewstow is derived from Dewi's Stow, the hamlet of David, from the church which once stood there.

In the Book of Llandaff it is recorded that Arthrwys, King of Gwent, gave the hamlet to the see of Llandaff in the sixth century.

Domesday Book refers to Sanctus Dewin which paid no rent except to the Saints, that is the profits were applied for the benefit of the priests.

At the time of Cromwell's rebellion the property of the see was confiscated, and Dewstow was sold to Sylvanus Taylour, in 1657, for £57.1.3. Taylour had already purchased the manor of Bishton and Llandewy Vach for £1,521.16.7., in 1650. He does not appear to have had any particular interest in Monmouthshire. He was one of thirty-seven people appointed by Order of Parliament, in 1651, to the High Court of Justice. He was referred to in another Order of Parliament, in 1659, when he was appointed as one of five Commissioners dealing with financial matters.

Dewstow was then the subject of many sales before becoming the property of Richard Vaughan Norman, Vicar of Magor, who died in 1797, and left the manor to John Kemeys Gardner Kemeys. It then passed to Susanna Gardner Kemeys, a spinster, who sold her interest to John Procto , a banker, of Chepstow. It remained in the Proctor family, until 1874, when it was sold to Theophilus Bevan, the owner of the iron works at the Pill. He conveyed the estate to Daniel Price, from whom} Henry Oakley bought it in 1893. The latter developed very attractive underground gardens and he lived in the house for many years.

Dewstow was a small compact manor consisting mainly of Great and Little Dewstow Farms and it changed but little in area from the 281 acres held by Charles Morgan in 1715.

XXI

LIFE AND CHANGES IN THE NINETEENTH CENTURY

THE beginning of the nineteenth century found local government very much as it had been for centuries. The affairs of the parish were in the hands of its inhabitants and the business was regulated by the Vestry meetings which had superseded the manor meetings at the Cross. The division of the parish into four manors was no longer apparent. The vestry meeting, or parish meeting, was held annually, at Easter, in the church vestry, and the notice of the meeting was affixed three days previously, to the church door. Most of those who attended would pass the Cross and then proceed along the tree lined lane, now known as Church Road, to the vestry. There they would be met by the vicar who acted as chairman of the meeting. They then discussed the parish problems and elected the following chief officers: churchwardens, overseers, and surveyor. The appointment of the constables was also confirmed. The main subjects they dealt with were church maintenance, the care of the poor, the upkeep of the roads, bridges, and certain reens, sanitary matters, and the maintenance of law and order through the duly elected constables. All the officers were unpaid and the parishioners were expected to render any assistance required.

There were occasions when the vestry was not large enough to accommodate all those who wished to attend the meeting, and the gathering consequently adjourned to a room at the White Hart Inn.

The water supply had been from wells and the Neddern Brook, but when the railway pumping station came into operation at the Severn Tunnel it had the effect of draining the whole area and all the wells dried up. The railway company had a large quantity of water available from this source which, though hard, was suitable for domestic purposes. The area was accordingly provided with a supply of water. In 1887 there was a largely attended vestry meeting to consider a letter from the Great Western Railway, at Paddington, in which they said they were not able to continue to permit a supply of water without proper terms and conditions. The terms of the railway company, of 2d. per 1,000 gallons, were later accepted, and continued for many years.

The century brought fundamental changes in the administration of parochial life as the central government became interested in local affairs, particularly with the introduction of the railways and the effect of the industrial revolution. More information and statistics became available for piecing together local history.

The first census was taken in 1801, and was followed by others at ten-yearly intervals. Before 1841, however, no attempt was made to return individual names, the official returns being purely mathematical, the number of persons enumerated in 1801 being 465. In 1831 John Hollis, one of the overseers, made the census and reported to the vestry meeting that there were 120 occupied dwellings in the village housing 583 people.

By 1841 the population had risen to 625, and after that there were large increases, to 962 persons in 1871 and 1401 in 1881. This reflected the effect of the railway developments such as the construction of the Severn Tunnel, the main railway lines, and the junction at Rogiet. As the temporary workers left the district Caldicot's population dropped back in 1901 to 1196.

The 1841 census can be taken as covering a typical year in Caldicot's agricultural epoch. The population of 625 occupied 130 dwellings, and was composed of 328 males and 297 females. They were the inhabitants of the old manors of Caldicot, Caldicot West End, Priory and Dewstow. By the diversity of their occupations they formed a community that was almost self supporting. The following were some of the trades and professions represented: Farmers and their labourers, shoemakers, tilers, masons, blacksmiths, grocers, butcher, tailor, innkeepers, wine-merchant, menservants, letter carrier, schoolmaster, and midwife. Physicians and surgeons lived for a number of years at the Grove, after Henry Wise vacated it. Of the 130 householders eighty-five were engaged entirely in agricultural operations. Details of the censuses are shown in Appendix H.

The registers of births, deaths, and marriages dating from 1717 are at the parish church.

In 1769 Thomas George, alias Thomas Shone Catty, died. He was purported to be the Robin Hood of Wales. Richard Withers "a monster in villainy" was buried in 1784.

Ann Stockham, aged forty-four, was killed by a cartwheel in 1841, and in 1849 the cause of the death of Major General Edmund Keynton Williams, K.C.B. was the removal of a musket ball. This gallant soldier received his wound in the Peninsular War.

Scarlet fever was prevalent in 1852, a number of children died, and in 1859 three children of Charles Hill died of the disease within three days. In 1870 three children of James Watkins died of convulsions on the same day.

The bite of an adder caused the death of young Withers aged five, in 1873, whilst he was gathering wild flowers in a field.

The Duchy of Lancaster had availed itself of its authority to sell its lands by disposing of the moors and commons, and also the common or open fields.

In 1853 an award was made under the General Enclosure Acts which made provision for the enclosure of Caldicot Moor, Rogiet Moor, Ben Acre, Caldicot Common Sea, Earlswood Common, Mynyddbach and Cwm Wood. The extent in Caldicot was approximately 1,650 acres, and was divided amongst many owners.

The enclosures of the common, or open, fields, of Beesditch, Mill Field, Great or West Field, Elmfield, Church Field, Little Field, Caerwents Brook, Shearfield, and Little Field at Whitehall were the subject of an award in 1859, made by John Peachy Williams, who had been appointed valuer by the Inclosure Commissioners. There were ninety enclosures.

It has been seen in other chapters how the social needs of the area were met by church, chapels, friendly societies, and other institutions. The ruined castle was still the centre of much activity, even as it had been in its early days.

The parishioners were ever ready to support the local events and to provide for their own entertainment. An archery meeting was held in the Castle in 1877, and in 1885 the Caldicot Quadrille Class Ball was held at the White Hart Inn. In the same year the Caldicot Glee Party gave a concert in the schoolroom. In 1886 the Glee Party sang at the wire mills and the proceeds went to a fund for providing a reading room and literary institute in the village.

In 1885 a branch of the Primrose League was set up. The league had been formed in memory of Benjamin Disraeli whose favourite flower was the primrose.

An interesting cricket match took place in 1874. Caldicot challenged the well established Chepstow Club to a match. Chepstow thought that a scratch Caldicot team would be poor opposition so they fielded a very weak team, but Caldicot borrowed some good players from the Lydney Club and they beat Chepstow by a handsome margin.

The nineteenth century commenced with the parishioners being mainly responsible for their own local government and well being. Their parish was as they made it, and the more they applied themselves to their parochial obligations and requirements the better was their lot. This century was, however, to see a gradual erosion of their powers. Parliament introduced legislation to set up bodies covering wider areas than the parish to carry out the services required by a developing society.

The Poor Law Amendment Act, of 1834, provided for the transfer of the parish overseer's duties in connection with poor relief and care to the Chepstow Board of Guardians. Rural sanitary matters followed.

The County Constabulary was formed in 1857.

The care of highways was transferred to a Highway Board, based on Chepstow, under the provisions of the Highway Act, 1862.

The Education Act of 1870 resulted in the establishment of the Chepstow and Shirenewton School Boards.

The major changes came with the introduction of the Local Government Acts of 1888 and 1894 when the County Councils, Rural District Councils, and Parish Councils were formed.

On the 4th December, 1894, a Parish Meeting was held in the schoolroom to elect 11 members to serve upon the newly constituted Caldicot Parish Council. There were 21 nominations and upon taking a poll the following were elected: W. Jones, E. R. Adams, J. Faulks, A.Cooper, W. P. Anstey, W. Howard, T. Carter, E. Jones, H. Thomas, H. A. Jones, and H. R. Hill. At the first meeting, held on the 31st December, 1894, Alfred Cooper, the retired school-master, was appointed chairman, and the clerk was the assistant overseer, Moses J. Squibbs. The Parish Meeting also elected A. Hillier, A. Cooper and E. R. Adams to represent the parish upon the Chepstow Rural District Council.

The adoption of the many reforms of this century resulted in a modern, and more efficient, system of local government to take the place of the old customs which had formed the basis of medieval and Tudor local administration.

The parish had its new power of electing representatives to look after their interests in the composite bodies of which they formed a part, and it retained its annual parish meeting, but much of the personal implication of the parishioners in their own affairs had disappeared, and they had to adapt themselves to entering the twentieth century as an integral part of the Chepstow Rural District.

Very few of the old houses of note still remain. All the West End farm-houses have gone to make way for modern development. A house still stands at Dewstow as a reminder of its past importance. Priory Farm House, the one-time home of monks of Llantony, still exists with its small windows looking towards the Church which the Prior of Llantony had built, and Court House, at one time the home of the Herberts, is now bounded by new houses. The cattle were a menace to Court House in Queen Katharine's time when she dug a ditch around the house to prevent the animals from damaging the low thatched roof. There is nothing to indicate the presence of the Cross. The new shopping centre obliterates the site of the first Wesleyan Chapel and the village well. The common fields are now densely built upon. The tree lined lane from the Cross to the Church is a modern thoroughfare, and other changes have taken place to reshape Caldicot from the agricultural village established by the de Bohuns.

APPENDIX A

EXTRACT FROM LIBER LANDAVENSIS
827–927 A.D.

Brockwael, son of Meurig, sacrificed two churches and for the redemption of his soul restored to Bishop Cyfeiliawg both the churches of Caldicot and St. Brides Netherwent with 54 acres of land with all their liberty, and all commonage to the inhabitants, in field and in woods, in water and in pastures and with free approach for ships at the mouth of Taroci (Troggy) and all its weirs for fisheries without any payment to any mortal man besides to the Church of Llandaff, and its pastors for ever. Their boundaries are: The influx of the Taroci, following Taroci along to the hollow, following the middle of the hollow upwards to its extremity, to the mound in the boundary of Tref Peren (Llanvihangel Rogiet), on the right to the other mound from the mound to the Carrieu in the boundary of Tref Peren, from one knoll to the other downwards to the Severn Sea, along the sea with its weirs for fisheries and shipwrecks and free approach for ships at the mouth of the Taroci where it began.

APPENDIX B

SURVEY of the manor of Caldicot and Newton made in September 1613, in the reign of King James I in the presence of Gerard Bromley, by the following:

Francis Harbert	William Blethin	George Parker
Henry Vaughan	Edward Reignoldes	Philip Robnett
John Walter	Roland Morgan	Philip William
Henry Pratt	Robert David Nicholas	William Howell
Philip William	Henry Philip	Thomas Lawrence
Thomas Leach	Charles Watkins	

Boundary (*Caldicott*)
They do present the circuit, length, breadth and boundaries of the said Lordship, and there is three Lordships more intermingled with the said Lordship of Caldicot, viz., the Lordship of Westende, the Lordship of

the priorie of Caldicot, and the Lordship of Dewstow. But the true bounds of those four Lordships, they present intermingled and do say it begins in length at the seaside called Severn and goeth up along the Somerwaye, between Yfton Wallpitts and Dewstow Wallpitts to Ffyrmyn Crosse. And from thence along the land to Hymors Hill, and fetcheth in the Pryorie Close by the Mynnetts. And so along Stubby Lane towards Woodcock Hill. And thence to James furlong and along James furlong hedge to the Pederhewle, and so along the king's highway to West bridge by Caerwent. And from West bridge down along a brook called Trogye Brook to Caerwents bridge. And from Caerwents bridge along Phills closes to Slowe house, and thence to the River of the Neden, and so along the Neden to Creeke Moore, and from thence along the hedge by the head acre in Creeke Moore to the end of the Slowe land and then along Creeke brooke to the Bridge at the house of William Jones (being the Alehouse there). And from thence along the lane called Bisshopps lane to Bassill hill, and then along the highway to Limekiln and so to fetch in Ufton hill and part of Pratt's farm, and thence up the hill again to the highway leading from Caldicott towards Shepstow. And thence down to Harpstone lane and thence to Portskewetts field. And to John Roberts hill and Taylors hill, and thence to the Cross Way, and so to Moor head, and along Moor head ledge to Sevalls house. And to Deep Weir, and from Deep Weir along the back Brook to William Lewis mead and the valley mead, and along the lake in Bysditch to the patches of the mead by Portskewetts ford called Base half-acre. And Alderfords acre. And then along that brook and water-course down to Sudbrook Mill. And from the Mill along Sudbrookes pill to the sea side called the Severn. And so along the seaside to Moors wrath. And is situate in the several parishes of Caldicot, St. Peere, Porscuett, and Caerwent.

Boundary (*Newton*)

The boundaries of all the lands within the Parish and Manor of Shirenewton being Duchy land, and begins at a place called the Garne Lloyde. And from the said Garne Lloyde to the Black Well and from thence to the Badwell. And from thence to Thomas Jones's barn of the Glyn, and from that barn along the lane towards a little common called Ducklesse. And from thence to the King's Mill called Curbyhyndes Mill. And from thence along the brook side to the Lady Mill. And from thence to a place called the Pulpit. And from thence to the house of John West, deceased. And from thence to Brodcroft and from thence to Dynham's Well in West Meade. And from thence to a lane called the Cross Way. And from thence to a place called the Garretts. And from thence to the Crooked Bridge. And from thence along the brook called Troggy to Williams Harris Mill. And there hence to the Garne Lloyde aforesaid.

Commons

And they do further present that there is one Common Moor called Caldicotts Common Moor for all manner of cattle commonable as a common appurtenant to the said Manor of Caldicot and Newton without number. And this Common doth contain in length from the West Wall in the West End of Caldicot down to Collistreete Pill. And in breadth between New Meade, Prickardes Meade, the Parson's seven acres, Great Twympill, and the sea called Severn on the south side, and the several Lordships of Undy, Llanvihangel Rogiet, and Yfton, and the Wallpitts on the West and North side thereof. And that there is four rivers or watercourses that do cross over athwart the same common into the sea called Severn, which are properly called by the several names of Westewarde Pill, Middle Pill, Newe Dicked ditch, and Poole Rough, and which are maintained by the tenants and parishioners of the Lordships and Parishes of Lanvihangel Rogiet and Yfton for their own good and wealth (otherwise all their lands lying between Caldicotts Common and their houses, and many of their houses also would be surrounded and overflown with high springs of the sea.) And that the tenants of Caldicott every man against his own lands by Somerway did and do always cleanse and scour the River or Watercourse from Poole Rough down to the Common Sea.

They do also present that they do also hold one other little Common in Caldicott as a Common appurtenant to the said Manor called by the proper name of the Common Sea containing in length from Caldicott Mill to Moore Warthe, and in breadth between the Marshes, Harbert's long forehead, and Severn on both sides thereof.

They do further present that they do also hold one other little quillett or Common in the parish of Caerwent and lordship of Caldicot and Newton called by the proper name of Ballon Moor. And one other little quillett or Common in the Parish and Manor of Caldicot called by the proper name of the Black Marlpits, which two little Commons are also without number for all beasts and cattle commonable to his Majesty's tenants, residents, and inhabitants within the said Manor of Caldicot and Newton.

Common Woods

They do also present that there is within the said Manor one little forest called Earles Woode, and one other little grove called Earles Grove belonging and appertaining to his Majesty's residents and inhabitants in Caldicott, Eastend or Upend and Newton and that there hath been waste done therein, but by whom they know not, for that waste was done long before the knowledge of this Jury.

Fines and Amercements

They further do present that the Right Honourable Edward Earl of

Worcester, and his officers under him, do receive, perceive, levy, and take all fines, amercements, perquisites of Court, waifs, strays, fellons goods, yearly happening within the said Manor.

The Castle

Ane Moreover they do present that there is an old ancient Castle in Caldicot, and that it is ruinous and decayed but the cause of the decay thereof they cannot present, for it was before the memory of this Jury or any of them, by whom or to what value they know not.

Demesnes

And they do present that the Right Honourable Edward, now Earl of Worcester, and his under-tenants do hold all the demesnes belonging to the same Castle. And that the said Earl doth receive the rents of his under tenants for the demesnes.

Mills

And further they do present that there is two Water Grist Mills within the said Manor of Caldicott and Newton, and one Fulfilling Mill also in Newton, which water mills are accounted his Majesty's Mills, and that they are holden from the said Earl by lease at an annual rent to his honour paid. And the Fulling Mill by Copy of Court Roll as a customary tenure with an annual rent to his Majesty and which the same Earl is to account for.

Royalties

They do present that his Majesty, and the said Earl under his Majesty hath the Royalties of hunting, hawking, fishing and fowling within the said Manor. But they say that all gentlemen do take their sports therein without any contradiction of the same Earl, and that there is no rent paid or answered to his Majesty in particular for the same royalties, for it was never accounted to be anything in particular value.

Encroachments

They do present that one William Price hath and doth enclose a common highway between Caerwents Bridge and Slowe house that containeth about two acres. And that one Edmond Morgan of Caldicot did encroach about thirty foot in length and two feet or thereabouts in breadth of his Majesty's waste land in Caldicot by a house in the occupation of Philip Robnett, or of his assigns, to a small value.

Customs

A presentment of all the Customs of the Manor of Caldicott and Newton given before the said Surveyor at this Court of Survey by the oaths of the said Jury, the day and year before said, as followeth:

1   They do acknowledge and confess their bounden duties as loyal subjects and poor tenants in all humility to our said sovereign lord

the King's Majesty, and to his heirs and successors for ever. And their duties and services to his Majesty's leets and law day in Caldicot twice any year, that is to say on the first Monday after May Day, and on the first Monday after Michaelmas Day, and no other day by custom without any summons.

2   They present that by their ancient custom those two days are their usual days wherein they ought to pay their rents.

3   They present that they ought to have fifteen days after to redeem their distresses if the bailiff distrain any of them for their rents.

4   They say and present that they ought to have a Steward and a Recorder sitting in their court together for that their records be their evidence.

5   At the first entering of a new Steward they ought to give no Court before they see and hear read the same Steward's Commission, and then also to have fifteen day after of respite before they do give Court.

6   That their Court ought always to be kept at the Cross in Caldicott, or near thereto, and that to be on a Monday, always monthly, and upon a lawful summons.

7   That the Bailiff ought not to take more of any tenant than 2d. for the arresting of the distress of any man.

8   That a freeholder may by our custom take 4d. of any man for the arresting of any man's goods within the Manor of Caldicot. And that arrest is as lawful as if he were a sworn Bailiff, the action being under ten shillings.

9   The Bailiff ought to take nothing for the poundage of any tenant's cattle.

10   Upon the surrendering of any tenement there is due to the King's Majesty for a fine 2s. 0d.

11   Upon the surrendering of every cottage or parcels there is due to be paid for a fine to his Majesty 12d.

12   Upon the death of every Customary Tenant in Caldicot being principal, there is due to the King's Majesty the best quick beast which the deceased hath. But if he have no quick beast then five shillings is due to his Majesty for and in the name of a herriott, and in Newton five shillings in the name of a herriott.

13   Upon the death of every freeholder being principal there is due to the King's Majesty double the rent of that freehold in the name of relief.

14   There is no herriott due upon a parcel.

15   They do present that their ancient custom is to have their house-bote, haybote and ploughbote, and all windfalls both in Earls Wood and Earls Grove, and also to have maste for their pigs and the herbage for their cattle both in the wood and in the heath. And also tile stones to build withall within the Manor.

16   That all tenants being residents and inhabitants there in Caldicot and Newton be free to Common with their cattle in the common called Caldicotts Common as it hath been used time out of mind.

17   That there ought to be freeholders upon the bench at every Court and lawday by their ancient custom.

18   That any tenant may surrender his lands by a letter of attorney in open Court there.

19   That the common there called the Common Sea is and ever hath been common to all tenants and residents being inhabitors of the East End of Caldicot and Newton.

20   That one common called the Ballon Moor is and time out of memory hath been common for all the tenants residents and inhabitors within the said Manor of Caldicott and Newton.

21   They present that the tenants by ancient custom ought to have the fold door unlocked.

22   It is lawful for a freeholder to deliver a tenants cattle out of the Pound being impounded for and in default or absence of the bailiff.

23   That the several of the common called Black Marlpitts is due unto the tenants of Caldicot and Newton.

24   That the custom is that no foster ought to be in Earls Wood unless he be a tenant.

25   That their common called Caldicotts Common ought to be driven but twice in a year. And the first driving shall not be before Whit Sunday and that the tenants without a bailiff may drive the common but not above two persons as well as the bailiff and tenants.

26   That a customary tenant may put out his customary lands from five years to five years for three score years.

27   They present that no woman can have any further right in their customary lands but during her life.

28   That the tenants of Caldicott do yearly pay and ever have paid about the Feast of St. Michael the Archangel 26s. 8d. to his Majesty called the Chence money, the which hath been called the Pill money for that it was gathered for boating there.

29   They present that there ought to be six substantial men being tenants, and sworn by the Steward in open Court for the chessing of the same 26s. 8d. called the Chence or Pill money, for that there is now but small boating used at the Pill.

30   They present that they have been accustomed to pay yearly 4s. for hay money for the grasing of the meadows there called Bisditch to his Majesty.

31   By their custom the Bailiff ought, so soon as the same meadow called Bisditch is open and common, to require or distrain one penny of every person which shall have any manner of cattle grasing in the said meadow towards the levying of the same 4s. to his Majesty.

32 They do also present that their custom is that the youngest son of any Customary Tenant is to inherit his father's customary lands and if no sons but daughters then the daughters as co-heirs to them and their heirs.

33 That the surrenders must pass in full and open Court before the Steward, Recorder and tenants, and not elsewhere.

34 They do present that a Customary Tenant having many sons, he may by surrender in Court pass his customary lands from the youngest son to his eldest or to any of his middle sons.

35 Likewise the custom is that a Customary Tenant having no son, may pass his land to any one of his daughters at his pleasure and bar the rest of his daughters.

36 And further they present that if any free tenant or customary tenant do make default of his appearance at any Leete or Law day, he shall be amerced and shall pay 6d.

37 If any Free or Customary Tenant be lawfully summoned to the monthly Court and make default upon the oath of the Bailiff he shall be amerced and shall pay 7s.

38 They do also present that if any Free or Customary Tenant be sworn on any Jury or view and a day given to bring in their verdict and make default he shall be amerced and shall pay 7s.

And further they do present that they, this Jury, are in great controversy, and divided into two parts, for and touching the presentment and setting down of the sixteenth article of their ancient custom for they whose names be hereafter written will and do allow, confirm present and pass that article in *hec verba*, viz:

That all being residents and inhabitants there in Caldicott and Newton be free to common with their cattle in the common called Caldicott Common, as it hath been used time out of mind.

Which article of custom these men whose names are subscribed did present it for that they were the Jury of Survey held for the said Manor of Caldicott and Newton in the 19th year of the reign of Queen Elizabeth (1578) before Ambrose Stevens and John Cartis, deputed for Sir Henry Knevett, Knight, and then and there it was presented as is before set down by the oaths of these gentlemen hereunder named, viz:

Henry Harbert	John Roberts
Henry David	John Mulgrey
William Base	David Nicholas
William Webb	William Rosser
Richard Base	David Lewis
William Martyn	Nicholas William David
Morgan Rice	Thomas ap Jeuan
John Cooke	William John ap Jeuan
William James	George David

John James   and
Richard ap Price   Roger Stephens

who were fathers to many of this now Jury, and were men of very good understanding and discreet men. And many of them had passed many years before that Survey in another Survey in the time of one Mr. Hillary's Survey, and before that Survey in the time of one Twymhoe and Mr. Morgan, two former Surveyors before Mr. Hillary. And now having an ancient record to lead them made in the time of Ambrose and Curtis, they proceed thereupon and do maintain that record, as by the same ancient record now shewed to concur with this Survey to Gerard Bromley, his Majesty's Surveyor there, it doth and shall apparently appear. And now divers of this Jury on the Survey of Mr. Bromley will not assent or agree with their fellows for the amplifying and confirming of that Sixteenth Article which is herebefore set down. And these be the names of them that stand out obstinately and will not agree with their fellows,

John Walter   Phillip William alias Glover
Rowland Morgan   Henry Phillips, and
Henry Pratt   William Jones de Park

And for the more explanation and true meaning of those that would have that the Sixteenth Article performed we do agree and our meaning is not to cut off any Free or Customary Tenant from having common in the said Common Moor and other commons aforesaid, if he do dwell out of the Manor of Caldicott and Newton. But we are grieved and do think it very unfitting and void of reason and good conscience that they those tenants dwelling out of the Manor and also their undertenants being residents and inhabitants there, should all common for one thing. But we agree that the one of them shall common and not both tenant and undertenant.

And we are well contented and do agree that if every Free Tenant and Customary Tenant dwelling out of the Manor will hold use and occupy his living and means himself, being a messuage or tenement, that then he is to common with his cattle as we do that are dwellers within the Lordship without any contradiction and gainsaying and none-else.

Whereupon we that be of this Jury of Survey and that do agree for the confirming of the said Sixteenth Article have hereunto every man set and subscribed his name.

And we humbly crave Judgement and Censure how that Article by this honourable Court shall be censured and decreed

Francis Harbert   Phillip William of Mathern
William Blythen   Robert David Nicholas
George Parker   William Howell
Henry Vaughan   Thomas Lawrence
Phillip Robnett   Thomas Leach
Edward Reynolds   Charles Watkins

APPENDIX C
HOLDERS OF CALDICOT CASTLE AND MANOR

Date holding ceased	*Holder*	*Reigning King*
1096	Durand	William Rufus
1125	Roger (brother of above)	Henry I
1127	Walter FitzRoger (son of above)	
1143	Milo Fitzwalter (son of above)	Maud & Stephen
1155	Roger (son of above)	Henry II
	Walter, Henry, and Mahel (sons of above)	
1182	Humphrey de Bohun (Third) Earl of Hereford through his marriage to Margaret daughter of Milo Fitzwalter	Henry II
1197	Humphrey de Bohun (Fourth) (son of above)	Richard I
1220	Henry de Bohun (son of above)	John
1275	Humphrey de Bohun (Fifth) (son of above)	Henry III
1298	Humphrey de Bohun (Seventh) (grandson of above)	Edward I
1321	Humphrey de Bohun (Eighth) (son of above)	Edward II
1336	John de Bohun, (son of above)	Edward III
1361	Humphrey de Bohun (Ninth) (brother of above)	Edward III
1373	Humphrey de Bohun (Tenth) (nephew of above)	Edward III
1397	Thomas Woodstock (youngest son of Edward III) through his marriage to Alianore, daughter of Humphrey de Bohun (Tenth)	Richard II
1400	Joan (daughter of above)	Henry IV
	Anne (sister of above) and her husband Edmund Stafford	Henry IV
1422	King Henry V	
1437	Katherine of Valois (wife of above)	Henry VI
1444	Henry VI	
1453	Sir John Beauchamp	
1461	Jasper Tudor, Earl of Pembroke	Henry VI
1469	William Herbert, Earl of Pembroke	Edward IV
1491	William Herbert (son of above)	Edward IV
	King Henry VII and Duchy of Lancaster	

APPENDIX　D

LESSEES of the Manor and Castle of Caldicot and Newton from the
Duchy of Lancaster.

Tenancy
commenced

1507	Charles Somerset	1st Earl of Worcester
1526	Henry Somerset	2nd Earl of Worcester
1549	William Somerset	3rd Earl of Worcester
1589	Edward Somerset	4th Earl of Worcester
1627	Henry Somerset	5th Earl of Worcester and 1st Marquis of Worcester
1646	Richard Watson	Granted by Commonwealth
1660	Edward Somerset	2nd Marquis of Worcester
1667	John Carye	
	Edward Carye	
1708	William Wolsley	
1759	Capel Hanbury	
1765	Jane Hanbury	
1773	John Hanbury	
1784	Jane Hanbury (later Stoughton)	
1790	Thomas Stoughton	
1812	Capel Hanbury	
1830	Thomas Lewis (St. Pierre)	

Charles Lewis purchased the Manor from the Duchy in 1857,
and in 1885 he sold the estate to Joseph Richard Cobb

APPENDIX E (i)

(a) Pedigree—Herberts

A true copy of an ancient Memorable Treatise of Record touching the Progenie and Descent of the honourable Name and Family of the Herberts, by Commission from Edward IV in the year 1460.

So it pleased the said King to raise to dignity such chief men as were partakers of his troubles and wars against his adversaries. And amongst others that he exalted he created William Herbert (who was before Lord Raglan) Earl of Pembroke and honoured him and made him Knight of the most noble order of the Garter, and after which creation the King commanded the said Earl and Sir Richard Herbert, his brother, to take their surnames after their first progenitor Herbert Fitzroy.

William Herbert, the son of William, the son of Thomas, the son of Gwilym, the son of Jenkin, the son of Adam, the son of Reginald,* the son of Peter,* the son of Herbert, the son of Herbert a noble lord descended of the Royal Blood of the Crown of England for he was the natural son of Henry I the first son of William the Conqueror. Peter the son of Herbert FitzHerbert had by his mother, the daughter of Milo Fitzwalter, had the lordship of Betsley, and his son Reginald was lord of Llanllowel (and so on).

Collected and set down by good authority by us

        Jenan ap Rytherch ap Jenan Lloyd
        Howell ap David ap Jenan ap Rys
        Howell Swrdwall ⎫
        Jenan Deulwyn   ⎬ Bards
        Jenan Brechifa   ⎭

*Peter and Reginald held Caldicot West End Manor.

(b) Pedigree—Herberts and Somersets

William ap Thomas m. Gwladys Gam
d. 1446 | d. 1454
William Herbert—Anne Devereaux

|

Earl of Pembroke d. 1461 in battle

|

William 2nd Earl of Pembroke
md. Mary, da. of Earl of Rivers

|

Elizabeth da. of above md.
Sir Charles Somerset 1st Earl of
Worcester d. 1526

|

Henry Somerset 2nd Earl of
Worcester d. 1549

|

William Somerset 3rd Earl of
Worcester d. 1588

|

Edward Somerset 4th Earl of
Worcester d. 1628

|

Henry Somerset 1st Marquis of
Worcester d. 1646

|

Edward Somerset 2nd Marquis
Worcester d. 1667

|

Henry Somerset 1st Duke of
Beaufort of Badminton d. 1699
Successive Dukes of Beaufort

Walter Herbert
md. Anne Stafford.
Children by his mistress Jenet
Llewelyn of Magor

|

Thomas Herbert
md. Bridget da. of Thos.
Kemeys

|

George Herbert d. 1539
md. Anne Moore of Crick

|

Henry Herbert d. 1592
md. Florence Robnet, St. Brides

|

Francis Herbert d. 1628
md. Susan

|

Richard Herbert d. 1664
md. Ann Perkins of Pilston

|

William Herbert d. 1749
md. Alice Andrews, Skenfrith

|

Ann Herbert da. of above
md. William Foord d. 1783

|

Mary Foord da. of above
md. James Hodges d. 1853

|

Elizabeth Hodges da. of above
md. Joseph B. Hillier

|

Arthur Hillier son of above d.
1894
md. Mary Ann Jones, Court
House

APPENDIX E (ii)

Pedigree—Gamage, Lewis of Van, and Van

Godfrey Gamages (from Gamages in France with William the Conqueror)
Payn de Gamages
Robert de Gamage of Rogiet (living 1271)*
William de Gamage. Sheriff of Gloucester.
Gilbert de Gamage of Rogiet md. Lettice da. of Wm. Seymour, Penhow.
He had Caldicot West End Manor.
William Gamage of Rogiet
Thomas Gamage
John Gamage
Morgan Gamage
Sir Thomas Gamage
Robert Gamage   Lewis ap Richard Gwyn

                    Edward Lewis of Van

Margaret Gamage (da. of above) md. Thomas Lewis of Van d. 1594
(Living in 1583 when they had Caldicot)

Sir Edward Lewis of Van d. 1628 (had Caldicot through his mother)

Sir Edward Lewis of Van d. 1630

William of Van (brother of above) d. 1661

Edward of Van (son) d. 1674

Catherine da. of Lewis ap Richard Gwyn
md. John Kemeys of Cefn Mabli

Their da. Cecil md. Lewis Van (Gilliber)

Thomas Van, Coldra d. 1643

Charles Van, Llanwern d. 1704 Had Cald.

Thomas Van

Charles Van d. 1755

Charles Van d. 1778
Caldicot property sold to H. Wise

*Robert Gamage witnessed a grant by Reginald son of Peter to Sir William de Valleys of West End, Caldicot.

APPENDIX F
DISPOSAL OF THE LAST HUMPHREY DE BOHUN'S PROPERTY

(*i*) *Portion to his daughter Maria* .

Manor of Walden, Essex
„   Depden
„   Quenden
„   Leighes
„   Dunmow
„   Masheby
„   Badewe
Castle and Manor of Pleshy
Manor of High Estre
„   Waltham
„   Wikes
„   Shenefield
View of Chishul
Court of High Estre
Manor of Farnham
„   Enfield, Middlesex
Tenement of Hakenoys
Blaunch Appulton, London.
Court of Hertford
Manor of Northamstead
View of Sauston, Canterbury
Manor of Fulmedestow, Norfolk
„   Longbenyngton
„   Haselea, Oxford
„   Kirtlington
„   Dadyngton
„   Periton
„   Ascote
„   Uphaven, Wilts
„   Nether Haven
Court of Monk Farley
Manor of Wokesey, Suffolk
„   Elmesete
„   Offon
„   Arnate, Notts.

(*ii*) *Portion to his daughter Alianore*

Manor of Wycombe, Bucks.
„   Crondon

Tenement of Westcote
Manor of Uplambourne, Berks.
  ,,   Speene
  ,,   Henton
  ,,   Pole, Wilts.
  ,,   Manyngford
Castle and Manor of Caldicot and Newton, Wales
Manor of Walton, Surrey
  ,,   Whitenhurst, Glos.
  ,,   Gwyffich, Dorset
  ,,   Yerkshull, Hereford
Castle and Manor of Brecknock, Wales
  ,,   ,,   ,,   ,,   Hay
  ,,   ,,   ,,   ,,   Huntingdon
Manor of Haresfield, Glos.
  ,,   Newnham
Courts of Hereford
Manor of Southam
Fees in Hereford
  ,,   Northants
Manor of Kneshale, Notts.
Tenements in West Greenwick, Kent
Manor at Hatfield, Essex
  ,,   Halynbury
  ,,   Wrytell
  ,,   Chiggenhale
  ,,   Ramesden
  ,,   East Lea
  ,,   Wakeryng
  ,,   Polmersh
  ,,   Southrop
  ,,   Haydon
  ,,   Fobbyng
  ,,   Norton
  ,,   Bermuersh
  ,,   Kymbalton, Hunts.
  ,,   Amondesham, Bucks.
  ,,   Sende, Wilts.
  ,,   Stratton
  ,,   Wylesford

APPENDIX G (i)
Vicars of Caldicot

Patron	Date	Vicar
Prior of Llantony, Glos.	1334	John
	1360	Nicholas Geoffrey
	1513	William Lewis
King Henry VIII	1535	Richard Johns
	1542	William Cheltnam
Richard Seaborne	1560	John Williams
John Seaborne	1590	John Griffith
	1591	Roger Jones
Edward Kemeys	1624	John Edwards
Nicholas Kemeys	1636	Howell Adams
	1638	Nathaniel Collington, B.A.
		Deprived by Puritans
Commonwealth	1649	Hopkin Rogers, put in by Puritans
Mary Kemeys	1660	Nathaniel Collington restored.
		Resigned 1664
	1664	John Williams
	1669	Morgan Lewis, M.A.
Charles Kemeys	1717	William Morgan, B.A.
		Lewis Jones
Charles Kemeys Tynte	1770	Edward Thomas
	1807	William Hurdman Jane, D.D.
Henry Sayce	1835	Henry Samuel Sayce, M.A.
Edmund Keynton Williams	1841	Edmund Turberville Williams, M.A.
	1885	Edward Vernon Collins, M.A.
	1892	Edward Trevor Bird, M.A.
	1893	Frederick William Clarke, M.A.

APPENDIX G (ii)
Rectors of Shirenewton

1323	William Seward
1397	John Kirketon
1399	Adam of Usk
1399	Thomas ap Adam
	Ranulph Brid
1438	William Colle
1438	Richard Spicer
1455	William
	David Paynod

1559 William Jones
1593 John Morgan
1596 Morgan Roberts
1597 Edward James, M.A.
1603 Francis Godwin, D.D. Later Bishop of Llandaff
1613 Philemon Blethin
1618 Thomas Williams
1640 Morgan Owen, M.A. also Bishop of Llandaff
     Richard Williams
1674 Marmaduke Hopkins, M.A.
1675 Joshua Hotchkiss, M.A.
1680 Edward Williams
1693 John Beavan
1727 Josias Prosser
1733 Lacon Lamb, M.A.
1743 James Birt, M.A.
1750 James Butcher
1760 John Parsons, M.A.
1773 Jeremiah Davies
     William Dyer
1816 James Ashe Gabb, M.A.
1844 James Davies, B.A.
1847 Edward Inwood Jones
1856 Charles Ranken Hall, M.A.
1884 Daniel George Davies
1891 George Platt Dew, B.A.

APPENDIX H
CENSUS STATISTICS

	CALDICOT		NEWTON	
Date	*Population*	*No. of Houses*	*Population*	*No. of Houses*
1801	465		519	
1811	414		522	
1831	583		791	
1851	661	133	933	199
1861	579	136	886	195
1871	962	185	859	194
1881	1401	256	773	177
1891	1293	271	648	158
1901	1196	259	779	177

REFERENCES

RECORDS

British Museum
Duchy of Lancaster
Monmouthshire County Archives
National Library of Wales:—
 Bishops Transcripts
 Badminton Papers
National Museum of Wales
Public Record Office:—
 Calendar of Patent Rolls
 Calendar of Fine Rolls
 Rentals and Surveys, S.C., and D.L.
 Inquisitions P.M.
 Court Rolls
 Duchy of Lancaster, Patents and Leases
 Institution Books
 Chancery Warrants
 Book Petitions
 Ministers' Accounts
 Census Records
 Assize Rolls, and miscellaneous documents

PUBLICATIONS

Adams, G. B.: Constitutional History of England, 1921
Annandale, C.: The Popular Encyclopedia, 1892
Barnes, Joshua: History of Edward III, 1688
Bradney, Sir Joseph: History of Monmouthshire, 1904-33
Busch, Dr. W.: Henry VII
Christie, Mabel E.: Henry VI
Clarke, G. T.: Genealogies of Glamorgan, 1886
Complete Peerage, ed. C. E. G., 1910
Cobb, G. W.: Story of Caldicot Castle, 1931

Coxe, William: A Historical Tour of Monmouthshire, 1801
Chronicles of Benedictus
Davies, Canon E. T.: Ecclesiastical History of Monmouthshire, 1953
Durant, Horatia: Raglan Castle, 1966
Froissart, Sir John: Chronicles of England
Gairdner, James: Richard III, 1898
Gough: History of Pleshy, 1803
Green, J. R.: Short History of the English People, 1985
Hyett, F. A.: Gloucester in National History, 1906
Jones, Theophilus: History of Brecon
Kingsford, C. L.: Henry V, 1923
Marsh, J. F.: Annals of Chepstow Castle, 1888
Morris, John E.: The Welsh Wars of Edward I, 1901
Nicholas, N. H., Siege of Carlavarock, 1828
Rees, Rev. T. Mardy: A History of Quakers in Wales, 1925
Rees, Prof. W.: South Wales and the Border in the 14th Century, 1933
Rees, Prof. W.: South Wales and the Marches, 1284-1415, 1924
Royal Historical Society: Handbook of British Chronology
Salzman, L. F.: Henry II, 1941
Sargeaunt, B. E.: Royal Mon. Militia, 1910
Somerville, Robert: Duchy of Lancaster, 1953
Tout, Prof. T. F.: Edward I., 1893
Vinogradoff, Sir Paul: The Growth of the Manor, 1904
Waters, I.: Chepstow Inns and Taverns, 1949
Waters, I.: Chepstow Miscellany. 1958
Webb, Sidney and Beatrice: The Parish and the County, 1906
Williams, Elizabeth H.: The Crosses of Monmouthshire, 1893
Willis, Browne: A Survey of the Cathedral Church of Llandaff, 1718
Wood, James G.: The Crossings of the Severn, 1914
Wright, Arthur: Church Bells of Monmouthshire, 1942
Notes of J. R. Cobb
Notes on Caldicot Castle by H. A. Tipping
Notes on Caldicot Castle by Octavius Morgan and Thomas Wakeham, 1853

ACKNOWLEDGEMENTS

I gratefully acknowledge information given and help afforded by the following: Mr. W. H. Baker, the County Archivist; Mr. and Mrs. T. M. Birbeck; Mr. W. J. Collett, the Newport Borough Librarian; Canon E. T. Davies; Professor R. R. Davies; Mr. Ellis Evans; Rev. Roy Hallett ; Mr. D. O. Liddell ; Professor W. Rees ; Mr. and Mrs. Ivor Waters; Mr. Bryan Woodfield; the Editor of Debrett; the staff of the Chepstow Branch Library, and many others who have given me the benefit of their knowledge of facts relating to Caldicot and Newton.

Thos. T. Birbeck

M

INDEX

INDEX

Abergavenny, 6, 16, 19, 49, 51, 65, 101, 126
Abrath, John, 65
Adam of Usk, 120, 164
Adam, John ap, 23, 59
Adam, Thos. ap, 120, 164
Adams, family, 92, 102, 104, 117, 148, 164
Advowson, 92-5
Agriculture, 57-60, 66, 69, 71-2, 84, 87-8, 94, 101, 108, 118, 124-5, 146-7, 151, 154-6
Albion, Inn, 117
Alderfords Acre, 150
Alderford, Francis, 68
Amondesham, 163
Andover, 8
Andrews, Alice, 160
Anglesey, 18, 49
Annandale, 23
Annesley, Sir John, 37
Anstey family, 137, 148
Applinsdene, Sir Ralf de, 26
Architecture, 76, 78, 82
Argoed, 123, 125, 128, 133, 138
Argot manor, 58
Arundel, 7, 39
Arundel, Earl of, 11, 27, 32, 33, 35, 39, 41-2, 44, 47
Astry, Sir Samuel, 55
Atkins, David, 90
Atkyns, Robert, 127

Badewe, 162
Badwell, 150
Bailiffs, 83, 86, 88-9, 141, 153-5
Baker, John, 86
Ballan Moor, 71, 151, 154
Ballyhorgan, 56
Balun, Hamelin de, 6
Balyn, Ivan ap, 60
Banbury, 51
Bands, 116, 135, 137
Barham, John de, 23

Base or Basse family, 68, 155
Base Half-Acre, 150
Basset, Ralph, Lord, 27
Bassill, Hill, 150
Bath, 95
Bayam, M.A., 72
Baynards Castle, 50
Bayons, Wm., 89
Beauchamp, Sir John, 50, 65, 84, 157
Beauchamp family, 7, 49
Beaufort, Dukes of, 55, 112, 130, 160
Beaufort family, 49, 50, 54-5
Beavan, John, 165
Becanshaw, Dr. Adam, 91
Beesditch, 58, 67, 109, 117, 142, 147, 150
Bells, 91, 95-6, 113, 137
Belyn, John ap, 23
Benacre Moor, 71, 108, 147
Benjamin family, 134-6
Berkeley, 26
Berkshire, 163
Berwick, 11, 34
Bevan, Theophilus, 110, 144
Bigod, Roger, 11, 20
Bird family, 164
Birkett, Alice, 122
Birt, James, 165
Bishton, 144
Bisshops Lane, 150
Black Marlpits, 71, 151, 154
Black Prince, 29, 31-3, 37
Black Rock, 90, 126
Black Tower, 76, 80
Blackweir, 124
Blackwell, 150
Bladesmere family, 28
Bladon, family, 128
Blaunch Appulton, 162
Blethin, William, 70, 122, 127, 130, 149, 156
Blethin family, 130, 133, 165
Blois, Charles de, 30-1
Boating at Pill see Pill Money
Bohun, Alianore de, 36-7, 41, 43, 46-7, 62-3, 79, 83, 157

Bohun, Edward de, 27-9
Bohun, Henry de, 12-3, 25, 91, 157
Bohun, Humphrey de (1), 8, 10
Bohun, Humphrey de (2), 9, 10
Bohun, Humphrey de (3), 10-1, 118, 157
Bohun, Humphrey de (4), 11, 157
Bohun, Humphrey de (5), 13,-6, 118,157
Bohun, Humphrey de (6), 16, 157
Bohun, Humphrey de (7), 16-9, 21, 59, 124. 157
Bohun, Humphrey de (8), 20-26, 157
Bohun, Humphrey de (9), 27-34, 157
Bohun Humphrey de (10), 35-7, 78-9, 86, 157, 162
Bohun, John de, 16, 18, 26-7, 157
Bohun, Maria de, 36-7, 39, 63, 162
Bohun, William de, 27-34, 37
Bohun, family, ix, 1, 9, 11-3, 16, 25, 36, 61, 65
Boleyn, Anne, 54
Bolingbroke, Henry, 39, 48, 63
Boundaries, 124, 149, 150
Bourchier family, 48
Bowen, Wm., 90
Brabant, 29, 30
Braose family, 10, 16
Brecon, 6, 7, 16, 21, 31, 35-6, 63, 78, 141, 163
Bren, Llewellyn, 25
Brendwode, 45
Brest, 30, 36-7, 44
Breteuil, Roger de, 3-4
Brewing, 61, 89, 114
Bridge (castle), 78-9
Bridgend, 109
Bridgenorth, 26
Bristol, 6-7, 9, 48, 50, 79, 80, 82, 84, 89, 90, 95
Briwer, Wm. de, 14
Broadcroft, 124, 150
Broad Leazes, 71
Brockwael, 2, 149
Brockwells, 67, 144
Bromley, Gerard, 149, 156
Brown, Wm., 123
Bruce, Robert, 23, 25
Bryme, John, 95
Buckingham, Earl of, 37
Buckingham, Duke of, 52, 54
Buckinghamshire, 23, 37. 162-3
Building work 79-85
Builth, 18-9
Burgh, Hubert de, 13

Burgundy, Duke of, 39, 44
Burroughs, Wm., 135
Bury St. Edmunds, 111
Butcher, James, 165
Butcher's Arms, 135
Butlershold, 123-4

Cae Pwcella, 120
Caerleon, 49, 78-9
Caerwent, 1, 5, 72, 89, 107-8, 112, 120, 125, 142, 147, 150, 152
Calais, 33, 36, 39, 43-6
Caldicot, passim
Caldicot Castle, 6, 11, 13-4, 40-2, 48-50, 54-5, 58-9, 61-2, 65-6, 70, 72, 74, 76, 78-85, 147, 152, 157
Caldicot Church, see Church
Caldicot Common Moor, 58, 147, 151, 154-5
Caldicot Common Sea, 71, 108, 147, 151, 154
Caldicot Cross, 62, 88, 90, 101, 107, 145, 148, 153
Caldicot Hall, see Great House
Caldicot Hundred, 103-4
Caldicot manor, see Manor
Caldicot Mill, 67, 70, 151
Caldicot Pill, 1, 59, 74, 78, 84, 107, 109-10, 144
Caldicot West End, see West End
Caradoc, 2-3
Carlisle, 21, 27, 34
Carmarthen, 18-9
Carnarvonshire, 25
Carpenter, John, 82
Carpenters, 78-81, 83, 85
Carpenters' Arms, 135
Carruthers, David, 126, 133-6
Carruthers, James Proctor, 133, 136
Carter, T., 148.
Carye, Edwd. and John, 55, 67, 69, 158
Castellan, Wm., 80
Castle Farm, 71
Cattbrane, 68
Census, 129, 134, 146, 165
Chapelhouse, 83-4
Chapels, 118, 123, 148
Charities, 94, 99, 133-4
Charles I, 55, 69, 92
Cheltnam, Wm., 154
Chence Money, see Pill Money

Chepstow, 2, 5, 20, 23, 40, 51, 55-6, 61, 72, 79, 81-2, 90, 93, 95, 101, 105, 107-9, 125-7, 130, 133, 142-4, 147-8
Chepstow and Caldicot Volunteer Infantry, 105
Chepstow Highway Board, 126
Chepstow Rural District Council, ix, 99, 130, 148
Chepstow School Board, 148
Chepstow Turnpike Trust, 126
Chepstow Union Workhouse, 101
Chester, 2, 16-7, 42
Chiggenhale, 163
Church, 12, 91, 94, 96, 99, 112, 120, 142, 149
Church, Geoffrey att, 35
Churches, The, 118
Churchesdon, Henry de, 35
Church Farm, 116, 141, 144
Church Field, 58, 68, 147
Church Hayes, 118
Church Road, 112, 145
Churchwardens, 92, 94, 95, 101, 104, 112, 116, 144-5
Cirencester, 7
Civil War, 69, 120, 142
Clappam, John, 51
Clark, Francis, 72
Clarke, F. W., 164
Clifford, James, 63
Clopton, John, 61
Clotherbox, John, 81
Cobb, J. R., 56, 85, 158
Cobham, Lord, 33
Cock-a-Roosting, 125
Coed Cumnor, 126
Coldra, 161
Colle, Wm., 164
Collins, F. V., 164
Collington, N., 93, 164
Combermere Abbey, 16
Commons, 58, 69, 71, 124, 147, 151, 154-6
Coniers family, 51, 89
Constable, 62, 90, 103, 105, 145
Constable of England, 6, 7, 10, 14, 16, 23-5, 27, 29, 34-5, 37
Conway, 17, 20
Cooke, John, 155
Cooper, Alfred, 113, 148
Cormeilles, 3
Cornwall, Earl of, 11, 14, 20, 24
Countess Tower, 78, 83

Court House, 160
Courts, 59, 61, 70, 84, 88-90, 103-4, 108, 148, 153-5
Courtyard, 76, 85
Crecy, 31-2
Cribba Mill, 123, 126-8
Crick, 67, 108, 112, 114, 125-6, 150, 160
Cricket, 147
Cromwell, Oliver, 55, 69, 142
Crondon, 162
Crooked Bridge, 124, 150
Cross, see Caldicot Cross
Crossway, 124-5, 150
Cross Hands Inn, 135-6
Crowley, Robert, 100
Croydon, 95
Culverhousetour, 79
Cumberland, 29
Curbehind Mill, 68, 70, 124, 127, 150
Curre family, 127-8, 130, 133-4, 137
Curtis, John, 155
Customary tenants, 60, 68, 72-3, 88, 124, 152-6
Cwm, 124-5, 128
Cwm Mill, 126
Cwm Wood, 71, 125, 147
Cyfeiliawg, Bishop 2

Dace, Clement, 141
Dadyngton, 162
Dangerfield, Philip, 61
Dangerville, Philip, 81
David family, 68, 90, 155
Davies, family, 108, 165
Davis family, 56, 72, 109
Dean, Forest of, 7-9, 18, 42
Deepweir, 1, 72, 107-8, 150
Demesne, 58, 67, 152
Denlwyn, Jenan, 159
Denny, 72
Depden, 162
Derby, Earl of, 33
Derehurst, Thos., 65
Despenser, Hugh le 25-6
Devauden, 126
Devereaux, Anne, 51, 160
Devizes, 9
Dew, G.P., 165
Dewstow, 57, 68, 107-8, 134, 144, 148, 150
Dinham, 125, 130
Domesday Book, 4, 5, 118, 144

Dore Abbey, 34
Dorset, 52, 163
Douglas, Earl of, 34
Dovecote, 59, 80
Dowle family, 95, 108
Duchy of Lancaster, 52, 54, 56, 62-3, 65-70, 72, 85-7, 124-5, 128, 130, 134, 137, 147, 150, 158
Duckless Common, 124, 150
Dungeon, 74, 83, 85
Dunmow, 162
Durand, 5, 9, 57, 118
Durham, Bishop of, 12, 20
Dyer, Wm., 134, 165
Dyers Mill, 127
Dynham's Well, 124, 150

Ealdgyth, 2
Earl Marshal, 13, 45-6
Earlswood, 58, 68, 71, 82, 84, 118, 123-6, 128, 133-4, 139, 147, 151, 153-4
Earl's Grove, 58, 118, 151, 153
East Lea, 163
Edmonde, T. W., 124
Education, see Schools
Edward I, 16-8, 20-1, 23-4, 60
Edward II, 24-6, 28
Edward III, 26-8, 30-7, 157
Edward IV, 50-2, 66
Edwards family, 90, 92, 111, 164
Eland, Sir Wm., 28
Elizabeth I, 54-5, 67
Ellis, Thos., 127
Elmfield, 147
Eltham, 46
Ely, Bishop of, 19, 41
Enclosures, 69, 71, 118, 125, 147
Enfield, 162
Engineer's Arms, 135
Engineers, Royal Monmouthshire, 116
Essex, 23, 34, 37, 39, 45, 162-3
Essex, Earl of, 12-3, 16, 23, 29, 34-5, 37, 78
Etkyns, David, 120
Evans family, 95, 128, 136
Evesham, 15-6
Ewyas, 9

Farms, Farmers, see Agriculture
Farnham, 11, 162

Farthinghill, 71
Faulks, J., 148
Ferney Cross, 99, 107
Ferry, 90
Fetes, 85, 116, 137
Ffryrmyn Cross, 150
Fiennes, Maud de, 16
Field, Phebe, 90
Fisheries, 2, 72, 59, 149
Fishpond, 59, 81
FitzAllan, Richard, 35
FitzHerbert, Herbert, 10, 159
FitzOsbern, Wm., 3
FitzRoger, Walter, 5-6, 157
FitzRoy, Herbert, 159
FitzWalter, Milo, 6-10, 58, 74, 91, 118, 139, 141, 157, 159
FitzWalter, Roger, 9-10
Five Bells, 134-7
Flanders and lords, 11, 20, 25, 30, 32-3, 36, 41
Flaxley Abbey, 10
Floods, 68-9, 151
Fobbyng, 163
Foliot, Gilbert, 7.
Font, 94
Foord, Wm., 70-2, 87, 95, 124-8, 160
Foresters, 51, 65, 70
Forests, 68, 125
Fox, George, 120, 122
France and French Wars, 3-5, 7-9, 11-6, 19, 20, 25, 27-8, 30-4, 36-7, 39, 43-6, 48-50, 52, 55, 63, 65, 83, 89, 157, 161
Frankton, Stephen de, 18
Freeholders, 58-9
Friendly Societies, 114-6, 134-6
Froissart, Jean, 43, 45
Fry, Wm., 127
Fryth Wood, 40
Fulling Mill, 126-7, 152
Fulmedestow, 162

Gabb, Rev. J. Ashe, 120, 128, 134, 165
Gaerllwyd, 123-5
Gam, Gwladys, 160
Gamage pedigree and family, 139, 141, 161
Gamage's Land, 124
Gaols, 59, 61, 70, 122
Garretts, 124, 150
Gascony, 14, 16, 20, 31

Gaunt, John of, 33, 37, 42 49 63
Gaveston, Piers, 24
Gawler, Francis, 122
Geffrey, Adam, 81
Geoffrey, Nicholas, 164
George, Thos., 146
Germany, 29, 32, 43
Giffard, John, 18-9
Gilberton, Sir Walter, 25
Glamorgan, Earl of, 55
Glass, 80
Gloucester, 4-5, 7-10, 12, 14-5, 25-6,
    34, 37, 41, 52, 55, 58, 91, 109, 118,
    141, 163
Gloucester, Earl of, 7-9, 14, 16-20, 25
Gloucester, Duke of, 41-6, 65, 80
Gloucestershire, 3. 6, 7, 10, 16, 23, 47,
    91, 95, 141, 163-4
Glover Philip. 156
Glyn, 150
Gogh, Wm., 89
Goldcliff, 89, 91
Goodbehind Mill, 127
Gorgevele Henry, 89
Gour, John, 83-4
Gournay, Sir John, 26
Gower, 50, 55
Grail, Wm., 116
Grantham, 29
Great Field, 147
Great House, 93, 128, 141, 144
Great Seal, 31
Great Tower, 78
Great Twympill, 151
Great Western Railway, 109, 145
Greenmeadow, 57
Griffith family, 68, 164
Grondra, 124, 126, 128, 133-6
Grosmont, 55
Grove, 146
Guardians, Board of, 101, 114, 147
Gwent, 144
Gwilym Ddu, 50
Gwyffich, 163
Gwyn, Lewis ap Richard, 161

Hadleigh Castle, 47
Hakenoys, 162
Hale, Geoffrey le. 60
Hall, Rev. C. R., 120, 133, 165
Halynbury, 163
Hanbury family, 56, 72, 107, 158

Hangingland, 68
Harbert family, 84, 90, 151, 155-6
Haresfield. 16, 163
Harlech, 51
Harpstone Lane, 150
Harris, Wm., 124, 150
Haselea, 162
Hatfield, 163
Haverfordwest. 16 52
Havering Bower. 45
Hawkin. John, 89
Hay, 8, 163
Hay, Thos. de la, 65
Haydon, 163
Hayward, 104
Hempstead, Richard, 141
Henton, 163
Hentsfoothold, 123
Henry I, 5-7
Henry II, 9-11
Henry III, 13, 15
Henry IV, 48
Henry V, 48-9, 65, 86, 157
Henry V, 49, 50, 65, 85-6, 157
Henry VII, 50, 157
Henry VIII, 54, 164
Herbert. Wm., 50-2, 54, 66, 157, 159, 160
Herbert family, 50-5, 66, 69, 74, 76, 89,
    94, 99, 104, 148-9, 159-60
Herbert's Charity, 94, 99
Hereford, 9. 141, 163
Hereford, Earl of 3, 4, 8, 10, 12, 14, 16,
    18-24, 29, 34-5, 37, 58, 63, 157
Herefordshire, 3, 8, 23, 52, 63, 163
Hertford, 23, 162
Hicks, Thomas, 94, 116
High Estre, 162
Highmoor Hill, 94-5, 150
High Tower, 74, 76
Highway Board, 108, 148
Hill family, 98, 146, 148
Hillier family, 148, 160
Hodges, James, 160
Holland, 20, 23, 42
Holderness, 42
Hollis, William, 126-8, 130, 134
Hollis family, 88, 101, 115-6, 128, 146
Hollis Mill, 127
Holme, Elizabeth, 122
Hooles, The, 67
Hope Chapel, 123
Hopkin family, 68
Hopkins family, 110, 165

Horsinden, Robert de, 35
Hotchkiss, Joshua, 165
Howard, W., 148
Howell family, 89, 124, 127, 149
Hughes family, 110, 133
Huntingdon, 23, 163
Huntingdon, Earl of, 52
Huntley, Thomas de, 23, 59

Ifton, 71, 99, 110, 150-1
Inns and innkeepers, 94, 114-7, 122, 134-5, 150
Ireland, 30-1, 41-3, 48, 55-6
Ironwork, 81, 110
Isabella, Queen, 26, 28, 139
Itton, 127, 130, 133-4

James family, 155-6, 165
James Furlong, 150
Jane, W. H., 164
Jeffreys, John, 130
Jenkyns, Hollapp, 89
Jenur, John, 61
Jeuan family, 155
Jeremy, Thomas, 135
John, King, 11-4
John of Gaunt, 33, 37, 42, 49, 63
John, Thomas ap, 101, 116
Johns, Richard, 92, 164
Jones family, 97, 108, 111-2, 114, 117, 120, 122-4, 127, 130, 133-5, 148, 150, 156, 160, 164-5
Joseph, John, 101, 116
Justices of the Peace, 103-4

Katherine of Valois, 49, 65, 83, 157
Kemeys family, 68, 70, 92-3, 95, 99, 103, 105, 112, 133, 142-4, 160-1, 164
Kenilworth, 15
Kent, 14, 26, 37, 163
Kildrummie castle, 24
King, Capt., 112
King's Head, 134
King's Mill, 150
Kirketon, John, 164
Kirtlington, 162
Knevett, Sir Henry, 155
Knewshale, 163
Knight family, 112, 116
Knowles, William, 127

Kymbalton, 163

Lackingay Sir John, 44, 46
Lady Mill, 68, 124, 150
Lamb, Lacon, 165
Lancaster, 25
Lancaster, Earl of, 24,-6 35
Lancaster, Duke of, 34, 36-7, 39, 41, 43-4, 63
  see Duchy of Lancaster for estates
Langley Edmund de, 37
Latrines, 79, 80, 82-3
Lawrence, Thos., 149, 156
Leach, Thos., 149, 156
Leicester, Earl of, 11, 15
Leighes, 162
Lewes, 15
Lessees of manor and castle, 158
Lewis, Morgan, 56, 72, 93, 164
Lewis, Thomas, 56, 90, 105, 161
Lewis family, 49, 56, 67, 72, 90, 112, 125, 141, 150, 155, 158, 161, 164
Liddell, C. O., 125, 128, 133
Lime and lime-kilns, 79, 83-4, 150
Lincoln, 7, 12, 37
Lincoln, Bishop of, 28-9
Lincoln, Earl of, 23
Litelhalle Tower, 83
Little Field, 147
Little Mill, 127
Little Moor, 71
Llandaff, 2, 57, 112, 120, 130, 144, 149, 165
Llandegelly, 70
Llandewy Vach, 144
Llandovery, 19
Llanfihangel Rogiet, 149, 151
Llanfrechfa, 95
Llanllowell, 159
Llanmelin, 1, 130
Llansoy, 126
Llantony Priory (Monmouthshire and Gloucestershire), 6, 9, 13 16, 47, 58, 91, 94, 141, 148, 164
Llanvair Discoed, 105
Llanwern, ix, 161
Llewelyn, 14-5, 17-8, 52-3, 160
Local Government, 145-8
London, 6-7, 27-8, 30-1, 34, 41-3, 45, 47-8, 50, 55, 67, 162
Longbenyngton, 162
Longcroft, 68

Longhouse, 83
Lord's Mead, 71-2
Lowe, family 130, 133, 137
Lower Coombe Mill, 127
Lowerfield, 67
Lower House, 128, 144
Lower Southfield, 68
Ludlow, 15
Lydney, 85, 116, 147

Madoc, Morgan ap, 49, 65, 89
Maesgwyneth, 1
Magor, 52, 107-8, 133, 144, 160
Malt House Inn, 117
Maltravers, Sir John, 26
Mandeville, Geoffrey de, 14
Mandeville, Maud de, 78
Manny, Sir Walter, 33-4
Manor, 52, 54, 57-8, 62-3, 69, 70, 88,
    105, 107, 125-6, 139, 141-2, 144-5,
    151, 158
Manyngford, 163
Maral, John, 23
March, Earl of, 26, 28
Marches of Wales, 3, 19, 26, 52, 66
Marshall, William, 13
Martel, Philip, 60
Martin family, 135, 155
Masheby, 162
Mason family, 80, 82, 84
Masons, 78-9
Mathern, 130, 156
Mears G., 95
Meurig, 2, 149
Middle Pill, 151
Middlesex, 23, 162
Middle Tower, 76, 82
Milford Haven, 109
Militia, 105-6
Millfield, 71, 147
Moat, 74
Molyneux, Thos., 105
Monk Farleigh, 11, 162
Monmouth, 65, 101, 107, 126
Montfort, Simon de, 15-7
Montague, Sir Walter, 69
Moore, Anne, 160
Moors, 69, 71, 125, 142, 147, 150-1
More, Nicholas, 103
Morehold, Wm., 81
Morgan family, 68, 90, 103, 127, 144,
    149, 152, 156, 164-5

Morris, Valentine, 107
Mortimer family, 10, 26, 28-9
Mount Ballan, 92, 112
Mounton, 125, 128
Mounton Brook, 68, 124, 126-8, 139
Mount Zion, 123
Mowbray, Thomas, 48
Mulgrey, John, 155
Musgrove, Samuel, 95, 101
Mynders Hill, 137
Mynnetts, 150,
Mynyddbach, 71, 123-5, 127, 134, 137,
    147

Nash, 89
Neddern, 1, 107-8, 145, 150
Nether Haven, 162
New Cut, 1
Newmarch, Bernard and Sybilla, 6, 9
Newmeade, 67, 142, 151
Newnham, 9, 163
New Passage roads, 125-6
Newport, 40, 79, 81-2, 90-1, 101, 107
Newton, see Shirenewton
New Tower, 81
Nicholas family, 110, 117, 122, 149,
    155-6
Nonconformist, 97, 123, 148
Norfolk, 162
Norfolk, Earl of, 3, 12, 20-1
Norfolk, Duke of, 48
Norman, Rev. R. V., 144
Normans and Normandy, 3-5, 7, 9, 31
Northampstead, 162
Northampton, 37, 50, 90, 163
Northampton, Earl of, 29-31, 34-5
Northfield, 57, 67
Northumberland, 34
Norton, 163
Norway, 43
Norwich, Ralph de, 13-4
Nottingham, 28, 133, 162-3

Oakham, 28, 42
Oakley, Henry, 144
Oaks, 68, 79, 81-2
Oddfellows, 115-6, 135
Offon, 162
Overseers of the Poor, 100-1, 104, 145
Owen, Morgan, 120, 165
Oxford, 8, 15, 37, 42, 162
Oxle, John, 79

Painted Tower, 76, 84
Palmer, John, 95
Pandy Mill, 127
Panteg, 120
Paper mills, 71, 127-8
Parish Council, 137, 148
Parish registers, 93
Parker family, 66, 90, 149, 156
Parkershold, 123
Parsons, John, 165
Parson's Grove, 118
Parson's Seven Acres, 151
Paynod, David, 120, 164
Pederhewle, 150
Pedigrees, 159-161
Pembroke, Earl of, 33, 50-2, 54, 66, 157, 159, 160
Penhow, 90, 104, 139, 161
Perce, Hugh, 68
Periton, 162
Perkins, Ann, 160
Peylewyn, Joan, 89
Philip, Henry, 149
Philippa, Queen, 30, 36
Phillips family, 83, 156
Piercefield, 107, 126
Pill, see Caldicot Pill
Pill House, 144
Pill Inn, 110, 117
Pill Money, 67, 84, 154
Pilston, 160
Plague, 62
Plantagenets, 23, 55
Pleshy castle, 14, 21, 34, 36, 43-7, 78, 162
Ploughing, 59-60
Plumbers, 78, 80, 82, 85
Pole, Michael de la, 41
Police, 104
Pollard, Mary, 93
Polmersh, 163
Pontyclyvon, 126
Pontypool, 56, 101, 107
Poole Rough, 151
Poor and Poor Laws, 100, 103-4, 114, 133, 147
Poorhouse, 101, 104
Poor's Allotment, 134
Pope, 14, 31, 33
Population, 109-10, 137, 146, 165
Porchester, 12
Porter, Arthur, 142
Portskewett, 2, 108, 110, 112, 116, 150
Pratt, Henry, 149, 156

Pratt's Farm, 150
Price family, 99, 101, 138, 144, 152, 156
Prickardes Mead, 151
Pride, Henry, 110
Prince of Wales, 31, 137
Prior family, 94, 101, 116
Priory Close, 150
Priory Farm, 148
Priory Manor, 58, 60, 68, 92, 95, 105, 107, 141-2, 144, 150
Prise of ale, 61, 114
Prittlewell Priory, 34
Proctor family, 112, 126, 133, 144
Prosser, Josias, 165
Prothero, Thos., 56
Pulpit, 124, 150
Puritans, 97, 120, 164
Putot, Wm. de, 13-4

Quakers, 120, 122-3
Quarries, 79, 83-4
Queen's Mill, 87
Quenden, 162
Quincey, Robert de, 16
Quinton, M., 138

Radcote bridge, 42
Raglan, 49, 50, 53, 55
Raglan, Lord, 159
Railway, 72, 101, 109-10, 116-7
Ramsden, 94, 163
Rates, 101, 109-10
Reading, 7
Rectors of Shirenewton, 164
Rectory Manor, 58, 118
Redmayne, Meurice de, 23, 60
Reece family, 101, 124
Reens, 108
Reeve, 61, 78-9, 86
Reeves family, 109, 138
Rents, 141, 153
Reynolds family, 124, 149, 156
Rhewl, 128
Rhuddlan, 18, 25
Rhys, 19
Rice, Morgan, 155
Richard I, 11
Richard II, 37, 41-4, 46, 48
Richard III, 52
Richards family, 134, 138
Richmond, Earl of, 52

Ridel, Geoffrey, 10
Rivers, Earl of, 160
Roads, 59, 107-8, 125-6, 148
Roberts family, 127, 150, 155, 165
Robnet family, 149, 152, 156, 160
Rochester, 6
Rochester, Earl of, 44
Rodge, 1, 68, 71-2
Rogers family, 55, 93, 97, 128
Rogerstone Grange, 130
Rogiet, 110, 146, 161
Rogiet Moor, 147
Rossen, Wm., 68
Rosser family, 70, 155
Rowlands family, 93, 112
Rushmeare, 68
Rutland, 29, 42
Rutland, Earl of, 43
Rykyll, William, 46

St. Arvans, 126
St. Brides Netherwent, 2, 149, 160
St. Briavels, 7, 9, 41-2
St. Pierre, 56, 67, 72, 95, 125, 133, 150, 158
Salisbury, 14
Salisbury, Earl of, 47
Sandwich, 31, 33
Sandy Lane, 99
Sapy family, 139
Sauston, 162
Sayce family, 90, 93, 164
Schools, 99, 112-3, 123, 134, 137, 148
Scotland and Scottish Wars, 8-9, 11-2, 21-7, 29-31, 34, 41, 52
Seaborne, John, 142, 164
Seaborne, Richard, 92, 142, 164
Senare, John, 89
Sende, 163
Severn, 1, 74, 124, 150-1
Severn Tunnel, 109-10, 116-7, 145-6
Severn Tinplate Co. 111
Seward, Wm., 164
Seymour, Sir William, 139, 161
Sharp, James, 108
Shenefield, 162
Shearfield, 58, 67, 147
Sheriffs, 4-6, 10, 57-8, 91, 118
Ship Inn, 116
Shirenewton, ix, 6, 10, 23, 49, 54, 58, 60, 67-8, 70-2, 104, 116, 118, 120, 122-8, 130-5, 137, 148, 150, 163-4

Shirenewton Church, 68, 118, 120
Shirenewton Hall, 128, 130, 133, 137
Shirenewton School Board, 148
Shrewsbury 7, 48
Shropshire 52
Simers Hill 71
Skenfrith, 160
Slade, 67
Slowe House, 150, 152
Sluys, Battle of, 30, 33, 37
Smith family, 51, 68, 81, 86, 89, 130
Smyth Moore 67
Somerset, 11, 52, 95
Somerset, Earl of, 54
Somerset, Duke of, 50, 54
Somerset, Sir Charles, 52, 54, 158, 160
Somerset family, 54-5, 66-7, 85, 158, 160
Somerway, 150-1
Somery, William, 39, 61, 78-82, 86
Southam, 163
Southfield, 57, 68
Southrop, 163
South Wales, 31, 50, 52
South Wales Borderers, 106
South Wales Railway, 72, 101, 109-10
Spain, 14, 17, 27, 33, 37
Speene, 163
Spencer, Isaac, 112
Spicer, R. and W., 164
Sport, 85, 116, 135, 137
Squibbs family, 95, 102, 148
Stafford family, 48, 52-3, 63, 86, 157, 160
Stanshaw, Alexander, 89
Star Pitch, 126
Steele, Rev., 112
Stephens, Roger, 156
Stevens, Ambrose, 155
Steward, 59, 61, 66, 70, 79-82, 88-90, 153
Stockham, Ann, 146
Stocks, 59, 62, 85, 103
Stoophill, 71
Stoughton family, 56, 158
Stradling, Wm., 65
Striguil, see Chepstow
Stubby Lane, 150
Sudbrook, 1, 110, 116, 150
Sudbrook Pill, 1, 2, 150
Sudbury, Simon de, 42
Suffolk, 162
Suffolk, Earl of, 29, 41
Surrey, 163
Surveys, 67-8, 70, 85, 88, 124, 127-8, 149, 155-6

Surveyors, 81, 104, 108, 145
Swansea, 109
Swynford, Catharine, 44, 49, 63
Sydeny, Robert, 90
Symon, Robert, 65

Talbot, Gilbert, 48
Talgarth, 139
Tan House, 134-5
Taylor, T. and S., 89, 144
Taylors Mill, 150
Tewkesbury, 52
Thomas, Sir Wm. ap., 49, 50, 65-6, 89, 160
Thomas family, 112, 127, 130, 134, 148, 164
Thomas Tower, 84
Tilers, 78, 85
Timber, 58, 61, 68, 81-2, 85, 90, 118, 124-5
Tin stamping, 87, 110-1
Tintern, 51, 61, 85, 95, 135
Tippling Philosopher, 94, 101, 115-6
Tollhouses, 108, 126
Towers, 76, 78-80, 82-4
Transport, 78-85
Tredegar Arms, 135
Trevella, 8, 125
Trinitycliff, 84
Troggy, 1 2, 68, 124, 126, 149-50
Trowbridge, 14
Tuck Mill, 127
Tudor, Edmund, 49, 50
Tudor, Jasper, 49, 51-2, 54, 66, 157
Tudor, Owen, 49
Turberville family, 18, 130
Turnpike acts, 107-8, 125-6
Tyler, Gregory, 80
Tynte, C. K., 164

Undy, 151
Uphaven, 162
Uplambourne, 163
Upper House, 134-5
Usk, 49, 50, 122, 125-6

Valers, Sir William de, 19, 23, 60
Valley Mead, 150
Valleys, Wm., 89
Valleys House, 60

Vallis Terrace, 60
Van family, 69, 141, 161
Vantotehall, 89
Vaughan family, 87, 91, 99, 149, 156
Vestry meetings, 101, 104, 145
Vicars of Caldicot, 89, 91-3, 164
Vychans, 18

Wakeryng, 163
Walden Abbey, 16, 21, 25-6, 34, 36, 47-8, 162
Wales and Welsh, 2, 6, 14, 23, 26-7, 51-2, 58, 74, 124, 136
Walewayn, John, 26
Wallace, Wm., 21
Wallpits, 142, 151
Walter, John, 149, 156
Waltham, 161
Walton, 11, 163
Warwick, Earl of, 24, 36, 42, 44, 47, 49 51
Warwick Wm., 95
Water supply, 74, 108, 145
Water Mills, see Mills
Water, John, 49, 65
Waters family, 122-3
Watkins family, 122, 146, 149, 156
Watson, Richard, 55, 70, 158
Waywardens, 108
Webb, Wm., 155
Webbs Lease, 68
Webleaze Farm, 71
Wedergrave, Nicholas de, 23
Well, 74, 145, 148, 150
Well Moore, 67
Weloc, 120
Welsh, Christopher, 130
Wentwood, 1, 79
Wesley, John, 90
West, John, 124, 150
West Bridge, 150
West End manor, 57, 60, 68, 107, 117, 124, 139, 141, 144, 148-9, 151, 161
Westcote, 163
West Field, 58, 67, 147
West Greenwich, 163
Westmead, 124, 150
West of England Hotel, 110, 117
Westmorland, 27, 29
Westward Moor, 71
Westward Pill, 151
Whitehall, 72

White Hart, 88, 94, 98, 101, 114-6
White Mill, 127, 147
Whitenhurst, Glos., 163
Whittyngton, Richard, 47
Wickliffe's Bible, 47
William the Conqueror, 2, 4, 10
William Rufus, 4, 5, 10
William, Philip, 149, 156
Williams family, 72, 93-5, 112, 138, 146-7, 164-5
Wiltshire, 10, 15, 23, 28, 37, 162-3
Winchester, 3, 7, 8
Winchester, Earl of, 16
Windsor, 16, 36, 42
Wine, 89, 93
Wireworks, 110, 147
Wise, Henry, 93, 110, 112, 141, 144, 146, 161
Wise family, 93, 102
Withers, Richard, 146
Wokesey, 162

Wolsley, Wm., 55-6, 158
Woodcock Hill, 150
Woodstock, Thomas de, 36-7, 39, 41-3, 45-7, 59, 61-3, 76, 79, 83, 86, 114. 157
Woodstock family 47-8, 65, 157
Woodville, Mary, 51-2
Worcester, Earls of, 54-5, 67-70, 127, 151-2, 158, 160
Worcester, Marquis of, 55, 69, 158
Worcestershire, 7, 9, 17, 52
Wordsworth, Wm., 51
Wreck, 59, 72, 90
Wronow Wyne, Jevan ap, 23
Wrytell, 163
Wycombe, 162
Wylesford, 163
Yatton, Somerset, 94
Yerkshull, 163
York, 13, 24-7
York, Duke of, 44, 49

A Suggested
GAMES SCHEME
For Juniors

A Suggested
GAMES SCHEME
For Juniors

By F. J. M. JOHNSON

Head of P.E. Dept. The College of Education, Loughborough

and M. D. Trevor

Assistant P.E. Adviser to Nottinghamshire

BASIL BLACKWELL · OXFORD

© Basil Blackwell 1970
Reprinted 1972
0 631 94820 1

Printed in Great Britain by Alden & Mowbray Ltd
at the Alden Press, Oxford
and bound at Kemp Hall Bindery

Primary School Games

All children play, and individual, group and team games are the outcome of play. Young children may go out into the play area for what the teacher terms 'Games' or in traditional parlance 'Organised Games' but it must be remembered that these children really play at playing games and it is with this in mind that many of these programmes are presented. Many children will later gain great satisfaction and enjoyment from major games but this thought must not be applied to all children. In consequence, to take out a typical junior class to play only major games would be to show a lack of understanding because they are not, from the point of view of maturation, ready, and premature training may do more harm than good.

To create the environment and provide all the necessary games apparatus is only part of the teacher's task. Praise and encouragement, and guidance from worthless practices into worthwhile skills are still essential. The children may originate the practices and the games and with practice they will surely gain in skill but this gain will be much greater if the teacher utilises his or her mature understanding of situations arising and helps the children with recommendations and suggestions. It cannot be over emphasised that for the child to benefit, success in junior games entails personal involvement.

Most of the necessary material for games lessons for the primary age range is given in the following pages. The first section is divided into programmes for the traditional junior range of seven to eleven years, although many twelve year olds would find the later work challenging. A section for rural schools is appended.

A programme, in the context of these pages, is a piece of work to be covered in about five or six weeks and from each programme a number of lessons can be drawn up. Many of the activities are worthy of much repetition. Thus 'with a partner, using any two pieces of equipment and a ball make up a moving target activity', will take about five minutes for several lessons, whilst again a game such as Commando Cricket will occupy fifteen to twenty minutes for a number of lessons. Some of the games will become very popular with the children, and with a wise teacher will often be included as 'children's choice'.

1

It may be worthwhile adhering to the sequence of programmes. Those presented for the latter half of the Autumn Term and those for the Spring (Winter) Term are generally vigorous, whilst those indicated for Summer and early Autumn take advantage, possibly optimistically, of warmer weather.

Every programme opens with 'free practice with available apparatus', and this may continue until the teacher and the whole class are ready to begin the main part of the lesson. Although all the apparatus needed in each programme is indicated at the beginning of that programme it is thought that the children would benefit from all the apparatus being taken out for every lesson. It can be loaded on an apparatus trolley or taken out in four team baskets. Apparatus dispersed around the playground and neatly stacked when finished with will facilitate class organisation. With simple explanation most classes can be relied upon to do much of the organisation involved.

Certain pieces of apparatus can be improvised. A tall tin, with a little sand or soil in the bottom makes an effective skittle. A long rope tied from the back of one chair to another makes a useful 'net' for some of the activities played over a net. Skipping ropes can often indicate floor markings, and a stout stick shaped to make a handle at one end can serve as a bat. Teachers and children will doubtless have greater ingenuity.

Sizes of pitches for many of the rounders variations will need to be modified with experience. If the batting or running sides score too easily the distance between the bases, islands or posts will be increased. But if they fail to score the pitch will be made smaller. For schools with boundary problems, i.e. nearby windows, greenhouses, main roads and low surrounding walls, most of the practices will still be playable and many of the games can be adapted. For instance rounders variations can be initiated by the striker throwing the ball or hitting a 'dead' ball instead of one pitched or bowled. Again, the teacher with experience of working in his or her own particular environment will be better placed to suggest modification.

Many of the activities suggested can be played on a hard surface or on grass, but some, e.g. bouncing variations will only succeed on the hard surface.

Finally, while you may find something new in these pages, you will certainly find something that you have played before. But we hope this little book may increase the enjoyment and satisfaction children can derive from games lessons. It is not necessary to be a gladiator to gain real delight or educational benefit from playing games.

F. J. M. J.
M. D. T.

YEAR 1—Autumn Term—Programme 1

Apparatus Needed

Balls of different sizes, Hoops, Skipping ropes, Coloured team braids.

1   Free practice with a variety of small apparatus.

2   *a* Free play with a small ball each.
    b How many different ways can you bounce the ball?
    e.g. bounce and catch, bounce, run under and catch, bounce, jump over and catch, pat bouncing.
    c Individual throwing and catching.
    N.B. For catching—hands together forming a cup.

3   *a* Free play with a hoop—any worthwhile activity to be developed for whole class, e.g. bowling, steering, guiding the hoop.
    b Can you run through a moving hoop?
    c How many activities can you discover using a moving hoop (jump over, run through, or round, spinning, spin and run round)?
    N.B. There are many more.

4   Hoops scattered about the playground. Free running—
    a Stepping into hoops (how many in 1 minute?)
    b Running around hoops (how many in 1 minute?)

5   Running around playground. Hoops on ground.
    'Twos!' means two people run and stand in a hoop. 'Threes!' and so on.

6   *Free and Caught*
    Ten hoops scattered fairly closely on ground. Five chasers wear braids. Children caught stand inside a hoop. These may be freed by being touched by free children. Stop after a set time. Count number caught. Change chasers.

YEAR 1—Autumn Term—Programme 2

Apparatus Needed

Balls of different sizes, Hoops, Skipping ropes, Play bats.

4

1   Free practice with available apparatus.

2   *Pairs Tag.*
    6 or 8 children holding hands in pairs chase the children
    who are free. Anyone tagged changes places with the person
    who touched him.

3   Small ball each—
    a Free practice.
    b Pat bouncing activities, e.g. with right hand and/or left
    hand.
    Alternate hands on spot.
    Alternate hands moving about.
    Bouncing high and low.

4   *a* Free skipping with rope each.
    b Rope stretched out on the ground. Jump over the rope in
    many different ways.
    Approach from different angles and show a variation of
    turns.

5   *Rolling Goals.*
    In pairs, rope each and a ball between two. Stretch the ropes
    out to form goals 4 or 5 yards apart. Try to roll 'goals' past
    each other (a goal is scored if the ball rolls over the rope).

Rope

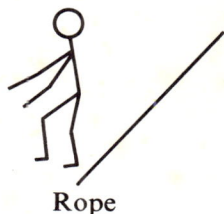

Rope

6   *Free and Caught* (Development of tactics).
    Place ten or twelve hoops close together in the centre of the
    playground. Choose five or six chasers. When caught
    children stand inside hoops but may be released if touched
    by 'free' children.
    Some of the chasers concentrate upon defending those
    inside hoops.

5

YEAR 1—Autumn Term—Programme 3

Apparatus Needed

Coloured Team Braids, Small balls, Large balls, Hoops and skipping ropes.

1   Free practice with available apparatus.

2   *Team Tag Variation.*
Eight catchers with braids chase those who are free, and each individual counts numbers tagged in a given time. Any child tagged remains free and in the game.

3   *Pairs practice with a small ball.*
a Catching with both hands, children stand a short distance apart.
b Standing a little further apart—different ways of sending the ball accurately to a partner, e.g. one-handed, rolling, bouncing, kicking, and other ways which come to mind.
c Moving freely bouncing the ball to a partner (encourage the use of space and sensible bounces).

4   A large ball and hoop between two.
a How many different ways can you use the hoop as a target in which to throw or kick the ball?
e.g. Hoop on floor. Throwing with bounce.
   Hoop held in air (vertically), ball thrown through.
   Hoop held in air (horizontally), ball thrown through, netball fashion.
   Hoop against wall—kicking or throwing ball through.
b Free play with a large ball or hoop (change after short interval).

5   *Snowball Tag.*
Two catchers wear braids and chase the rest. When anyone is tagged he puts on a braid and joins the catchers.

6

YEAR 1—Spring Term—Programme 4

Apparatus Needed

Hoops, skipping ropes, Variety of balls, Coloured braids.

1 Free practice with available apparatus.

2 Free practice with ropes or hoops, followed by—
   a Trying to skip 20 times.
   b Running through a rolling hoop.

3 Hoops scattered—ropes scattered, but stretched out straight.

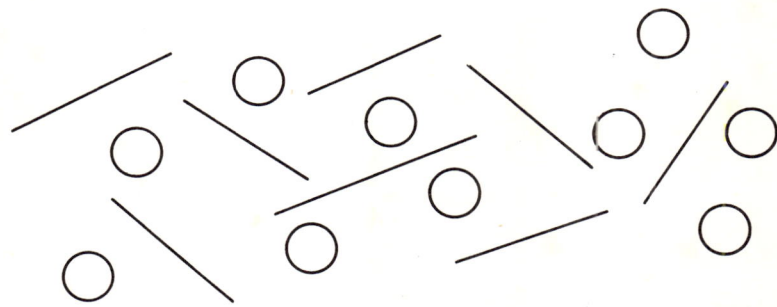

Free running (pretend ropes are high hedges), jumping over the ropes and running around the hoops.

4 Contest to jump into the most hoops and over the most ropes in a given time.

5 Ball each—Free play.
   a Run and bounce and catch.
   b Dribble the ball like a footballer.
   c Jump over a rolling ball.

6 *Twos and Threes.*
   Four pairs of children hold hands and chase the others. When another is touched form a three, but when the number reaches four, split into two separate pairs.

7

YEAR 1—Spring Term—Programme 5

Apparatus Needed

Variety of balls, Coloured braids.

1   Free practice with available apparatus.
2   Make up running games using 2 pieces of apparatus.
3   *a* Hard bouncing, running under the ball several times.
    b Jumping over a bouncing ball as many times as possible before it dies.
    c Find out what other running, jumping and turning activities can be done with a bouncing ball.
4   Snowball Tag Whole Class (Programme 3).
5   In threes, large ball between three, passing on the move, using hands or feet, and using a large area.
6   Free play with a partner using any available apparatus.

YEAR 1—Summer Term—Programme 6

Apparatus Needed

Hoops, skittles, ropes, playbats, shuttlecocks, shinty sticks, variety of balls.

1   Free practice with available apparatus.
2   *a* In threes using a hoop, skittle or rope as a target at which a small ball is thrown.
    b As in (*a*) except 1 player defends the target with bat, feet, hands, etc., 1 player bowls an easy underarm with bounces, from behind a rope laid out 8–10 yards from the target; other player fields.
    c As above except that if the ball is hit try and run to the bowler's rope before he can field the ball and return.
It may be possible to introduce simple runs or points. If this is successful, try playing in fours and fives introducing the idea of fielding.

8

3 In threes, large ball, bounce passing on the move; teacher coaching for running into spaces.

4 Pair activities devised by the children using—
Bats and shuttlecocks, Bats and balls, Shinty sticks or hockey sticks and balls.
These activities can be used as group practices over more than one lesson to give children a variety of experience.

5 Numbers race in a circular formation.
Children standing in a large circle are numbered one, two or three. When they hear their number called they race in one direction around the outside of circle and back to their place. Try not to be last.

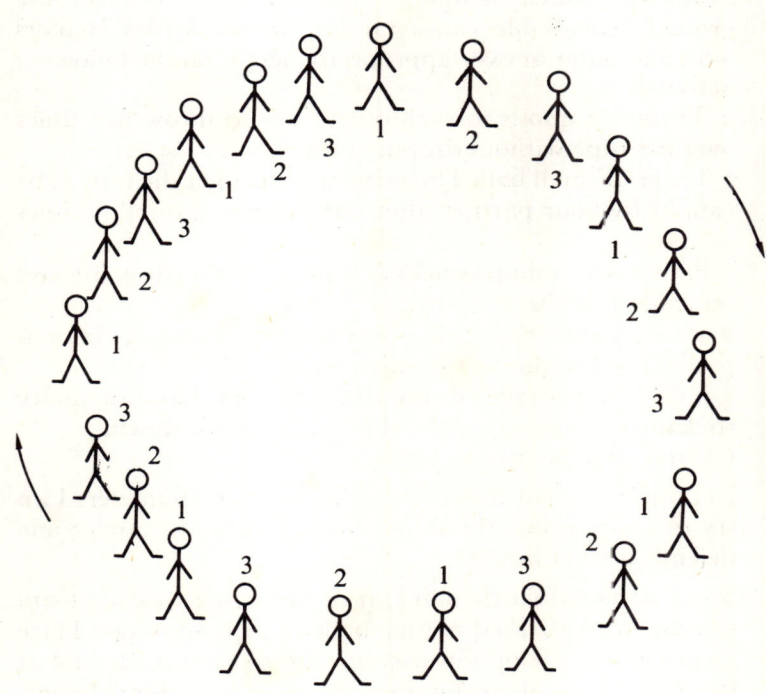

YEAR 1—Summer Term—Programme 7

Apparatus Needed

Ropes, variety of balls, playbats, shuttlecocks, skittles, canes, quoits, shinty sticks, hoops, chalk.

1 Free play using available apparatus.

2 Ropes stretched out on ground.
   a In pairs push passing football fashion across the rope.
   b In pairs pushing small ball over the rope to each other with shinty stick.

3 Ropes at various heights scattered about the playground, e.g. ropes tied across pairs of chairs, clothes lines tied to any available points, skipping ropes stretched out on the ground. If available, canes standing on two skittles. In pairs working under or over appropriate height on the following activities—
   a Throwing quoits to each other. Try to throw five times over the rope without dropping the quoit.
   b Large or small ball. Throwing the ball over the rope to be caught by your partner after one bounce (target: 5 times as above).
   c Playbats and shuttlecocks. Keeping the shuttle going and remembering the best score.
   d Playbat and small ball—over the rope as many times as possible (allow one or two bounces).
   e Balls being propelled to partner by foot, hand or shinty stick through the gap without knocking skittle down.
   Change groups around periodically.

4 In threes with ball and skittle in circle 10 foot diameter. Two try to knock down the skittle from outside the circle; one defends it from inside.

5 Small games of skittle ball four or five a side wearing team braids. Areas marked out in chalk or skipping ropes. Place skittle in large hoop towards the end of each pitch (not at the very end—allow for two yards or so behind hoop). Teams pass ball and attempt to knock down opponents' skittle.

10

Rules

  i Person with the ball cannot be touched.

 ii No running with the ball.

iii No one allowed inside hoop. A skittle knocked down accidentally by a defender counts as a goal.

 iv Game starts and re-starts by alternate teams taking a pass from the centre.

6   Numbers Race variation—bouncing the ball in a circular formation (Similar to Programme 6, Number 5).

YEAR 2—Autumn Term—Programme 8

Apparatus Needed

Ropes, hoops, variety of balls, quoits, skittles.

1   Free practice with available apparatus.
2   Originating activities using two different pieces of apparatus.
    e.g. Throw or kick a ball at a skittle.
        Throw a ball through a moving hoop.
        Stand in a hoop—bounce small ball around outside.
        Throw large ball up—head into hoop.
        Bounce a large ball from side to side along the length
        of a skipping rope on the ground.
        Throw at a skittle.
        Keep a ball bouncing with the aid of a bat.
3   Hoops, skittles and quoits scattered around the playground.
    Find out three methods of dribbling around these objects.
    e.g. i Large ball, football fashion or pat bouncing.
         ii Small bat and shinty stick.
        iii Small ball pat bouncing.
4   One small ball between two standing a few yards apart.
    Different ways of sending the ball to a partner.
    e.g. One hand; Two hands; Underarm; Overarm;
        Bouncing; Rolling.
5   In pairs with a small ball standing about six yards apart.
    The child with the ball bounces it hard vertically. The
    other child runs to try and catch it.
6   *Tower Ball Variation.*
    Groups of five, one large ball, 12 foot diameter circle formed
    with skipping ropes, and one skittle. In the circle a child
    defends a skittle. The ball must be rolled by the other four
    children standing outside the circle. Change the child in
    the centre every minute or every hit.
7   *Bounce Passing Game*
    Groups of five, one large ball, two ropes. A and B attempt
    to pass to C and D by bouncing ball in E's area. E attempts
    to intercept pass. Can you make three successful passes?
    Change E so that all have a turn.

 C

 D

Rope

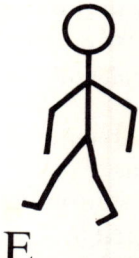 E

Rope

 A

 B

13

YEAR 2—Autumn Term—Programme 9

Apparatus Needed

Variety of balls, quoits, beanbags and ropes.

1   Free practice with available apparatus.

2   *a* In fours. Three players passing by hand and one trying to intercept changing with the person whose pass he stops. No physical contact is allowed. Emphasise moving into unguarded spaces and suggest use of bounce pass.
    b Two versus two. Team passing trying to reach five consecutive passes. No physical contact is allowed.

3   *a* Large ball between two. One rolls the ball underarm without bouncing to partner standing about six yards away. Stop the ball with your foot in such a way that it stays close to you—find out the best ways.
    b As above except ball is rolled to left or right of partner in order to make him run to trap the ball.
    c As in (*a*) except run forward to meet the ball and trap it.

4   Tracing shapes such as circles, figures of eight, zig-zags, snakes, etc., by:
    a Pat bouncing large or small ball.
    b Dribbling football fashion.
    c Dribbling small ball with shinty stick.

5   In twos with a ball each. Two skipping ropes joined together and placed on the ground with various loops, curls and zigzags. Let children decide shapes. Pat bouncing from side to side or into loops without touching rope.

6   *Competitive Chain Tag.*
    Start with three or four separate catchers. When touched children join hands with catcher and keeping inner hands joined try to catch a third child. See who is first to catch a total of four. Start again choosing catchers from those who are still free.

14

YEAR 2—Spring Term—Programme 10

Apparatus Needed

Variety of balls, hoops, skittles, ropes, shinty or hockey sticks.

1 Free practice using any available apparatus.

2 Working in twos making obstacle courses using hoops, skittles and ropes.

   e.g. Jump into hoops.

       Jump over ropes.

       Run around skittles.

3 In twos standing one yard apart either side of a line made by a skipping rope on the ground.

   One child dodges from side to side along his side of the rope trying to lose his partner and the other, also keeping to his own side, tries to stay opposite to his partner.

   The following are variations of the Dodge and Mark activity:

   a One bouncing and catching a ball the other without a ball keeping opposite.

   b One pat bouncing a ball, the other keeping opposite.

   c One dribbling a football and the other trying to stay opposite.

   d One dribbling with a shinty stick—other with stick but no ball.

   Children should be instructed on feinting to left—moving to right, etc.

4 *a* Large ball between two. One throws ball vertically above head. The other runs forward and tries to trap the ball under one foot and stand still.

   b Small ball between two. One throws the ball vertically above head. The other runs forward and tries to catch the ball, after the first bounce.

5 In fours, one large ball. Three standing in chalk circles as shown. A throws ball to B and runs immediately pass is made to stand in B's circle. B throws to C and runs to C's circle, etc.

   Coach passing and running very quickly, so that there are never two players in one circle.

15

6 *In fours*. One large or small ball.
   a Free passing—any method but children must all be on
   the move.
   b Keep passing in a variety of ways.
   e.g. One handed bounce pass.
   　　 Two handed bounce pass.
   　　 One handed without bounce.
   　　 Two handed without bounce.
   　　 One handed roll.
   　　 Two handed roll.
   　　 Pass through legs.
   　　 Football passes.

7 *Touch and Run*.
   In Twos. Two skipping ropes placed parallel about 8 yards
   apart. Children face each other across one of the ropes. The
   child on the outside holds one hand forward and the other
   touches this hand and tries to run back to his rope before
   he is tagged by the other. Take turns to chase.

YEAR 2—Spring Term—Programme 11

Apparatus Needed
Variety of balls, shinty sticks, play bats, hoops, coloured team
braids.

1　Free practice with available apparatus.

16

2   *a* Free practice large or small ball each.
    b Keeping the ball in the air for three successive hits.
    i Using any part of the body.
    ii Using three different parts of the body.

3   In threes. One ball of any kind. Standing in a line behind the leader who holds the ball and stands behind a short starting line. He starts by running, carrying the ball around a skittle placed about ten yards away. He may pass the ball to the next in the team at any point in his return to the end of the team. Next one repeats.
Use this for
    i Carrying or pat bouncing.
    ii Dribbling and passing football fashion.
    iii Using shinty or hockey sticks.
    iv Using rugby ball or quoit.
    v As a relay, if distances and type of ball are same for each team. Decide on a set finishing position.

4   In threes. Free passing on the move. Each group may decide on the type of ball and method of passing.
e.g.   i Dribbling and passing football fashion.
      ii Running and passing rugby ball.
      iii Running and passing netball fashion.
      iv Using shinty or hockey sticks and small ball.

5   *Hoopball.*
Games of three *v.* three. One large ball per game. Two hoops placed about 8–10 yards apart, no defined areas but organise games parallel to each other. A goal is scored if you can bounce the ball inside your opponent's hoop.
Rules
No running with the ball.
No physical contact with opponents.
Discuss with children other rules which may arise.

6   *Free Dodgeball.*
Use two large balls. Four throwers wearing coloured braids throw the balls to hit the dodgers on the legs. When hit these children put on braids and join the throwers. N.B.— Throwers are not allowed to run whilst holding the ball.

17

YEAR 2—Summer Term—Programme 12

Apparatus Needed

Variety of balls, hoops, quoits, beanbags, ropes, shinty or hockey sticks, playbats, shuttlecocks.

1   Free practice with available apparatus.

2   In twos. Making a moving target at which a ball, beanbag or quoit is aimed. Free choice of apparatus.
    e.g. Roll hoop—throw ball through it.
         Roll small hoop through larger rolling hoop.
         Throw or roll small ball at larger rolling ball.
         Spin a hoop—try and throw small ball through it.
         Roll ball to partner who aims a push pass (soccer) at it.
         Throw hoop in the air—partner tries to throw quoit through.

3   In twos using any suitable apparatus (small ball, playball, shinty or hockey sticks, netball, football or rugby ball). The activity is pass and run. The child in possession of the ball stands still. The one without the ball runs as quickly as possible into a space to receive the next pass. (Emphasise passing and then running immediately into a space.)

4   *Group Work.*
    a Target bowling—in twos standing behind hoops about twelve yards apart. Bowling from behind one hoop to pitch first bounce inside the other. Competition—first to score three hits.
     i Underarm.
     ii Overarm.
    b In pairs with a playbat each and a shuttlecock between two. Two chalk circles three yards diameter and two yards apart (use skipping rope as Compasses). Stand in own circle and hit the shuttlecock to make it land in your partner's circle; partner defends his own circle and tries to return shuttlecock to the other circle.
    c In fours, one defending a target with any suitable piece of apparatus, one bowling, two fielding. Let children invent their own rules.

5   *Game—Chinese Wall Game.*

Two parallel lines 10 feet apart are drawn across the centre of the field to represent the wall. One or more players stand on the wall to defend it. The other players try to run from one boundary to the other to cross the wall without being touched by the defenders. Those touched join the defenders on the wall.

Wall

A variation can be played by the runners counting the number of times they get to and from the boundaries.

6   *Net Games.* (A net may be a length of thin rope or string attached to netball posts, high jump stands, drainpipes, chairs, railings and so on. These can be arranged at differing heights from say 2 ft. to 6 ft.).

In pairs selecting from bats, balls, shuttlecocks, quoits, beanbags and large balls.

Originate a game across a net selecting what you consider to be the appropriate height. (At this stage most children will originate a co-operative game, i.e. keeping rallies going. Later they can be encouraged to beat their own record.)

19

Apparatus Needed

Variety of balls, ropes, hoops, skittles, beanbags.

1 Free practice with available apparatus.

2 In pairs using a skipping rope, a hoop and any size ball making a moving target.
   Answers to this problem may have arisen from previous programme.
   e.g. i Tie rope to hoop. Swing around in circle on ground, partner stands still and bounces ball into hoop as it passes.
       ii As above—move hoop more slowly—partner runs around after hoop, trying to bounce ball in it.
       iii As above—one child running holding rope, others follow trying to bounce ball in moving hoop.
       iv Suspend hoop. Allow to swing.

3 *Progression Ball.*
   Ball (any size) and hoop between two. Marks as shown below about 2 feet apart.

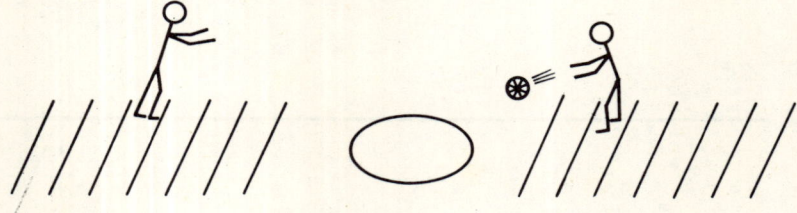

   Alternate aiming at the hoop for say 20 shots. If you hit the target move one place backwards. If you miss, move one place forwards. The winner is the one furthest away after a set number of shots.

4 Make up a pairs game using circles made up of chalk, hoops or ropes. A ball may be used.

5 *Target Ball.*
   Use markings as for progression ball (above). Place small ball in centre of chalk circle. Players stand opposite and throw a small ball at the target ball—one point each time you knock the ball out of the circle.

20

6   *Dodge Ball Rounders*. Teams of 6 to 8.

One team are fielders, the other team in pairs are runners and dodgers. The first runner throws the ball anywhere in the direction of the skittles. He runs around the 4 skittles while his partner dodger runs into the circle. The fielders retrieve the ball and try to hit the dodger below the knee, keeping outside the circle. If they succeed before the runner completes the course no score is made, but if they fail the runner scores a point. When all have had a turn at being runners *and* dodgers teams change over. (See later rule in Programme 14 Number 7.)

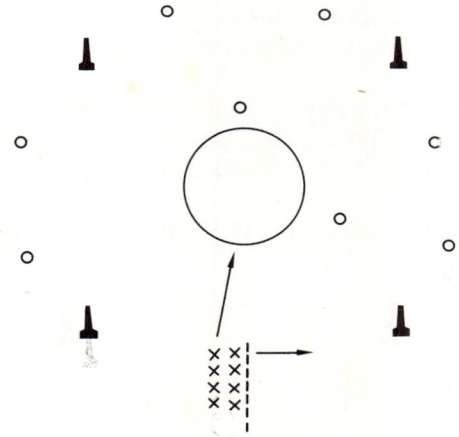

7   *Shuttle Relay*.

Teams of 6, divided into two groups of 3 facing each other as below, with space of about 20 yards between.

No. 1 runs and gives beanbag to No. 2 and stands behind No. 6. No. 2 runs with beanbag to No. 3 and stands behind No. 5 and so on, until teams return to original positions.

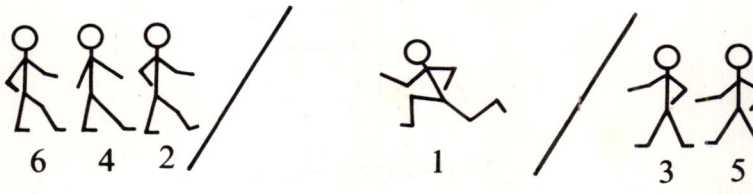

6   4   2   1   3   5

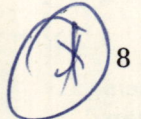

8 *Tunnel Ball Rounders.*
The pitch is marked out as below.
A large plastic ball is struck and the striker tries to run a complete rounder. Meanwhile the fielding team, having retrieved the ball, stand in a line and tunnel it through their legs to the last child who holds the ball above his head. If the team succeeds in doing this before the runner returns, no score is made.

Children are not out because each member of the team has one attempt. The score is totalled and the teams change.

Adjust the bases so that the children have a reasonable chance of scoring.

If the teacher discusses the basis of this type of rounders with his class and asks the following questions, many games will be devised.

a What other activity could the striker do on his way around the bases? (Dribble a ball, pat bounce a ball, etc.)

b What activity could the fielding team do?
Later.

c Is it possible to involve the whole of the batting team on each strike?

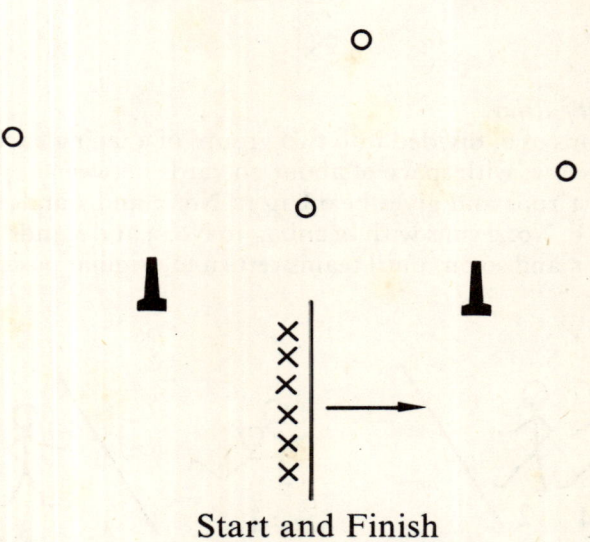

Start and Finish

22

YEAR 3—Autumn Term—Programme 14

Apparatus Needed

Variety of balls, skittles.

1   Free practice with available apparatus.

2   Ball each—any size. Hit the ball into the air several times, using different parts of the body (e.g. knee, foot, arm, hand, head), and catch.

3   Dribbling the ball (any method, any parts of body) in large and small figure eights.
Large means filling the area available.
Small means about 3 ft.
Try and continue for two minutes without losing control of the ball.

4   Large ball 3 *v.* 3 catching and passing. Five successive passes count 1 point. 3 *v.* 3 passing as above except only bounce pass may be used.

5   *Running Circle Bounce Ball.*
Four players around 6-ft. diameter circle, one with large ball. The ball is bounce passed into and across the circle while the players keep moving. Aim for the greatest number of consecutive passes.

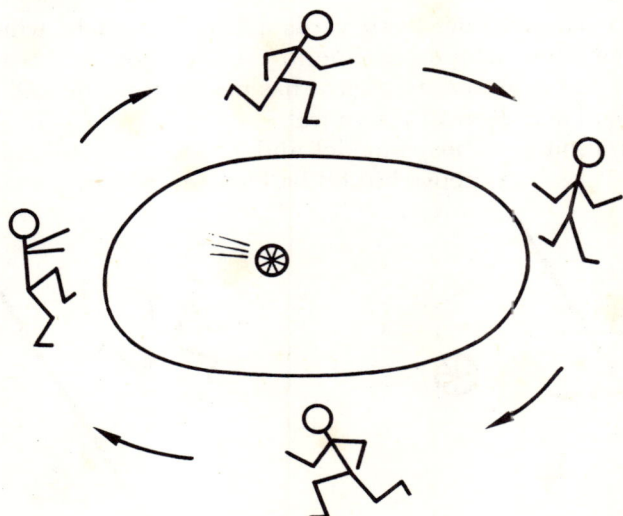

6   *Roll Ball Relay.* (Teams of 4).
No. 1 rolls ball and runs after it. When it crosses **TURNING LINE** he is allowed to pick it up and return it to No. 2. (The game can be played kicking and passing.)

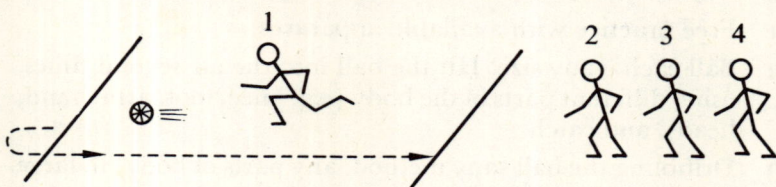

7   *Dodge Ball Rounders.* Variation in Teams of 4.
(See Programme 13.)
Later, if the fielding side can bounce the ball inside the circle before the dodger arrives, it counts as a hit, and no score is made.

YEAR 3—Autumn Term—Programme 15

Apparatus Needed

Variety of balls, skittles, hockey or shinty sticks. Coloured team braids.

1   Free practice with available apparatus.
2   Two parallel lines 8–10 yards apart. Ball each, which is rolled from behind one line in the direction of the other. The ball is picked up after it has passed this line and then rolled back. Repeat ten times.
Variation—as above but kick and stop ball football fashion.
As above but hit ball hockey or shinty method.

3   Ball passing. Three players versus one—trying to reach ten passes. Groups may decide to pass soccer, netball, shinty or hockey fashion. Emphasise running into position—looking for spaces.

4   *a* Several games of skittle ball three- or four-a-side. Using small pitches (about 20 ft. by 40 ft.).
  i   Try to keep this a non contact game.
  ii Coach passing and running into a space.
  iii Do not run with the ball.
  iv No one to enter circles.
  v   Goal scored by knocking down opponents' skittle.
If crowding occurs use centre line, players keeping to their own side of the line.

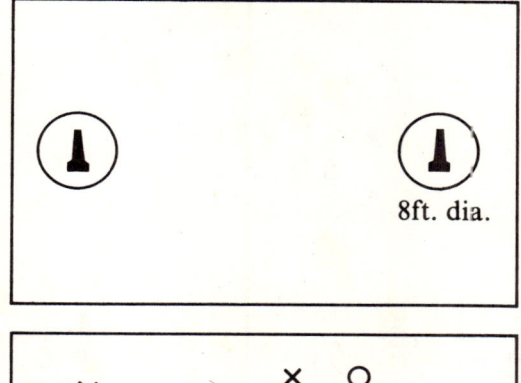

8ft. dia.

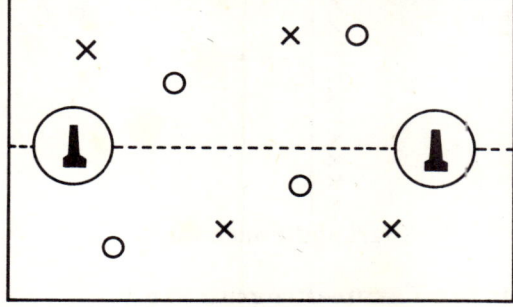

Skittleball Variations.
b Rules as above but play soccer fashion—put several skittles inside circles.
c Rules as above but play shinty or hockey fashion—put several skittles inside circles.

5   *Whole Team Skittleball Rounders.*

Half class fielders, half class runners. Pitch marked out as below. Runners' captain throws the ball forwards, and his whole team run around the course. The fielders retrieve the ball and keeping outside the circle try to knock down as many skittles as possible before the last runner completes the course.

1 point awarded for each skittle knocked down.

This game can be played football fashion for both fielders and runners.

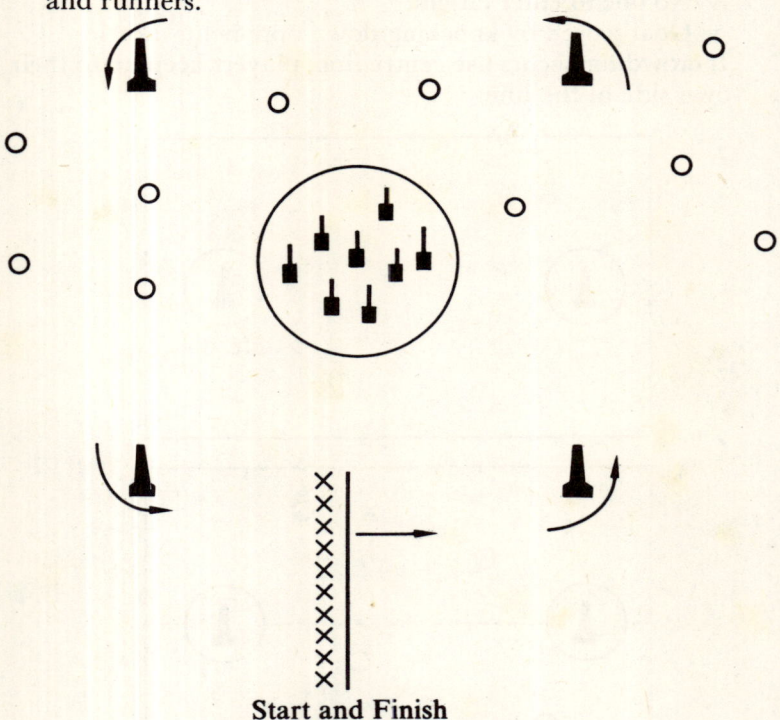

Start and Finish

YEAR 3—Spring Term—Programme 16

Apparatus Needed

Variety of balls, shinty or hockey sticks, canes, skittles, coloured braids.

1   Free practice with available apparatus.

2 Four- or five-a-side football, shinty or netball using groups of skittles as goals as in Programme 14, 4*b* and *c*. Emphasise idea that some players ought to concentrate on attacking and some on defending.

3 Repeat dodge and mark activities as in Programme 10, concentrating on the football and shinty practices. Coach feinting to left or right.

4 *a* Simple heading practices in twos.
i Head ball back to server who stands still.
ii Head ball back to server who moves after having thrown the ball.
b Shinty in twos. Passing and running encouraging quick returns.

5 *Team Tag.*
A quarter of the class wearing coloured braids try to tag the rest of the class who, when touched, crouch down. At the end of one minute the number crouching is counted and this is the team score. Change teams and repeat.

6 *Speed Bouncing.*
A large ball each. Pat bouncing a set distance, e.g. the length of the playground in as few pat bounces as possible. Do not catch the ball until the course is completed.

7 *Circle Speed-bounce Relay*
The class forms a large circle in pairs, one behind the other, with a ball between two. On the signal the children in the outer circle run in an anti-clockwise direction bouncing the ball as in 6 above until they return to their original places where they pass the ball to their partners who repeat the procedure. This is done for a given number of circuits (say 6).

8 Six- or seven-a-side games of football, shinty, skittleball or netball, similar to item 2 but with slightly more involved teamwork. (Helpful organisation for this type of activity is indicated in the Small Schools Scheme Programme B, No. 6).

Apparatus Needed

Variety of balls, shinty or hockey sticks, coloured team braids.

1   Free practice with available apparatus.

2   Dribbling a ball with hands, feet or stick, showing variation of speed and changes of direction.

3   Choice of activity as above passing in pairs, followed by 1 *v.* 1 dribbling and tackling. Aim to keep possession of the ball as long as possible.

4   *Circle Tag.*
    Two circles of four children, hands joined. Keeping hands joined, each circle chases the remainder of the class. Any child touched by the arms or shoulders of the chasing circle, joins that circle. The first circle of seven is the winner. Repeat with different children.

5   Teams of 4 *v.* 4 team passing, all passes to be bounce passes. Aim: to make the greatest number of consecutive bounce passes.

6   *Rugby Touch.*
    Teams of four. Players are allowed to run with the ball, but when touched by an opponent must immediately pass the ball. Aim: to score a try by placing the ball beyond opponents' line. (Size of pitch should be varied according to ability of children.) Later all passes would have to be made backwards.

7   Soccer, shinty or hockey 5- or 6-a-side. Coaching for width in attack—use of wingers.

8   *Whole Team Football Rounders.*
    Teams of 4- to 7-a-side. Pitch marked as shown in diagram. The x's line up as in diagram, each with a football. The o's spread out in the playing area.
    On a given signal every x kicks his ball somewhere between skittles 1 and 4. They then run around all 4 skittles and back to the starting line. Meanwhile the o's retrieve one ball each, football fashion, and dribble into the centre circle where the ball is trapped. When the last runner completes the course the number of balls in the circle is counted. Teams then interchange.

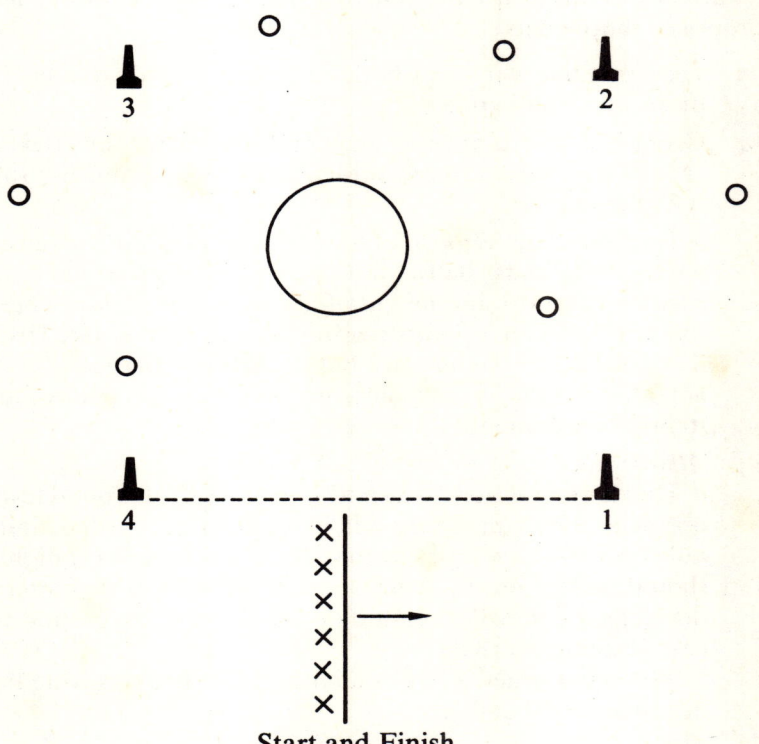

3

2

4

1

Start and Finish

YEAR 3—Summer Term—Programme 18

Apparatus Needed

Variety of balls and bats, shuttles, quoits, skittles and canes, ropes or simple nets.

1 Free practice with available apparatus (individually, in pairs or in small groups).

2 Groups of four practising striking for rounders or cricket. (Make easy serves to encourage hard hitting and use soft balls for safety.)

3 *a* Half the class. Groups of four (2 *v.* 2) playing net games with quoits, bats, balls, shuttles, etc. (Children make up own size of court and height of net and some children may like to decide on a points scoring system. Games like Deck Tennis, Padder Tennis and Batinton may emerge.)
   b Half the class. In pairs devising games which use any four items of equipment.

4 *Athletics Practices.*
   a Hurdling practices. Running over a flight of ground level obstacles achieving 3 strides in between each 'hurdle'. Suitable obstacles are ropes, canes, chalk lines—several flights should be laid out to avoid queuing. As this stride pattern develops the 'hurdles' should be raised from the ground in easy stages up to 18 ins.
   b Throwing practice. Pairs facing each other throwing for distance (small balls).

5 *Skittle Ball Rounders* (2 games).
   Two teams, fielders and batters. The batters are in pairs, one behind the other. Pitch as in diagram. The front batsman throws, hits or kicks a ball forward at the line AB and runs round the 4 skittles ABCD. Meanwhile his partner runs into the circle to defend the skittle. The fielders retrieve the ball and keeping outside the circle, try to knock down the skittle. If the skittle is knocked down before the runner completes the course no score is made. If the runner completes the course before the skittle is knocked down, a point is scored.

30

When each pair in the batting team has changed its role the teams change over.

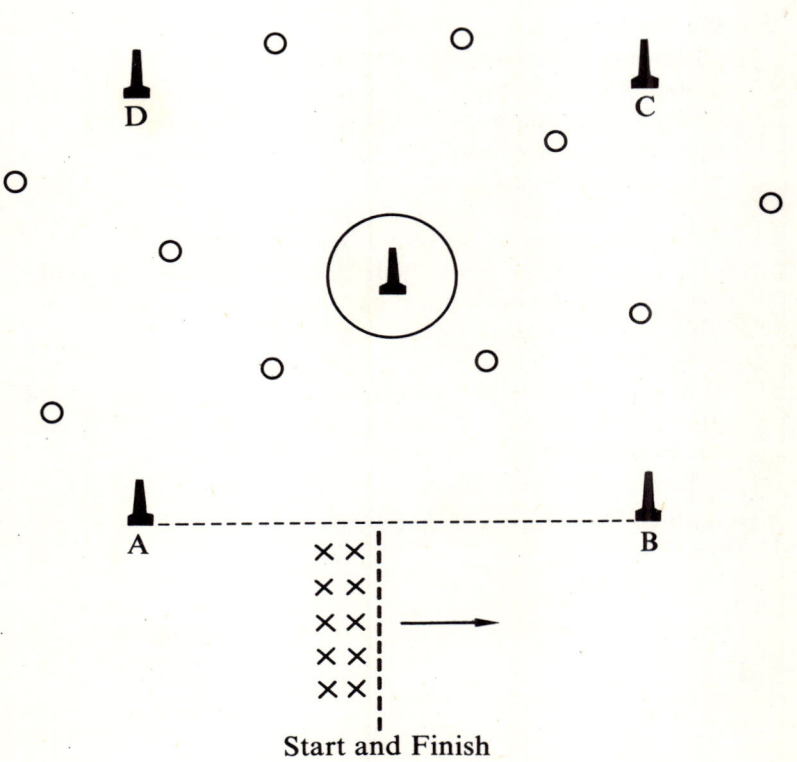

Start and Finish

YEAR 3—Summer Term—Programme 19

Apparatus Needed

Variety of balls, bats, skittles, hoops, relay batons.

1 Free practice with available apparatus.

2 *Athletics Practices.*
  a Jumping. Class activity in several groups:
   i Running, long step.
   ii Running, long hop.
   iii Running, long jump.
   iv Standing, broad jump.
   v Three successive spring jumps.
   vi High jumping at 2-ft.-high bar.
   a from the front; *b* from the left side; *c* from the right side;
   d experimenting with hopping, turning and striding.
  b Running. Relay practices teams of 4.
   i Shuttle touch relay.
   ii Relays. Four runners in a line, 10 yards between each
   runner. On the start, A runs to touch B, B to C, C to D, and
   D to finishing line.
   iii Repeat ii with a baton.

3 Games of Non-Stop Cricket or Commando Cricket.
  Non-Stop Cricket.
  Teams of 5 or more.

The bowler bowls a large light ball to the first batsman who strikes it with his hand and runs around the skittle and back to defend the target. The fielders return the ball quickly to the bowler who bowls at the target as soon as possible without necessarily waiting for the batsman to return. A run is scored each time the batsman succeeds in returning to the target.

The batsman is given out if:

i He is run out at the target; ii He is caught out; iii He is bowled out.

When the umpire shouts OUT! the next batsman runs as quickly as possible to defend the target and once again the bowler need not wait for the incoming batsman to arrive at the target before he bowls.

Batsmen must not cross the batsman's line before the umpire shouts OUT!

Teacher.

Targets may be mats, ropes, hoops, a group of skittles in the playground, perhaps markings on a wall.

The bowler should always have a defined area in which to stand, e.g. mat, hoop, chalk mark, stump.

Commando Cricket.

Teams of 5 or more.

The game is the same as non-stop cricket except that both teams are numbered. The game commences by No. 1 in the bowling team bowling to No. 1 in the batting team. When No. 1 is out No. 2 in the bowling team bowls to No. 2 in the batting team, and so on.

This is a more complicated version of non-stop cricket and its fun lies in the quick thinking and team work required.

Apparatus Needed

Variety of balls, shinty and hockey sticks, coloured team braids.

1 Free practice in pairs or small groups for football, hockey, netball, shinty.

2 Small groups as above—first time passing.
   Main coaching point is to ensure that children look where they intend passing the ball *before* they receive it.

3 3 *v.* 3 (or small groups as above). Team passing—any method. Five consecutive passes = 1 point.

4 5 *v.* 5 soccer, hockey, shinty.
   Conditioned games—'Two touch' means each player must not touch the ball more than twice when he receives it.
   In netball—Introduce simple rules.

5 *Running Dodgeball.*
   One ball, 2 lines, about 20–25 yards apart.
   One of the x's hits a ball served by one of the o's. The x's run to the far line and back. O's field the ball and throw to hit x's legs.
   Count number of hits.
   Each team bats five times.

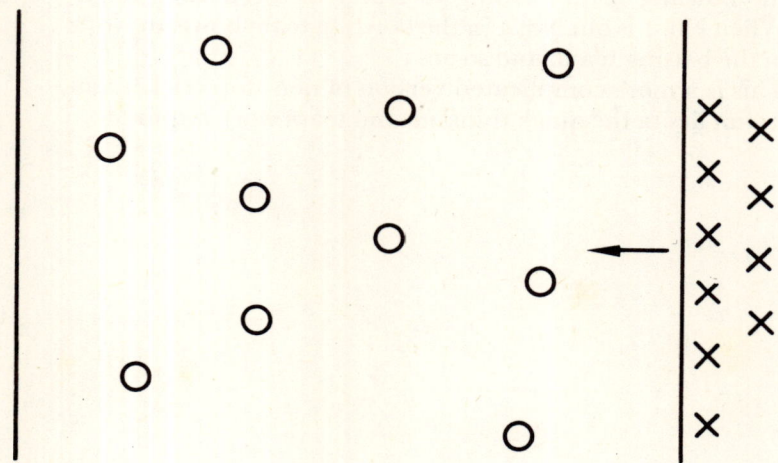

6   *Danish Rounders.*

Children are divided into 2 teams, fielders and batsmen. Pitch marked out as below. The posts should be areas marked out on the ground allowing enough room for several children to stand in them at once. One player of the fielding team bowls the ball (underarm throw) and the first batsman hits the ball with his fist, forwards of the batting line and sets off round the course. The fielders retrieve the ball and return it to the bowler who jumps quickly into the bowling square, holds the ball up in the air and shouts 'STOP!' Any members of the batting team who are running between 2 posts when the bowler calls 'STOP!' are out. If a batsman has reached the safety of any post he may remain there until he judges a hit to be sufficiently hard to continue round the course. Each member of the batting team who succeeds in completing the course (regardless of stops at posts on the way round) scores a point for his team. When a batsman hits a ball which is caught without bouncing, he is out and also any other runner who has decided to run between any 2 posts on that hit. If a runner has made no attempt to run on a catch but remains at a post he is not out. After a set time the teams change over.

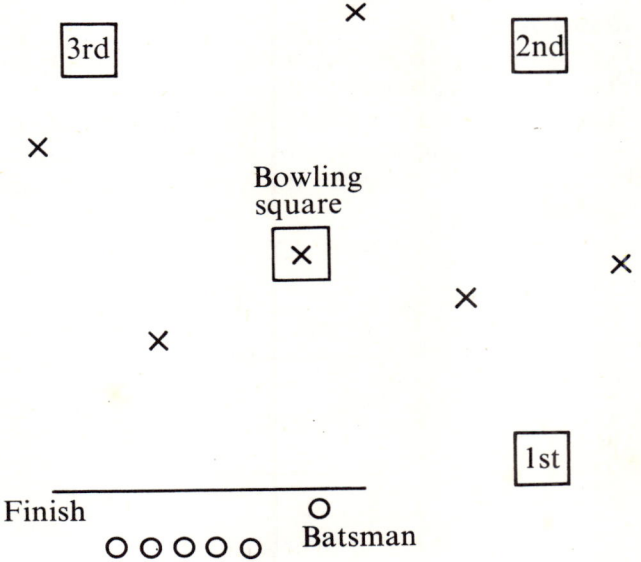

YEAR 4—Autumn Term—Programme 21

Apparatus Needed

Variety of balls, shinty sticks, coloured team braids, skittles.

1 Free practice of known skills in football, hockey, netball or
   shinty.

2 *Team Dodge Ball.*
   Four teams in different coloured braids. Two light plastic
   balls are used.
   One team throws the balls at the other three teams and each
   hit is recorded.
   The player with the ball is not allowed to run and a time
   limit of two minutes is suggested. The winning team is the
   one scoring the greatest number of hits.

3 Practices in pairs.
   a Heading—soccer.
   b Goal shooting—netball.
   c Stopping and hitting—hockey and shinty.

4 *Boys and girls mixed.*
   Hockey, netball, shinty. At 5-a-side level. Emphasise first
   time passing.

5 *Release Tag.*
   Four teams with coloured braids. One team as catchers.
   Players caught placed in Prison (square).
   Some catchers should guard prison since prisoners may be
   released by being touched by those children who are still
   free. Each team chases for three minutes, when number in
   Prison is counted.

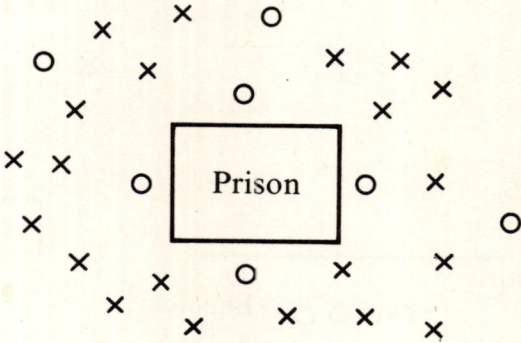

Apparatus Needed

Variety of balls, ropes, beanbags, coloured team braids. Hockey and shinty sticks.

1   Free practice with available apparatus.

2   In pairs, one braid between two. Circular course made up of folded ropes or beanbags. One person from each pair runs one lap around circle and passes braid on to partner. Continuous run for 3 or 4 minutes. Pair with most laps wins.

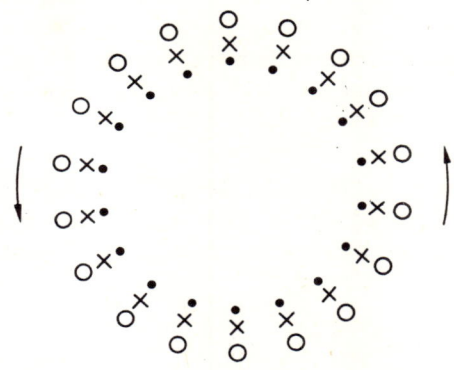

3   Variations of the above may be played by introducing dribbling for soccer, hockey or shinty, or pat bouncing.

4   *Four Team Skittle Ball*
Four skittles are set out in a square 15–20 yards apart. The game is played between four teams wearing different coloured braids. Each team has one skittle to defend and three to attack. The normal rules for skittle-ball apply but the children should be coached to switch their attack to the least crowded skittle. Teams of 5 are suggested. Two simultaneous games will occupy 40 children.
The game is started by the ball being thrown up at the centre. After a goal is scored the game is restarted by a throw from the defending team.

5   Five-a-side Soccer, Rugby touch, Hockey, Netball.
Coach marking in defence.

YEAR 4—Spring Term—Programme 23

Apparatus Needed

Variety of balls, coloured team braids, shinty and hockey sticks, skittles.

1   Free practice with available apparatus.

2   *Competitive Team Tag.*
Four teams wearing braids. Each team in turn chases for a set time. When touched the individual runs a complete circuit of the play area and thereby gets back in the game. When the set time is up, all stop and the number running round the circuit is counted as the chasing team's score.

3   *Team Passing.*
Four passers *v.* two opponents for shinty, netball, soccer, hockey. Try to make as many consecutive passes as possible. Children take turns to be opponents.

4   *Dribbling Relay.*
Teams of three. Hockey, shinty, soccer dribbling, or pat bouncing around skittle. Pass at any time on the return to the next player who must receive the ball behind the starting line.

5   *Hockey, Netball, Soccer, Rugby touch.*
Six-a-side games. Emphasise width in attack, i.e. wingers encouraged to play wide apart, and defence to follow up behind its attacking forwards.

6   *a* Girls—variation of 4-ring skittle ball (prog. 22 No. 4) to be played with hockey or shinty sticks (several skittles in each circle may be used). Rules to be developed by the children.
b Boys—Rugby Touch (see prog. 17 No. 6). Coach the backward pass.

38

YEAR 4—Summer Term—Programme 24

Apparatus Needed

Bats, small balls, wickets or skittles. Variety of balls. Apparatus required for the game selected in 3.

1   Free practice with available apparatus.

2   *Circular Cricket*—several games.
Cricket ball—tennis ball—wickets (for the better players—perhaps cricket ball, pads, gloves, etc., if available).
A game suitable for up to 10 players, the ideal number being about 7.

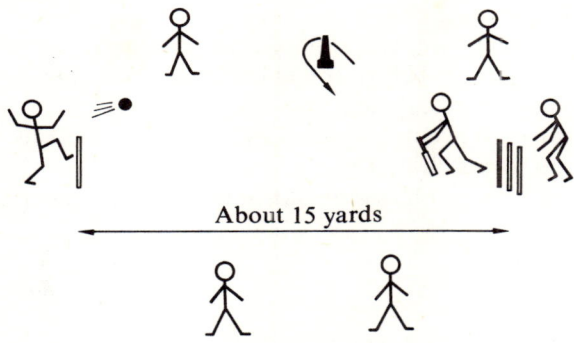

About 15 yards

At the commencement of the game each of the seven players has 10 'runs'. No. 1 bowls 10 times to No. 5, who may score runs by running around the stump X and back to his batting line. He adds those runs to the 10 with which he started. If under normal cricket rules he would have been given out (bowled, caught, run out, etc.) he merely subtracts 3 runs from his total and continues batting until he has received his 10 bowls. All of the players then move one place around in a clockwise direction and the game continues with No. 7 bowling to No. 4.

The bowler is awarded 3 runs if he:

  i   Bowls a player out.

  ii   Has a player 'caught' from his bowling.

  iii   Has a player 'stumped' from his bowling.

A fielder may also be awarded 3 runs if he:

  i   Catches a batsman out.

  ii   Throws in the ball which 'runs' a batsman out.

39

A stumper may be awarded 3 runs if he:

i Stumps the batsman out.

ii Runs the batsman out.

iii Catches the batsman out.

This is an individual game and the winning player is the one with the highest number of runs after the last man has batted.

Teacher.

Leg before wicket is always a doubtful decision and is not included. The game may involve bowling 'unders' or 'overs'. If a hard ball is used pads and batting gloves, etc., will be needed.

3 *Netball Rounders.*

The batsman hits the soft plastic ball and tries to run a complete circuit before the fielding side can retrieve it and score in the netball ring.

The batsmen are never out. Each batsman has one hit and then the teams change over.

Adjust size of pitch to give batsman a fair chance of scoring.

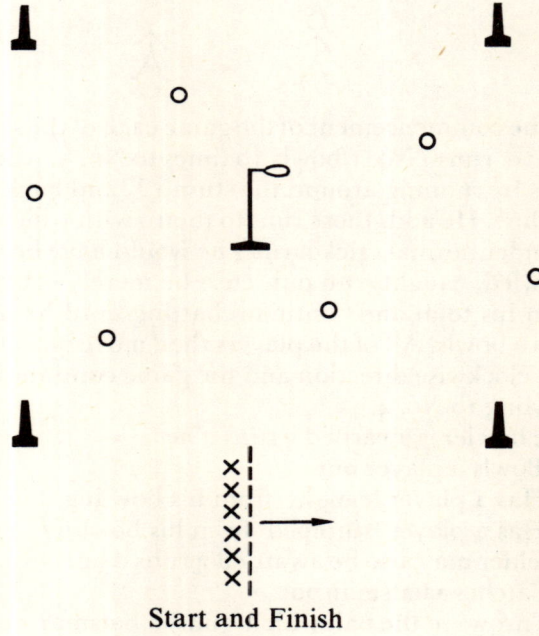

Start and Finish

4   *Pairs Rounders.*
    Several games with 6 pairs of children in each game. A light
    plastic ball is used. The game is played as normal rounders
    except that the ball is struck by hand. All field except the
    batting pair who continue until they are both out and the
    next pair take their place. The pair with the highest score
    win. Several innings may be played.

5   Any game from the previous programmes which the children
    choose.

As a variation for one or two lessons the following Potted Sports
programme might be used.
Potted Sports. Teams of 4 or 5 children. Blackboard for recording
scores. Four minutes each activity—team leaders keep scores—
record at each change.

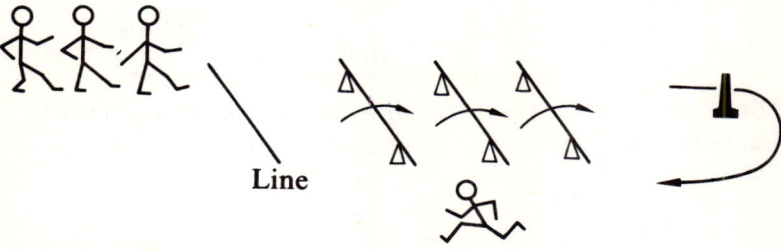

Line

Hurdling. The team runs one at a time. Each time a person completes a circuit 1 point is scored.

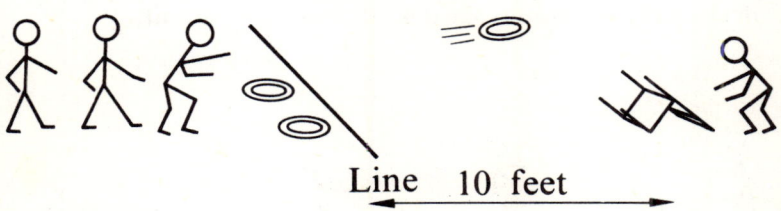

Line   10 feet

'Hoopla' ring a chair leg to score 1 point—use 3 quoits (take
turns).

41

Dribbling, pat bouncing or football method, around skittle. Pass at any time on return after reaching 'passing line'. One point per circuit.

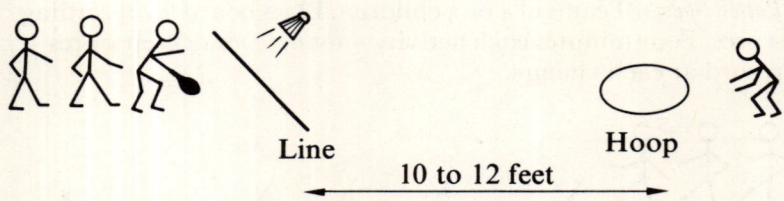

Hit shuttlecock with playbat into hoop—use 3 shuttlecocks. Each successful hit scores 1 point (take turns).

Hockey dribble around skittles—1 point per circuit.

Passing backwards and forwards along row—1 point each time the ball returns to leader.

42

The activities in programme 24 can be continued and the following additional suggestions can be used.

Apparatus Needed

Variety of balls. Playbats, long ropes for nets, quoits. Skittles, canes, hurdles.

1   *a Half class*—allow children own choice, e.g.

Examine possibility of devising wall games—players in pairs or doubles strike, throw, kick, etc., ball at wall over net line to rebound and land inside court lines. A high wall is usually required. In all of the above games devise simple ways of scoring.

b Half class.

   i Bowling cricket fashion at a grid marked on floor. Have 10 bowls—record score.

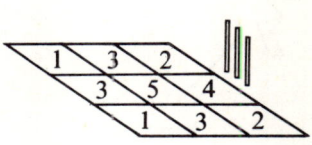

ii Bowling rounders fashion at markings on wall at appropriate height. Ten bowls, record score.

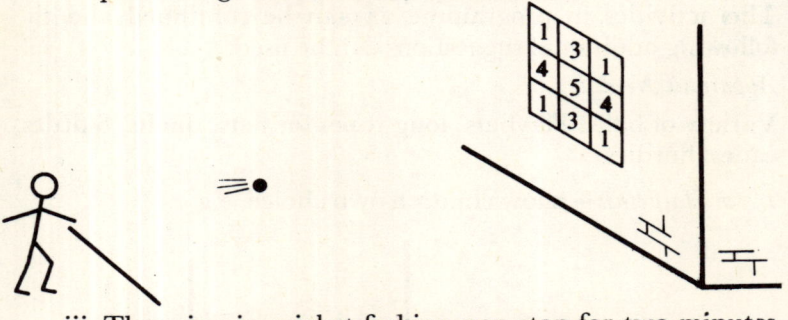

iii Throwing in cricket fashion non-stop for two minutes. Record scores.

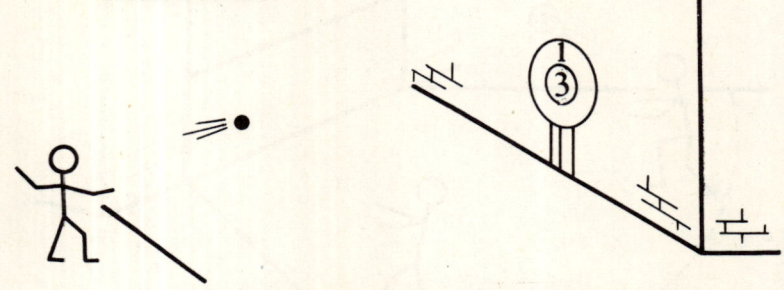

i, ii and iii will interchange freely. After about 10–15 minutes half classes will interchange.

2 Teacher's and children's choice of any games or activities which have been of particular interest in the preceding programmes.

As an alternative the following activities may be attempted.
Simple Athletics standards competition.
Arrange distances, heights and times, so that least able performers can score and most able cannot reach maximum.

1 Six consecutive standing broad jumps. Points awarded according to lines cleared.

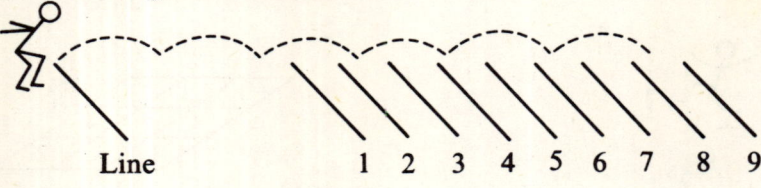

Line   1 2 3 4 5 6 7 8 9

2   *Running long jump* (only if sand pit available).

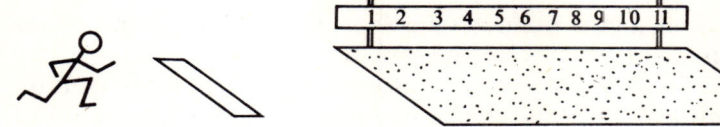

3   *Throwing for distance.*

   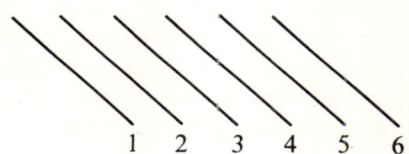

4   *Running and jumping* (hurdling) competition—course around edge of playground—hurdles made from skittles and canes. Points awarded according to time, e.g.
20 seconds scores 1 point
19 seconds scores 2 points
18 seconds scores 3 points, etc.

5   *High Jump*. Score points according to height, e.g.
2 ft. 6 ins.=1 point
2 ft. 7 ins.=2 points, etc.

6   *Zig-Zag Sprint Race* (if space not available) around pegs.
Time: 20 seconds scores 1 point
        19 seconds scores 2 points, etc.

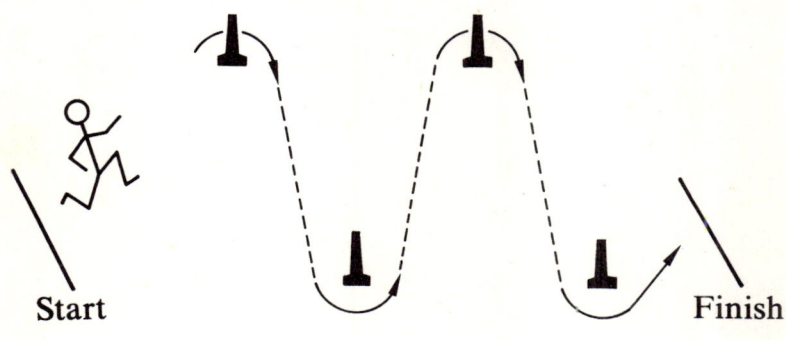

Playground Sessions for Small Schools

In playing games in small schools we have to face the problems which arise from a wide age spread.

The following programmes are offered as a possible solution to these problems although it must be emphasised that much of the material in the programmes which is in the earlier part of the book is appropriate to small schools.

It may be that after, say, quarter of an hour, the infants could continue with free activity while the older ones develop techniques and skills. The teacher will know how much activity these infants can sustain in any one session.

Many of the activities and games originated by the children or suggested by the teacher will prove worthy of practice over a considerable period of time.

Programme A

1 Free practice with available apparatus.

2 Ropes, hoops, skittles, beanbags, canes scattered around the playground. Free running and jumping over obstacles.

3 Propelling a ball of any size, by any method, dodging all over the play area (e.g. dribbling with feet, hands, stick or bat, pat bouncing, throwing and catching). Stopping and starting under control.

4 Making up activities with combinations of any two pieces of apparatus (e.g. rope and hoop, skittle and ball, cane and hoop, cane and beanbag, hoop and ball).

5 Throwing and catching individually with a ball (e.g. 1 hand, 2 hands, high, running, after a bounce on floor or wall).
(*Teacher:* Small children will find a larger ball easier to catch.)

6 This section may not be suitable for infants and where infants and juniors work as one group, it is suggested that the infants revert to free play with available apparatus or free practice in any of the previous activities.
   i Two versus two teams passing any method (5 consecutive passes score a point).
   (*Teacher:* Coach children to run into an open space.)
   ii 3- or 4-a-side skittle ball. Rules to be developed as children suggest them.

Programme 7 No. 5 suggests some basic rules if required.
Programme 15 No. 4*a* gives a further development.

Programme B.

1   *Introduction.* Free practice with available apparatus.

2   Ropes, hoops, skittles, beanbags, canes scattered around the playground. Jumping as high as possible over apparatus.

3   Propelling a ball of any size, by any method, dodging all over the play area (e.g. dribbling with feet, hands, stick or bat, pat bouncing, throwing and catching). Tracing large and small circles.

4   In pairs making up activities with combinations of any three pieces of apparatus.

5   In pairs stopping a rolling or bouncing ball (persuade children to adjust distance and speed of ball according to skill).

6   Not suitable for infants.

Small team games (5-, 6- or 7-a-side) of hockey, shinty, football, informal netball. Rules to be developed as children suggest them.

Where there is a wide range of ability the teacher may place children of similar ability in the same area. This will solve the problem of the stronger players dominating the game.

If crowding occurs in these games the following pitch markings may be used.

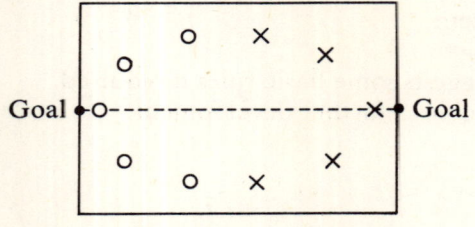

5-a-side players keep to their side of a line drawn from goal to goal.

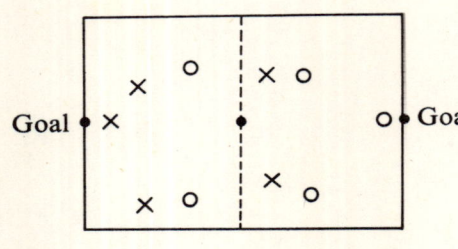

5-a-side (or 6-a-side) players keep to their side of halfway line except at restarts.

48

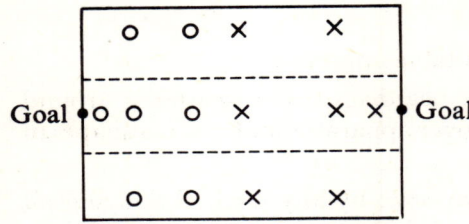

7-a-side players keep to their strip of the field.

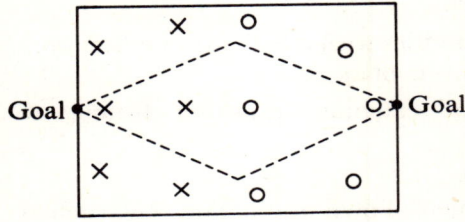

Later.

7-a-side. Players keep to their own area except when in possession of the ball. This pattern ensures that teams play wide during mid-field play and more scope is given to wing and full-back play.

Marking is more easily understood by the children when using these lines.

Programme C

1 Free practice with available apparatus.

2 Ropes, hoops, skittles, beanbags, canes scattered around playground. Jumping over apparatus and making shapes in the air.

3 Propelling a ball of any size, by any method dodging all over the play area (e.g. dribbling with feet, hands, stick or bat, pat bouncing, throwing and catching). Tracing large and small figures of eight.

4 In pairs making up activities with a ball and combinations of two or three other pieces of apparatus.

5 In pairs throwing and catching, adjusting distance to ability.

6 Not suitable for infants.
   In pairs aiming at targets of own origination (e.g. such as hoops, skittles, marks on walls, hoops against walls, chalk marks on playground, throwing, rolling, kicking, hitting a ball, throwing a beanbag, throwing or rolling a quoit, rolling a hoop).

7 Dodge Ball variations, e.g.
   Circle Dodge Ball
   Snow Ball Dodge Ball
   Team Dodge Ball **Prog. 21** No. 2
   Free Dodge Ball **Prog. 11** No. 6
   Running Dodge Ball **Prog. 20** No. 5
   Circle Team Dodge Ball as below.

Circle Team Dodge Ball
The children are divided into teams of 5 or 6. One team stands inside the circle and the other team standing outside roll a large plastic ball at the legs of those inside the circle. These children may run, dodge and jump to avoid being hit. The number of hits scored is recorded for a given length of time, e.g. 1 minute, and then teams change.

Programme D

1   Free practice with available apparatus.

2   Ropes, hoops, skittles, beanbags, canes scattered around playground. Jumping over each piece of apparatus in a different way (e.g. taking off one foot, both feet, landing on one or both feet, trying to jump high or far, turning, twisting, jumping in different directions).

3   Propelling a ball of any size, by any method dodging all over the play area (e.g. dribbling with feet, hands, stick or bat, pat bouncing, throwing and catching). Child originated shapes in the play area (e.g. curves, waves, letters, figures). Zig-zags and other shapes with sharp turns.

4   In pairs throwing a ball to a partner in many different ways (e.g. one hand, two hands, between legs, underhand, overhand, round the body, over the shoulder, etc.).

5   As in Section 6 of Programme 3 but with moving targets (e.g. rolling hoops, quoits or balls, hoops or quoits towed on ropes).

6   Not suitable for infants.
Rounders variations, e.g.
Tunnel Ball Rounders **Prog. 14** No. 8
Dodge Ball Rounders **Prog. 13** No. 6
Skittle Ball Rounders **Prog. 18** No. 5
Netball Rounders **Prog. 24** No. 2
Whole Team Football Rounders **Prog. 17** No. 8
Whole Team skittles Rounders **Prog. 15** No. 5
Danish Rounders **Prog. 20** No. 6.

Programme E

1   *Introduction.* Free practice with available apparatus.

2   Ropes, hoops, skittles, beanbags, canes scattered around playground. Making up sequences of jumps, using different pieces of apparatus (e.g. into a hoop, out of the hoop, side to side over a rope, round a skittle or beanbag). Later this can be combined with the variety suggested in section 2 of **Programme 4.**

3   Propelling a ball of any size, by any method, dodging all over the play area (e.g. dribbling with feet, hands, stick or bat, pat bouncing, throwing and catching). All previous practices in Section 3 of previous programmes with variations of speed.
(*Teacher:* Encourage children to vary their choice of apparatus and method of propulsion from lesson to lesson.)

4   In pairs using a variety of apparatus, making up games based on a theme of under or over or through.

5   In twos or threes keeping moving, throwing and catching a large ball.

6   Not suitable for infants.
    i *Cricket variations,* e.g.
      Non-stop Cricket **Prog. 19** No. 3
      Circular Cricket **Prog. 24** No. 2
      Commando Cricket **Prog. 19** No. 3.
    ii *Net Games*
      (probably played over a rope), e.g.
      Catch Tennis
      Quoit Tennis
      Hand Tennis
      Shuttlecock and Playbats
      Padder Tennis
      and any other net game selected by children.

See **Prog. 12** No. 6 and also **Prog. 18** No. 3*a* for development.